The
Politics
of
Voice

SUNY Series
in
American Literature

David R. Sewell, Editor

Malini Johar Schueller

The
Politics
of
Voice

*Liberalism and Social Criticism
from Franklin to Kingston*

State University of New York Press

Published by
State University of New York Press, Albany

© 1992   State University of New York

Printed in the United States of America

For information, address State University of New York
Press, State University Plaza, Albany, N.Y. 12246

Production by M. R. Mulholland
Marketing by Terry A. Swierzowski

Library of Congress Cataloging-in-Publication Data

Schueller, Malini Johar, 1957–
      The politics of voice : liberalism and social criticism from
   Franklin to Kingston / Malini Johar Schueller.
         p.   cm. — (SUNY series in American literature)
      Includes bibliographical references and index.
      ISBN 0–7914-0855–8 (CH : alk. paper) . — ISBN 0–7914-0856–6 (PB :
   alk. paper)
      1. American prose literature—History and criticism. 2. Social
   problems in literature. 3. Capitalism and literature—United
   States. 4. Politics and literature—United States. 5. Literature
   and society—United States. 6. Liberalism in literature.
   I. Title. II. Series.
   PS366.S62S38   1992
   320.5' 0973—dc20
                                                                90–25941
                                                                CIP

10 9 8 7 6 5 4 3 2 1

For
John K. Schueller

Contents

Preface   ix

Acknowledgments   xiii

1. Introduction   1

2. Franklin's *Autobiography:* Revolutionary Liberalism
    and Authorial Control   17

3. Carnival Rhetoric, Aestheticism, and Transcendence
    in *Walden*   31

4. Democratic Capitalism and the Role of Culture:
    The Identity of Multiple Observers in *The American Scene*   47

5. The Artifice of Boundaries: Language Intersection
    in *The Education of Henry Adams*   67

6. Class and Gender: The Divided Voices of
    Twenty Years at Hull-House   87

7. Language and Ideology: Linguistic Depoliticization
    in *Let Us Now Praise Famous Men*   103

8. Toward a Politics of Difference: Linguistic Otherness
    in *The Armies of the Night*   123

9. Polemics and Dialogics in *The Woman Warrior:*
    A Radical Challenge   143

Postscript   157

Notes   161

Index   193

Preface

This is a study of a number of American personal-political narratives from the Enlightenment to the present which are argumentative in nature and in which we see the potential subversiveness as well as the limits of liberal thought: Franklin's *Autobiography, Walden, The American Scene, The Education of Henry Adams, Twenty Years at Hull-House, Let Us Now Praise Famous Men,* and *The Armies of the Night.* In these texts, writers use personal narrative as an occasion for political commentary and conscience raising and present themselves as cultural spokespersons. My thesis is that the manifest politics and rhetorical structure of these texts dramatize an ambivalent critical stance toward the liberal consensus. Although writers of the personal-political narrative undertake radical critiques of bourgeois homogeneity and the consensual culture of capitalism, their radicalism is limited by their inability to give up two of the fundamentals of liberal thought: individualism and universalism.

The Politics of Voice examines the beginnings of what is perceived as liberal discourse with Franklin's subversion of class privilege and his proposition of an individualistic selfhood and republican citizenry in the *Autobiography.* It then moves on to examine the subversive parodies of business and commerce culture in *Walden,* parodies tempered by Thoreau's aesthetics of transcendence. We have more self-conscious and conflictual social critiques in the early twentieth century: Henry James's equivocal liberalism positioned against the uniformity of capitalist democracy and fearful of the threat of immigrants, Henry Adams's aesthetic radicalism manifested in his critique of universalism and his search for differences, and Jane Addams's complex questioning of class lines along with a promotion of high culture. With Agee and Mailer we have two politically different versions of aesthetics after modernism. In Agee's *Let Us Now Praise Famous Men,* stylistic subversions and romantic transcendence create a problematic aestheticization of human subjects, whereas in Mailer's *The Armies of the Night* postmodern aesthetics and ideology provide a radical impetus to liberal thought and generate a politics of difference. In the last chapter I examine Maxine Hong Kingston's *The Woman Warrior* in order to look at some of the issues raised in personal-political narratives of a radical tradition which are inspired by the experience of marginalization.

A major focus in all these texts is on what might be called the "politics of form." This refers to ideologies implied by the use of certain narrative strategies realized as "voice" in these texts; most importantly, it means the politics implied by the manner in which the polemical authorial voice is positioned within these texts; it also means the politics that emerges from possible differences between the positioning of voices and the overtly thematized agenda. A continual strategy of the book is therefore to relate the manifest politics to the politics as it emerges from form. Particular attention is paid to the writers' dialogue with an endemic feature of American capitalism: the need for ideological conformity and, resulting from it, the denial of the ideological difference represented by marginal groups and a belief in the naturalness of existing class structures. What I hope to illuminate is the idea of form as political voice, as a way of speaking and a means by which, to various degrees, cultural hierarchies are both questioned and maintained. I have found the insights of Mikhail Bakhtin particularly useful because they provide means of formulating ideological analyses that do not rely on reflection theories of literature.[1] Another important influence on this study is Fredric Jameson.[2]

This politicization of form is one way of overcoming the separation between intrinsic and extrinsic approaches which concerns theory even today. It also attests to my conviction that ideological analysis must be integrally related to formal concerns. The question of history should not be hastily settled (as it has been with some historicists) by going back to the historical approaches of the 1930s even if by way of Foucault. Instead we must make use of, and push to the limits, the political implications of theory. My approach, then, is a move against formalism, which assumes the political neutrality of aesthetics, and also a move against pure historicism. We can no more think of a literary work as a text than we must think of letters, diaries, and so forth also as texts. To assume a simple connection between primary "extrinsic" ideological positions as shown in letters or other political writing of the period and their secondary reflections in the literary work is to aggressively reinscribe the disciplinary boundaries (and reinstate the autonomy of the text) it has been the task of theory to question during the last thirty years. It is also to reduce the complexity of ideological analysis to a simple homology.

I write, moreover, as a critic with an agenda. I focus specifically on the points of rupture in these texts, where the illusion of harmonious unity is shattered and where the conflictual liberal-radical politics of these texts create multivoicing at the center of the narrative. Bakhtin, the theorist of struggle and antagonism between discourses both social and textual, therefore provides an appropriate working methodology with his vision of the text as a structure of differently positioned voices.

The social analyses in this book have been greatly influenced by the observations of Alexis de Tocqueville in *Democracy in America*. Tocqueville's astute insights into the pressures for patriotism and conformity in America are relevant today. Equally important are Tocqueville's analyses of the alienation caused by the emphasis on individualism. Louis Hartz's *The Liberal Tradition in America* confirms Tocqueville's interpretation of American "equality" as conformity. I have found particularly useful Hartz's thesis that American liberalism lacked a truly radical component because, unlike Europe, it had no feudal structure to oppose. Hartz sees a fundamental complicity between liberalism and democratic capitalism. American liberalism has often positioned itself against the competitive business culture and the uniformity of capitalism, but it has been restricted by its inability to give up the individualistic social framework endemic to capitalism. Thus even those who are fundamentally opposed to liberal capitalism are implicated in the assumptions of individualism. It is partly the belief in a unified, autonomous self independent of social influences that has hindered the most critical of literary liberal thought in America from gaining radical insights.

Despite its weaknesses, liberal thought has been an important aspect of the American intellectual and literary experience. My purpose in this book is to examine the complexities of the liberal polemics in these texts, to deconstruct, if you will, their hidden political workings, not to simplify or impoverish them. Another book remains to be written about the politics of form of radical personal-political narratives in America, narratives which do not support their politics on appeals to universalism and which question the validity of an authoritative, autonomous self. Such a book would include titles such as Margaret Fuller's *Woman in the Nineteenth Century*, Du Bois's *The Souls of Black Folk*, and Johnson's *The Autobiography of an Ex-Colored Man*. The last chapter, devoted to Maxine Hong Kingston's *The Woman Warrior*, briefly examines some of the issues raised in texts of marginal, radical writers.

What follows is an introduction which discusses the main ideas of liberal thought and analyzes theories of ideological analysis. The subsequent chapters discuss forms of political voicing in Franklin's *Autobiography, Walden, The American Scene, The Education of Henry Adams, Twenty Years at Hull-House, Let Us Now Praise Famous Men, The Armies of the Night,* and *The Woman Warrior.*

Acknowledgments

When I began work on this book, I was a member of Virgil Lokke's study group on theory at Purdue University and I am grateful to the participants of the group for the intellectual insights they provided. I also wish to thank Leonard N. Neufeldt and Virgil Lokke for reading and commenting on several versions of this manuscript. Over the years, for help and guidance far beyond the call of duty I am grateful to Leonard N. Neufeldt. Lee Quinby provided the most constructive criticism for this book. For her friendship, encouragement, and insightful suggestions I am thankful to her.

I am grateful to my colleagues at the University of Florida for reading portions of this book. Brandon Kershner, in particular, helped me greatly with the theoretical aspects of my work. Daniel Cottom, Andrew Gordon, Anne Goodwyn Jones, David Leverenz, Brian Richardson, John Seelye, and Gregory Ulmer were all kind enough to critique parts of the book. Russell J. Reising discussed crucial revisions with me and I am thankful to him and to the two anonymous readers for their readers' reports for SUNY Press.

I want to acknowledge the following for permission to quote from their editions:

Houghton Mifflin for excerpts from *Let Us Now Praise Famous Men* by James Agee and Walker Evans. Copyright 1939 and 1940 by James Agree. Copyright 1941 by James Agree and Walker Evans. Copyright © 1960 by Walker Evans. Copyright © renewed by Mia Fritsch Agee and Walker Evans.

New American Library, a division of Penguin Books USA Inc. for excerpts from *The Armies of the Night* by Norman Mailer. Copyright © 1968 by Norman Mailer.

Portions of this book, in different versions, were published earlier as follows:

"Carnival Rhetoric and Extra-Vagance in Thoreau's *Walden*" *American Literature* 58 (March 1986), pp. 33–45.

"Authorial Discourse and Pseudo-Dialogue in Franklin's *Autobiography*" *Early American Literature* vol. 22, no.1 (1987), pp. 94–107.

"Questioning Race and Gender Definitions: Dialogic Subversions in *The Woman Warrior*" *Criticism* vol. 31, no.4 (1989), pp 421–37.

I am truly appreciative of the enthusiasm and support of my mother and my family. My son, Divik, sustained me throughout this project by his cheerfulness and good humor. I cannot even begin to thank my husband, John, who looked after both Divik and me and kept my spirits up. This is his book as much as mine.

1

Introduction

The alienation of the American intellectual from politics has long been noted by literary and cultural historians. Dramatizing this separation, studies of American literature have, until recently, emphasized the quest of writers to create "world[s] elsewhere."[1] In the last decade there has been a turnabout in the scholarship, and critics are suggesting that worlds elsewhere cannot be apolitical and are integrally related to the social and political ideas of their times.[2] But whatever the critical turn, it has been recognized that in every generation many American writers have conceived of themselves as vaguely belonging to some oppositional party. I say "vaguely" because there are often similarities in styles of opposition even where there is little similarity in content. Compare, for example, the oppositional stance of the hermit Thoreau and that of the cosmopolite Henry Adams. The politics and ideas that these writers have criticized are related in one way or other to the dominant force in American cultural politics since the revolution—liberalism. But precisely because liberalism has been so pervasive in American culture, many writers who have undertaken radical critiques of aspects of liberal ideology, and who are committed to a radical or revolutionary politics, have found themselves unable to dissociate themselves from features of liberalism which are so entrenched that they have become synonymous with being American. This book is about the politics of form in personal-political narratives by such liberal and reluctantly liberal writers.

American literature has a long history of personal narratives which are highly political and in which writers have positioned themselves as cultural spokespersons whose task is to guide national values. In prerevolutionary America this use of personal narrative as exemplary and as a means of guiding the nation was limited to legislators and priests. Diaries like William Bradford's *Of Plymouth Plantation* no less than John Winthrop's sermon aboard the *Arabella*, both authored by powerful governors, were designed to consolidate the powers of the theocratic state. Private and public writing was invested with clerical and political authority. Later, revivalists like Jonathan Edwards and Michael Wigglesworth looked back to this mode of writing. Edwards not only used public sermons to chastise his auditors but also used personal narrative to record exemplary Christian conversions and to condemn the immorality of his flock. Personal narrative was thus also a means of social instruction.

The political persuasiveness of Puritan writing depended greatly on the role of the speaker. Thus, whether writing sermons, personal narratives, or exemplary lives of other men as in Cotton Mather's *Magnalia Christi Americana*, Puritan writers emphasized their speaking voices. When writing with a primarily political and argumentative intent, later American writers have favored using prose narrative in similar ways by foregrounding personal experiences, emphasizing their speaking voices, and attempting to address the culture at large. Thus the tradition of using personal narrative for socio-political concerns continued long after the tradition of letters was established in America.

But although there are cultural paradigms like Puritanism under which to examine the politics of these early personal-political narratives, there are no similar paradigms for postrevolutionary ones. I suggest that liberalism is such a useful paradigm. Liberalism emerged as the dominant political ethos during the revolutionary period. *The Declaration of Independence* made reference to "natural and inalienable rights" which were universal and beyond history, and in the writings of Jefferson and Paine liberal individualism emerged as political dogma. The American constitution, too, was "an authentically Lockean statement" about individual rights.[3] It was not that Puritanism disappeared from the cultural horizon. Sacvan Bercovitch, in *The Puritan Origins of the American Self*, demonstrated its remarkable persistence. However, the tendency of many scholars, following the lead of Perry Miller, to see all American writers as Jeremiahs of Puritan origin bemoaning the loss of the original promise of America is problematic because it denies the possibility of any radical or dissentful impulses in American literature. The continuity thesis also ignores the definite political shifts of the revolutionary period. As John P. Diggins points out, "While we see the conscience of Puritanism persisting in certain aspects of American intellectual history, in political history we see the emergence of Lockean individualism. What preoccupied the thoughts of major statesmen from Jackson to Lincoln was not so much the political duty of the citizen as the economic opportunity of the worker and entrepreneur."[4]

Many American writers from the revolutionary period till the counterculture sixties were deeply concerned about, and interested in, this ideology of American political life. When they turned to personal-political narrative, they dealt in one way or another with the legacy of liberalism, and their narratives formed an important strand in American letters. We see this debate around liberalism within personal-political narrative in Benjamin Franklin's *Autobiography*, Henry David Thoreau's *Walden*, Henry James's *The American Scene*, Henry Adams's *The Education of Henry Adams*, Jane Addams's *Twenty Years at Hull-House*, James Agee's *Let Us Now Praise Famous Men*, and Norman Mailer's *The Armies of the Night*. Liberalism was both an energizing and limiting ideology for these writers. Radical individualism, paradoxically, gave impetus to critiques of bourgeois homogeneity and the liberal-capitalist consensus while at the same time transcendent individualism or the belief in values beyond historical contingency limited these critiques from affirming radical difference. Literary liberalism within personal-political narratives is thus not a simple acceptance or rejection of the dominant liberal ideology but an agonized debate within it which has taken diverse forms for nearly two centuries.

What explains the peculiarities and resilience of liberal thought in America? In order to answer that we need to look briefly at liberal theories and their particular applications in America. Liberalism in Europe was a response to a feudal order which was experiencing dissolution in the sixteenth and seventeenth centuries. Hobbes and Spinoza initiated the theorizing about modern individualism and the belief in governments designed to ensure the liberty of all men.[5] But the most important thinker for American liberalism was John Locke. Locke's notion of property as a "natural right" that guaranteed liberty to the individual became the basic tenet of liberal thought in America. Behind Locke's formulation lay three important concepts: individualism, which extolled the importance of a person's will and responsibility to himself; universalism, which assumed that all human beings had similar rights and concerns irrespective of their historical situations; and capitalism, which in both theistic and patriotic versions glorified the quest for property.

Thus, although liberalism was potentially subversive because of its egalitarian belief in the equal status of all people irrespective of class, it acquired a conserving, stable image in America, where it became a handmaiden to capitalism and competitive individualism, which were idealized as national virtues. One of the earliest and still the most astute of social commentators who analyzed the paradoxical problem of a free, egalitarian society with fixed beliefs was Alexis de

Tocqueville. "As the American participates in all that is done in his country, he thinks himself obliged to defend whatever may be censured in it.... America is therefore a free country in which, lest anybody should be hurt by your remarks, you are not allowed to speak freely of private individuals or of the state."[6] Because America was a free country in which every individual aspired to be a property owner or capitalist, homogeneity of opinion was inevitable. Tocqueville lamented, "I know of no country in which there is so little independence of mind and real freedom of discussion as in America."[7] This complicity between liberalism, democratic capitalism, and bourgeois homogeneity was later seen by Louis Hartz in *The Liberal Tradition in America*. Hartz postulated that because America lacked a feudal tradition, it also lacked a revolutionary tradition. In America there was only a "fixed, dogmatic liberalism of a liberal way of life."[8] Thus, continued Hartz, "'liberalism' is a stranger in the land of its greatest realization and fulfillment.... Here is a doctrine which everywhere in the West has been a glorious symbol of individual liberty, yet in America its compulsive power has been so great that it has posed a threat to liberty itself."[9] Along with political homogeneity and the compulsion for consensus, Lockean liberalism also influenced concepts of community. Tocqueville had already foreseen the privatizing and alienating power of capitalism which confined people "entirely within the solitude of [their] own heart[s]."[10] But, more importantly, the uniformity of liberal-capitalist ideas created a new kind of consensual society. As Hartz points out, "a sense of community based on a sense of uniformity is a deceptive thing. It looks individualistic, and in part it actually is.... But in another sense it is profoundly anti-individualistic, because the common standard is its very essence, and deviations from that standard inspire it with an irrational fright."[11] Another manifestation of this paradoxical consensus is a faith in a radical "American way of life" which has remained unchanged through history. As Daniel Boorstin puts it, Americans have "become exemplars of the continuity of history and of the fruits which come from cultivating institutions suited to a time and place, in continuity with the past."[12] Instead of community, then, liberal capitalism inspires consensual society or mass society.

Many American writers have been concerned about the unanimity of thought generated by liberal capitalism and have criticized both the uniformity and alienation of American society. However, like Hartz, they have been unable to give up the basic tenet of liberal capitalism—individualism. Hartz criticizes American individualism for being anti-individualistic, but he does not criticize the concept of indi-

vidualism itself. However, individualism assumes and prizes an ahistorical, autonomous self that presumes a culture of consensus. Consensual society demands the conformity of its isolated, autonomous
members, whereas society as community recognizes the differences
and interrelationships among them. That is why the concept of community has always been a liberative one for radical and utopian
thinkers, Marxists and feminists alike. For thinkers on the Left, community is a necessary corrective to alienation. Marcuse, for example,
views solidarity as a precondition for liberation, and Jameson celebrates the social collective. Feminists like Chodorow and Gilligan, on
the other hand, offer models of community based on woman-centered
values such as nurturance and interconnectedness as alternatives to
an oppressive patriarchy.[13] Feminists, in fact, reveal the ironic truth
that individualism, rather than fostering social diversity, is intolerant
of it. Herein lies the limiting factor of the quasi-radical yet liberal
social critics of America. These critics offer alternative social visions in
place of the liberal social consensus, but they are also limited by their
adherence to individualism and universalism, a belief in values
beyond history and culture.

I particularly choose to deal with liberal discourse in personal-
political narratives because in these narratives writers are most conscious of their roles as cultural spokespersons who have the task of
guiding the moral values of the nation. Because these texts are, in the
largest sense, polemical, the writers emphasize their speaking voices
and dramatize their social criticisms by having imaginary debates
with their readers. Many of these writers were, in fact, public figures
who were accustomed to lecturing their audiences. Franklin was a
household name by the time the *Autobiography* was published; Thoreau had traveled the lecture circuit; Jane Addams had addressed gath-
erings of labor unions, women, and political leaders; Mailer had
always performed for his public and had also run for public office. So
when these writers turned to personal-political narrative, they
retained many argumentative rhetorical strategies and kept their
speaking voices dominant.

The complexities, paradoxes, and limits of the social criticism in
these texts can be seen as much in the rhetorical strategies used by the
writers as in the manifest politics. Because these writers, in one way or
another, oppose forms of cultural consensus, they create different
kinds of dispersive rhetorical situations. They attempt to bring in the
voices of different Others as challenges to the dominant culture; they
often question the autonomy of their own voices; and they address the
voices of different textualized readers by decentering their own voices.

But, on the other hand, their inability to give up the bourgeois notion of the unified, individualistic subject puts limits on the dispersiveness of these rhetorical strategies. Rhetorically, then, we can see a changing pattern of what we may call "dialogic" dissent in these texts as these writers challenge different forms of the liberal-capitalist consensus.

Because of the controversy surrounding Bakhtin's concept of the dialogic it is necessary to clarify our usage of it here. Dialogism does not simply refer to a rhetorical exchange between speakers (although it can include it) but to a radical, politicized view of language. Dialogic thinking is based on intersubjectivity. It celebrates the Otherness of language, the potential of words to always carry echoes of other words. Bakhtin sees the novel as the most democratic of literary forms because it nurtures this dialogic potential of language. The novelist welcomes speech diversity and the inflections of other voices in his/her narrative. The novel develops the "dialogic essence" by which "fewer and fewer neutral...'rock bottom truths' remain that are not drawn into dialogue."[14] It will be our purpose to see the politics of the dialogic rhetorical strategies in these texts.

An analysis of rhetorical strategies, particularly the modes of address chosen by the authors, the authors' conceptions of their own voices and subjectivities, and the interaction between the authorial voice and other voices thus reveals the buried politics at work in these texts. At times this politics strengthens the manifest political agenda; at other times it puts it under question. But whatever the relation, the style of the politics is as important as the overtly stated agenda. And this is true not only in literary texts but in the world of everyday politics as well. Advertisements are perhaps the most obvious cases of political persuasion. However, the question of the relationship between form and ideological purpose has been addressed in many diverse areas, particularly by Foucault. *Discipline and Punish,* for instance, examines the politics of different forms of executions— public or private—and the politics of different kinds of prisons. Foucault's philosophical endeavor throughout his career was to demonstrate that forms and structures of institutions had as much to do with their political allegiances as did their overtly stated politics.

Although literary theory has always reserved a special place for analyses of form, it is only within the last fifteen or so years that rhetorical and formal analyses have been used for more than comments on aesthetics alone. Both New Criticism and structuralism had attempted to protect a sacred territory of art. Whereas New Critics demarcated the text as an autonomous entity severed from sociopolitical reality by the aesthetic canons of good taste, many structuralists viewed the text as a relationship of signs within a hermetic aesthetic system. They viewed ideology in criticism as evidence of vested interests of which their own methodologies were free.[15]

In poststructuralist thought, however, ideology both in literature and criticism has been viewed with less than suspicion. Ideology has been reinscribed into the text, but without resort to the problematic classic concept of the subject and the reflection theory of art (both of which structuralists also repudiated). Poststructuralists have demonstrated that there is no writing that is ultimately free of ideology. Critical neutrality has thus become a dated notion. However, the reintroduction of ideology into criticism has taken varying forms. Here it will suffice only to mention two camps: that of Marxists both American and British, and those that are referred to as Continental theorists. Marxists like Jameson begin with the premise that "there is nothing that is not social and historical—indeed that everything is" in the last analysis "political."[16] Unlike classical Marxists like Lukács, however, these thinkers do not posit a direct, unmediated relation between text and referent. "The notion of a direct, spontaneous relation between text and history," Terry Eagleton points out, "belongs to a naive empiricism which is to be discarded."[17] The idea of reflection or homology is challenged for Williams by the concept of mediation and for Jameson by dialectics itself.[18] For these Marxists, then, the aesthetic act is ideological, and "form," even more than content, is the bearer of ideology.[19] Jameson's concept of ideology of form is a way of seeing texts as socially and culturally significant *because* of the way they are constructed. Jameson sees "formal processes as sedimented content in their own right...carrying ideological messages of their own, distinct from the ostensible or manifest content of the works."[20] The text refracts ideology, although it cannot be reduced to it. Such critics have been contrasted with those that supposedly fetishize the text (and by implication ignore ideology), notably Jacques Derrida, Paul DeMan, and Gilles Deleuze.

To postulate, as many critics have, a crude extrinsic-intrinsic opposition between the schools, however, is to oversimplify a complex critical picture. The so-called textualists also begin with the presumption of ideology. In fact, Deleuze and Guattari's endeavor throughout *Anti-Oedipus* is to question and bring to light ideologies and power relations in psychoanalysis which remain hidden from its surface formulations. Similarly, Derrida's deconstructing of philosophy involves working through its concepts to see "what this history may have concealed or excluded, constituting itself as history through this repression in which it has a stake."[21] Derrida demonstrated the metaphysical presuppositions in philosophical works by treating these works like literary texts. The analysis of language was in fact an analysis of logocentrism and ethnocentrism.[22] The differences between the two camps lie elsewhere. Most importantly, the textualists are marked in their refusal to view any social vision as absolute. If anything is venerated, it is the process of deconstruction. But that process itself continues to undercut its own discourse. The formulation of some kind of utopia or positive hermeneutic is therefore alien to textualism. Marxists, however, are able to postulate a utopia and an absolute methodology. Marxism, for Jameson, is an untranscendable horizon.[23] No less significant, possibly, is the fact that though the textualists see themselves as implicated in ideology, even in the very act of criticism, they (particularly Derrida and DeMan) seldom deal overtly with ideology. They therefore give the *appearance* of being concerned with language only.

In the context of this ideological-linguistic problematic, Mikhail Bakhtin is an important figure.[24] At once a Marxist and poststructuralist, Bakhtin is "a paradox from the standpoint of literal dating."[25] One of Bakhtin's major accomplishments is his ability to combine a textualist awareness of the linguistic (textual) nature of all value systems with a Marxist awareness of the social nature of language. "The study of verbal art," Bakhtin insists, "must overcome the divorce between an abstract 'formal' approach and an equally abstract 'ideological' approach."[26] His own works are successful attempts at doing so. Like the sophisticated Marxists, Bakhtin emphasizes the ideology of form but retains the textualist emphasis on relativity and difference. He examines the various nuances of a single word, but his unit of study is not a linguist's sentence but language in social use—an utterance; he emphasizes the socio-political bases of words but insists that words are not transparent reflections of a "reality" beyond language. David Carroll sees Bakhtin's importance in his deconstruction of the intrinsic-extrinsic problematic, in his refusal "to accept the 'inside' and 'outside' as separate and uncommunicating opposites at all."[27] It is no wonder that Bakhtin used his literary criticism—his analysis of Rabelais and Dostoevski, and his theories of the novel—to express his antiauthoritarian values and his belief in the social nature of the self. Celebrations of the polyphonic novel and carnival are obviously political. In order to make stylistic analysis ideological, Bakhtin begins by socializing linguistic concepts themselves. Instead of a study of "language," a grammatical category, he substitutes "discourse"; instead of analyzing the linguist's "sentence," he analyzes the "utterance." Language and ideology, in other words, are not contestatory but mutually constitutive realms because each is implicated in the other. As V. N. Volosinov/Bakhtin points out, "The domain of ideology coincides with the domain of signs. They equate with one another. Whenever a sign is present, ideology is present too. *Everything ideological possesses semiotic value.*"[28]

The significance of the linguistic-ideological equation becomes clear when we realize that 'ideology'as used by Bakhtin is a liberating rather than a repressive concept. Ideology does not refer to the false consciousness of the bourgeoisie, to doctrinal illusions that must be exposed and eradicated (the vulgar Marxist usage); neither does it refer to a repressive structure as evident in Barthes's statement "Ideology can only be dominant."[29] Ideology in Bakhtin's works refers primarily to the omnipresence of social organizations, to the fact that signs are always constructed only within such organizations. Because Bakhtin sees individual subjectivity as constituted by the social, signs cannot be autonomous. A word means something because of its socially constituted nature, and every word is contextual. Ideology in Bakhtin's usage can be explained as an idea system, socially determined, "something that *means.*"[30] Susan Stewart emphasizes the dynamic nature of Bakhtin's concept of ideology, both a "product and producer of social practices." "One's speech both reveals *and produces* one's position in class society."[31] No text, in this sense, can be separated from ideology, although every text is ideological in a different way.

For our purposes, here, the most important of Bakhtin's concepts is that of 'voice'. Because language for Bakhtin is not a set of grammatical categories but a system in social use, he conceives of words as inseparable from the speaking voices that utter them. Caryl Emerson explains, "For Bakhtin, words cannot be conceived apart from the voices who speak them; thus, every word raises the question of authority."[32] This notion of the speaking voice is far more complex than (although it includes) related concepts used by narratologists and reader response critics.[33] At times *voice* can simply refer to the words of a character or the implied voice of the author.[34] But voices and speakers, for Bakhtin, are not compositionally marked. "Voice zones," for instance, may only be stylistically designated.[35] Shifts in syntax and tone may indicate different voices even within passages demarcated as direct speech. On the other hand, because a word is "born in a dialogue as a living rejoinder within it," there are different interacting voices within each word.[36] Each word participates in a network of social interactions. *Voice* thus refers to an ideological speaking presence in the text, whether broadly thematic (though these are not synonymous) or minutely lexical. At no point, however, is it possible to identify all the voices in a text or an utterance so that it has a definite social or ideological referent.[37] But language is not merely communicative but polemical, and hidden polemic is pervasive in literary speech. "Every literary discourse more or less sharply senses its own listener, reader, critic, and reflects in itself their anticipated objections, evaluations, points of view."[38] Dostoevski's works, "taken as utterances of their author, are the same never-ending, internally unresolved dialogues among characters (seen as embodied points of view) and between the author himself and his characters."[39]

Hidden and overt polemic are central features of the personal-political narratives we are discussing here, because in these narratives writers are engaged in a liberal polemic with forms of cultural authoritarianism and standardization that they seek to dialogically question. Rhetorically, this polemic manifests itself in different ways. At the most fundamental level the polemic is present in parodies and subversions of cultural unanimity. It is also present in the writers' methods of including political and cultural difference into the narrative, the manner in which voices of Others are included.[40] Although, in the Bakhtinian sense, language is always fundamentally dialogic, that does not mean that language cannot be used in a coercive or authoritative manner. Whether the voices of Others are included in order to be marginalized or whether these voices create a productive indeterminacy will therefore indicate an extremely different politics. Finally, the polemic is implicitly present in the way the authorial voice is presented. Because a textual voice is an important way in which subjectivity is represented, modes of authorial voicing are in themselves significant political statements about conceptions of self, society, and community.

The study begins with an analysis of Benjamin Franklin's *Autobiography*. Franklin chronicles his life story in order to emphasize the unique development of self and society necessary for the founding of the new country. He continually subverts the privileges attendant upon heredity and acquired culture and proposes a society based on republican simplicity and a sense of self based on individual success. The rhetorical strategies of the text reflect a need to consolidate and unify a new world citizenry. Franklin speaks as a moral purist, a bold adventurer, a cunning businessman, and a respected statesman; he brings in voices of various others—litterateurs, poets, actors, priests, educators—and uses this multiplicity to polemically institute an individualistic self conducive to a society of emergent capitalism.

Literary liberal discourse in the mid-nineteenth century begins the critique of the business and commerce culture that continues till today. Thoreau questions the capitalist consensus legitimized by

Franklin and envisions a culture constituted by differences and a radical individualism. He undermines the culture of work and success by parodying its slogans, proverbs, and language, and thus creates a double-voiced discourse that shatters the hegemony of a singular culture. It is in *Walden* that we also see the emergence of an aesthetic culture based on a separation of the material and the spiritual which makes problematic the politics of difference that liberal discourse takes as its agenda.

In the early twentieth century the debate within liberalism becomes more self-conscious and conflictual but takes diverse forms even though the participants are three patricians: Henry James, Henry Adams, and Jane Addams. In *The American Scene*, James uses the separation between the material and spiritual in order to work out his conflictual liberal politics. He positions himself against the standardization of American capitalist democracy and astutely analyzes the reification of human relationships within capitalist society. On the other hand, James is ambivalent about giving up the consensual notion of a cultural and national identity. James speaks through a narrative voice that takes on multiple identities and protean qualities even as he fears the radically disruptive voices of the immigrant and the Jew which challenge the idea of an essential and singular American identity.

Adams's liberalism works by radicalizing and relativizing intellectual inquiry. Although Adams in the *Education* presents himself as a lone survivor of eighteenth century rationalism seeking certitudes in the world of twentieth century multiplicity, he delineates a process of education that is motivated by a search for caveats within seemingly proven systems of knowledge. Instead of staying within the rhetoric and language of a particular discipline, Adams questions the validity of disciplinary boundaries. Evolution, physics, history, politics, and religion are not autonomous modes of inquiry that the author follows but voices that dialogically interact, intersect, interpret, and thus modify each other.

Jane Addams is the most radical of the three patrician liberals and the one with the most agonized and divided political voices. *Twenty Years at Hull-House* begins as a narrative of Addams's marginalization as a bourgeois woman and becomes a narrative of an objective social scientist. Addams emphasizes the primacy of economic and cultural differences and simultaneously retains the concept of universal cultural values. But despite these dichotomies, which reflect Addams's paradoxical position as a bourgeois resident of the inner-city slums, Addams makes important contributions to the political effectiveness of radical, liberal discourse. Hull-House, both as project and metaphor, breaks the boundaries between culture and the masses and culture and the market which plagued thinkers like Thoreau and James and would again surface with James Agee's documentation of tenant life.

With Agee and Mailer we see two politically different versions of liberalism after the introduction of modernist aesthetics. In *Let Us Now Praise Famous Men*, a highly subjective documentary about three tenant families, Agee attempts to depict the tenants in all their variety and not simply as economic integers within capitalist society. What emerges is a problematic aestheticization of human subjects that results from a separation of the religious-aesthetic from the political. By asserting that a quasi-divine truth about the tenants exists prior to socio-ideological violation, and by claiming a mystical insight into this divinity in the tenants, Agee effectively depoliticizes the tenants and denies them a voice. Mailer, on the other hand, uses postmodern politics and aesthetics in *The Armies of the Night* to radicalize the liberal critique of consensus. Although he tends to romanticize a past of absolute virtues, Mailer, like Adams, welcomes the entry of other voices into his political analyses. Convinced of the necessity of a politics of difference, Mailer both celebrates the dispersive politics of the New Left and speaks through a voice that questions its own autonomy and singularity.

In contrast to the writers who participate, even if ambivalently, in the liberal consensus, Kingston offers a compelling instance of the fact that personal-political narratives of radical writers, who speak consciously from positions of marginality, dramatically reformulate conceptions of selfhood and authority. Marginal writers who seek to be radical have to question concepts of unity and coherence because their own political efficacy depends upon forcing a recognition of the values of difference and diversity upon the dominant culture. In *The Woman Warrior* Kingston writes polemically as a Chinese-American woman battling with a patriarchal, white American culture but does so from a radically unstable position. She writes as a woman but destabilizes the concept of gender; she speaks as a Chinese-American but questions racial definitions. The authorial voice in *The Woman Warrior* is thus highly provisional, always full of echoes of other voices, and never autonomous.

By analyzing the politics of voice in these texts, we see how ideologies such as liberalism are not simply present or reflections of inherent "American" values but exist in a state of struggle and tension that must not be overlooked. The problem, as Cecil F. Tate rightly points out, is that many works in American studies follow the dictates of "holism" (which in turn generates cultural monoliths), which is viewed not only as methodological but ontological.[41] Concepts such as 'the American tradition' or 'the American dream' or 'the American myth' are taken as self-evident, as if they indeed do represent the history and beliefs of an entire people, while the social conflicts, power struggles, and dominance exerted in order to maintain such cohesive social myths are neglected. In an examination of the totalizing impulse in studies of American literature, Russell J. Reising aptly observes that these "symbolic" analyses "deny the possibility...of studying American literature as a vehicle of social knowledge."[42] However, in recent years, American literary scholars have recognized that the very notion of a cultural center is in itself ideological and cannot be accepted as naturally present. Cathy N. Davidson, for instance, describes the constructed nature of literary tradition and points out the pernicious effects of a reductive theory of American identity on pedagogy.[43] John Carlos Rowe and Myra Jehlen have questioned the assumptions of coherence and unity that underlie many studies.[44] My study, having no investment in maintaining a homogenous American identity, gestures in a similar direction. It questions the idea of an accepted cultural center and a singular "American" identity in several ways: by examining highly politicized texts of major writers as quasi-radical critiques which exist in tension with the writers' participation in the dominant culture; by dramatizing the confrontation of major American writers with issues of otherness, difference, and social diversity; and by emphasizing the conflictual rhetorical strategies in these texts.

Some of the personal-political narratives under discussion here have been analyzed under the rubrics of other generic categories. Despite the fact that these categories are largely formalistic and ignore the politicized nature of these texts, it is necessary to examine the the-oretical premises of these categories and explain why I have chosen not to operate within them. By far the most numerous attempts at classifying these texts have been what we might call the "mixture" theories. Responding primarily to the works of Capote, Mailer, and Wolfe, critics have formulated theories to explain what has been vari-ously termed the "New Journalism" or the "Nonfiction Novel." Observations common to these critics are the following: that around the sixties there appeared a number of works embodying a new genre—the Nonfiction Novel or the New Journalism; though there were precedents to these works of the sixties (in works like *Life on the Mississippi* and *Walden*), the earlier works were of an essentially different nature;[45] these works were not merely "documentary" but employed "fictional" techniques. It is the use of conventions of "fiction," yet the "documentary" nature of these works, that has most preoccupied the critics.[46] While describing them variously as mixtures of fiction and journalism (Holowell), "fables of fact" (Hellman), "literary nonfiction" (Weber), or "fictual" (Zavarzadeh), critics have attempted to quantify the generic mixture of these "hybrid" texts.[47]

Obviously such criticism relies on and thus reifies several traditional taxonomies. Most importantly, it assumes the purity of forms such as "fiction" and "journalism" which are intermixed in the works of the sixties. Genres, in other words, are seen not as constructed categories but as essences. But the concept of a pure, inviolate genre is extremely problematic. Because texts always exist in social, cultural, and aesthetic relationships to other texts, the semantic and generic boundaries of any work are far from clear. To base an analysis on generic mixtures is therefore to invoke a purity that does not exist.

Moreover, most of these critics continue to invoke terms like *fact*, *fiction*, and *mimesis* without adequately questioning them. A major portion of these studies is still devoted to proving that, despite their being based on "real" experiences, these works are not really documents. Again, one is compelled to ask what a "mere document" really is. Narratologists like René Wellek, Robert Scholes, and Northrop Frye have, of course, offered classifications based on the fact-fiction dichotomy.[48] However, the very concepts of fact and fiction confidently used by narratologists and mimesis theorists have been effectively challenged both by historians and speech-act theorists.[49] To categorize texts according to factuality and fictionality is therefore to oversimplify language. Further, because any transcription of an experience involves selection, order, and weighing, the value of such an approach to genre is questionable.

Another category used to classify some of these works is that of autobiography. Although studies of autobiography are more diverse than those of the New Journalism, most are also dependent on assumptions of generic purity or cultural continuity. Robert F. Sayre, for instance, emphasizes the need to analyze distinctions between "fiction" and "truth."[50] He defines autobiography according to breadth of perspective and the importance given to childhood. Albert E. Stone views autobiography as a means of exploration rather than definition but still invokes differences between autobiography and "art" and uses formalized content definitions or "occasions" to examine the genre. Adams's *Education* thus takes as its occasion an old man looking back at a long career.[51] G. Thomas Couser, on the other hand, emphasizes cultural continuity. He sees the American autobiographical enterprise as a sacred one, a continuation of the Old Testament prophetic tradition. In all cases, autobiography is seen as a way of creating unity, and genre is treated as an essence.[52]

My decision to focus on liberal discourse within personal-political narratives has been dictated by the fact that in these narratives the clear foregrounding of an authorial voice and the strong political emphasis provides excellent grounds for the study of the ideology of form. There are obviously many works of fiction that are vehicles of liberal discourse and also many personal narratives that are not as overtly political as the ones discussed here.[53] My purpose in the following chapters is to deal with personal-political narratives in terms of both relationships and differences. I will focus both on their major characteristics and on the changes created among them by the varying relationships of voices in the texts.

2

Franklin's *Autobiography:*
Revolutionary Liberalism and
Authorial Control

Few persons in revolutionary America could have been as multifaceted as Benjamin Franklin. Scientific inventor, shopkeeper, printer, journalist, revolutionary politician, and elder statesman, Franklin was as much at home in Philadelphia as he was in England or the courts of France. As a writer Franklin used guises as various as those of the matronly Silence Dogood and the young, impecunious Poor Richard. But perhaps the most revealing of guises was one he used only once in his writing career. In May 1751 Franklin wrote a letter to his own newspaper, the *Gazette*, in which he attacked the British government for continuing its policy of exporting its criminals to the colonies. The letter was signed "Americanus."[1] Whether he was speaking about the virtues of thrift, frugality, and industry or satirizing contemporary fashions and conventions, Franklin emphasized that he spoke from the perspective of an emergent revolutionary society that challenged the status of the aristocracy and traditional class structures and the power of imperial Britain. As Americanus, he was the political voice of this new society.

This new society was moving from the goals of classical republicanism and Calvinism toward a new liberalism. Franklin, who had read and greatly admired John Locke, mythologized himself as a particularly American liberal, a "practical idealist and Protestant folk hero."[2] Franklin had little respect for hereditary privilege, a premise on which the English social order was constructed. In a letter to his daughter Sarah he joked about how honors based on heredity logically decreased with every generation.[3] And as early as 1769 he insisted that the only power that the King of England had over America was a legislative one and not a sovereign one.[4] Thus, despite the fact that he advocated moderation in the country's dealings with England prior to the revolutionary period, Franklin's vision was forward looking. That is why whether critics have criticized Franklin's cult of success or praised his philosophies, they have, following Vernon L. Parrington's lead, associated him with a line of thought antithetical to that followed by men like John Cotton, Jonathan Edwards, and Alexander Hamilton.[5] But whereas revolutionaries like Jefferson concluded that one could never, in all surety, prescribe a certain way of living because ethical values and social structures were always relative, Franklin could, in the guise of Americanus, propagate a particular lifestyle and set of values that would stay in the American liberal imagination.[6]

The basis of Franklin's philosophy was the liberal idea that ownership was the key to happiness. While in Ireland and Scotland he had spoken of the "happiness of New England where every man is a freeholder."[7] But Franklin was not interested in the peculiarities of the frontier or agrarian theories because he was an urbanite and saw urban America as the future of the country. He aimed, therefore, to make ownership in the city possible and desirable to all. This goal was at once one of radical equality and a demand for social unanimity. Franklin mythologized the solitary individual bound by no ties of dependency and motivated by the single need to achieve business success. And because business success could be best achieved by watchful personal habits like frugality, industry, and temperance, he mandated these virtues as necessary for an aspiring capitalist. That is why Franklin had to make the story of his material success in his *Autobiography* resemble a conduct book.[8] Wealth and virtue were not separate in Franklin's scheme because acquisition was a virtue, and, conversely, virtue was dependent on acquisition. As Franklin explains in the *Autobiography*, he wished to convey a certain type of instruction. He filled his almanac with "Proverbial Sentences, chiefly such as inculcated Industry and Frugality, as the Means of procuring Wealth and thereby securing Virtue, it being more difficult for a Man in Want to act always honestly."[9] That is why Max Weber, who gave Franklin a central place in his study of the emergence of capitalism, noted how persistently in the *Autobiography* the "duty of the individual toward the increase of his capital" was presented as a "peculiar ethic." The infraction of its rules was treated "not as foolishness but as forgetfulness of duty."[10]

Franklin's conception of an egalitarian society of virtuous, individualistic citizens bettering their material lives was both subversive and consensual. It reflected the dual inclinations of the revolutionary nationalist and of the incipient patriarch occupied with governance and control. Nowhere is this dual impulse in Franklin's liberalism more evident than in the narrative of his life, in which the author both dialogically subverts traditional class structures and positions of power and also uses a political voice that attempts to create consensus (and control differences) within the new republic. Franklin clearly conceived of the *Autobiography* as a public, political document, and it was used as such both by educators like Noah Webster and by businessmen like Thomas Mellon. Mellon attributed his own success as a financier to his reading of the *Autobiography* and recommended it to all young, aspiring men.[11] Franklin did not conceive the narrative of his life to be an outpouring of personal confessions in the manner of Rousseau or a spiritual journal in the manner of the Quaker pietist John Woolman. It was to be a polemical public document, meant to instruct young persons to worldly success.

The political intent of the *Autobiography* is evident in a letter by Benjamin Vaughan which Franklin requested be prefaced to Part II of the text. Vaughan clearly saw Franklin's life as an analogy to the life of the new republic. Vaughan requests the author to complete and publish the story of his life because it will "present a table of the internal circumstances of [his] country, which will very much tend to invite to it settlers of virtuous and manly minds" (BF 135). Again he reiterates the parallel: "All that has happened to you is also connected with the detail of the manners and situation of a rising people" (BF 135). Vaughan also emphasizes the subversive polemical thrust of the *Autobiography*: "Your account of yourself...will shew that you are ashamed of no origin; a thing the more important, as you prove how little necessary all origin is to happiness, virtue, or greatness" (BF 137).

When he wrote Part I of the *Autobiography* in 1771, Franklin had been in England for seven years working for the American cause and was beset with doubts about his success as an American agent.[12] His decision to address this portion of his autobiography to his son is part of his creation of a complex political voice. Franklin's son William was at this time an experienced public official and scarcely needed advice, but the assumption of a paternalistic voice made writing a manifesto of ethics more possible.[13] The opening paragraph of the *Autobiography* finds the narrator apparently groping for justifications for addressing the narrative to his son. In the vein of a family chronicler he writes, "Imagining it may be equally agreeable to you to know the Circumstances of my Life, many of which you are yet unacquainted with...I sit down to write them for you" (BF 43). But soon the narrator confesses to other motivations:

Having emerg'd from the Poverty and Obscurity in which I was
born and bred, to a State of Affluence and some Degree of Reputation in the World and having gone so far thro' Life with a considerable share of Felicity, the conducing Means I made use of,
which, with the Blessing of God, so well succeeded, my Posterity may like to know, as they may find some of them suitable to
their situations, and therefore fit to be imitated. (BF 43)

Franklin's purpose in writing the story of his life, then, was to celebrate the mythology of new America—the privatized individual's rise
to success in the marketplace. That he chose to retain the pretext of
addressing his son even nineteen years later when he was completing
his memoirs is politically significant. William, Franklin's illegitimate
son, was a Tory and had openly sided with the British during the revolutionary war. Contemporary readers would have been aware that
Franklin was trying to address and include in his readership British
loyalists whom he hoped to challenge. The fact that the loyalist was
his son, and could thus be addressed paternalistically, reversed and
subverted the popular revolutionary image of England as the parent
and the colonies as dutiful children.[14]

    The narrative of Part I of the *Autobiography* is also structured
around a series of subversions of forms of authority. The young
Franklin continually breaks relationships of dependency and powerlessness and, like an urban American Adam, sets out on his own each
time, becoming more independent than before. Franklin images his
yearnings for freedom as a young boy as his love for the sea. The
young Franklin works as assistant tallow chandler and soap boiler to
his father, but he "dislik[es] the Trade and has a strong Inclination for
the Sea" (BF 53). Because Franklin likes to read, his father tries to create a vocation for him as a printer. But as apprentice printer to his
brother James he chafes against the terms of his employment, where
"Tho' a Brother, he [James] considered himself as my Master, and me
as his Apprentice" (BF 68). In a later note to this part Franklin added,
"I fancy his harsh and tyrannical Treatment of me, might be a means
of impressing me with that Aversion to arbitrary Power that has stuck
to me thro' my whole Life" (BF 69). The description of Franklin's
apprenticeship with his brother clearly dramatizes the young boy's
subversion of this arbitrary power and his assertion of his individuality. Given the management of the newspaper for a short period while
his brother serves an unfair term in prison, Franklin makes haste to
initiate changes in the newspaper and soon also finds means to break
the indentures with his brother. His next job also involves a similar

egalitarian leveling of figures of authority. While working for Keimer's printing house in Philadelphia, the young Franklin has the satisfaction of being singled out for a meeting with the governor, Sir William Keith, while his employer looks enviously on; and while Franklin's fortunes continue to rise, Keimer daily accumulates credit till he is forced to go to Barbadoes. In these instances the author speaks subversively, demonstrating the triumph of the single individual over circumstances and structures of social power.

Franklin's emphasis on industry and frugality should not be interpreted to mean that he advocated a life of Spartan simplicity and saw luxurious living as sinful. He was, in fact, enough of a modern capitalist to see that the demand for luxuries would create employment for the next generation of Poor Richards. In the *Autobiography* he records his own satisfaction at having earned well enough to be able to eat with a silver spoon. What Franklin criticized was the class significance of luxuries as they were associated with taste and culture in traditional class-structured societies. That is why he liked to parody signifiers of class. The older statesman reveled in the sensation he created in France by wearing a fur cap and scandalizing the "powdered heads of Paris."[15] Franklin liked to think of himself as a radical egalitarian and successfully projected that image to his admirers. When John Adams arrived at Passy, he noted that Franklin's reputation was familiar to all—coachmen, peasant, chambermaid. "When they spoke of him they seemed to think he was to restore the golden age.... His plans and his example were to abolish monarchy, aristocracy, and hierarchy throughout the world."[16] In the *Autobiography* Franklin wished to create a similar subversive and egalitarian consciousness. That is why he repudiates luxuries insofar as they are signifiers of class status, and he demonstrates the folly of those who try to acquire the habitude of the upper classes. Franklin describes, for example, the downfall of his rival, the owner of another printing shop, not so much in economic terms as in terms of class. Franklin proposes a partnership to this rival owner, David Harry, which the latter rejects with scorn. Franklin then goes on to explain why Harry becomes destitute. "He was very proud, dress'd like a Gentleman, lived expensively, took much Diversion and Pleasure abroad, ran in debt, and neglected his Business, upon which all Business left him; and finding nothing to do, he follow'd Keimer to Barbadoes" (BF 126). The author uses David Harry's decline to symbolize the end of aristocracy and to advocate an egalitarian order.

But although Franklin's liberal individualism questions inherited social structures, liberalism as ideology also works as a means of creating social homogeneity. New England statesmen like John Winthrop, William Bradford, and, later, Cotton Mather had always been concerned about the threat of anarchy from rough settlers.[17] The stringent rules of these theocratic states were formulated in part because of this threat. In prerevolutionary America, Franklin stood at a similar threshold of political dissension and thus used his writings to provide ideological coherence to the new republic. Franklin was aware that he was addressing not only people who were looking for means of creating their fortunes but also many to whom this liberal-capitalist ideology was unacceptable. These readers would include the devout Christians who questioned the ethics of capitalism and the aristocracy who feared the breakup of traditional classes. Franklin explains his own techniques of persuasion in the *Autobiography* when he writes, "If you would inform...a positive, dogmatical Manner in advancing your Sentiments, may provoke Contradictions and prevent candid Attention" (BF 65). A more workable method would be to give the appearance of being dialogically open to other voices and of admitting other ideological voices into the narrative.

In the opening paragraphs of the *Autobiography* the narrator delineates what appear to be the diverse voices in which he will speak. To his son, who might want to know the circumstances of his life, he speaks as a father; to his posterity, who might want to imitate his success, he speaks as a statesman and teacher. And when he justifies the preoccupation with his career, his "indulg[ing] the Inclination so natural in old Men," he speaks as a forgetful old man (BF 44). But in all these apparently different voices Franklin valorizes the ethos of capitalistic individualism. As his friend Abel James discerned, the *Autobiography* would promote a "Spirit of Industry and early Attention to Business, Frugality and Temperance" (BF 134). In order to impress this singular message upon his readers, Franklin had to appropriate and control all other ideological voices.

The most apparent technique used to control and subordinate other voices in the *Autobiography* is that of the instructive episode followed by a direct address to the reader. The voice of the potentially hostile reader, in these cases, is not dramatized enough to create ideological multiplicity or to question the ideology of the authorial voice. It is introduced in order to be appropriated and contained by the authorial voice. An example of this kind of containment of other voices occurs in the 1778 section of the *Autobiography*. Franklin describes his unsatisfactory business dealings with an honest though careless South Carolina printer. After the printer's death, his widow, a much better accountant, keeps good records and augments the business.

The instructional value of the story, Franklin informs us, lies in its applicability to women whose education has largely been frivolous. They are the readers to whom this particular episode is directed:

> I mention this Affair chiefly for the Sake of recommending that Branch of Education for our young Females, as likely to be of more Use to them and their children in Case of Widowhood than either Music and Dancing, by preserving them from Losses by Imposition of crafty Men, and enabling them to continue perhaps a profitable mercantile House with establish'd Correspondence till a Son is grown fit to undertake and go on with it, to the lasting Advantage and enriching of the Family. (BF 166–67)

The above paragraph is a masterful example of reader manipulation and control. Franklin attempts to draw the attention of women by resorting to the traditional image of women as part of the "weaker" sex and trying to appeal to their needs for independence. On the other hand, it is obvious that Franklin is not questioning the hierarchies of patriarchal culture. The widow is encouraged to continue keeping shop only till the next adult male in the family can assume control. The woman without thoughts of practical education is therefore not endangering her emancipation but rather the culture of nascent capitalism. The voice of the woman averse to business is introduced not as a challenge to the values of individualism and profit making but as the voice of folly. Franklin is also careful to associate business success with domestic happiness, the "lasting Advantage and enriching of the family." The frivolous woman pales in comparison to the "real" woman, the businesswoman who augments the finances and thus, it is suggested in true Lockean logic, the happiness of her family. In like manner, Franklin uses the instructive episode to instill the values of capitalist culture into teachers of Latin and people fond of disputation.

As we mentioned earlier, Franklin was one of the revolutionary statesmen who formulated a liberal discourse that moved beyond both Calvinistic notions of sin and depravity and classical republicanism, which stressed virtue as the fundamental quality of a good citizen. John Diggins reminds us, "The idea of virtue was not even mentioned in the Declaration."[18] But Franklin could not ignore the appeals of these former ideologies for his readers, and in a moment of authorial double-voicing he tells us that he considered titling the narrative of his life *The Art of Virtue*. Actually, *The Science of Virtue* would have been a more appropriate title because Franklin, in true Enlightenment fashion, conceived of virtue as an estate that could be achieved once a reasonable

plan had been formulated. Franklin's plan was to tabulate a list of thir-
teen virtues which could be sequentially acquired. Readers looking for
classical reverence for virtue or for strict Calvinist and Puritan morality
would find it in the *Autobiography* but in such a manner that it was sub-
ordinated to and made to serve the liberal-capitalist ideology.[19]

Franklin's attempt to contain the ideology of classical republicanism is evident in the manner in which the task of arriving at moral perfection is framed in the narrative. He wants to devise the project of
virtue, Franklin tells us, because he distrusts the narrowness of particular creeds and instead of striving to make people good Presbyterians,
for example, wants to make them "good Citizens" (BF 147). The thir-
teen virtues of good citizenry, in order, are "Temperance," "Silence,"
"Order," "Resolution," "Frugality," "Industry," "Sincerity," "Justice,"
"Moderation," "Cleanliness," "Tranquility," "Chastity," and "Humili-
ty." The order of the virtues is perhaps as revealing as the list itself. It
obviously prioritizes those that are conducive to individual success
over those that maintain bonding within the community. "Sincerity"
and "Justice," the virtues that enhance relationships between citizens,
are ambivalently placed in the middle of the list. Further, Franklin's
intention to acquire only "the *Habitude* of all these Virtues" is clearly
antithetical to Calvinist and classical notions of good citizenry (BF
150). Following the description of the project of arriving at moral perfection, Franklin outlines its usefulness. Franklin's project leads to the
"early Easiness of his Circumstances," the "Acquisition of his For-
tune," "some Degree of Reputation among the Learned," and finally
"honorable Employs" (BF 157). With the project of moral perfection,
then, Franklin appropriates some of the rhetoric of Puritan moralism,
and even though he puts it to different use, it creates some double-
voicing in the text.

Another way in which Franklin both appropriates and subverts
Calvinist notions of sin and repentance is by emphasizing the key
"errata" of his youth. Although Franklin notes the errata in the manner of a repentant sinner (so that he can instruct youth on the necessity of virtue), he simultaneously embeds the ethical implications of the
errata by using the language of profit and loss. Take, for example,
Franklin's account of his attempts to seduce Mrs T., the lover of his
friend Ralph. When Ralph borrows money from Franklin and moves
to a Berkshire village to teach, Franklin, in Ralph's absence, attempts
"familiarities" with Mrs T. Here Franklin momentarily adopts the
voice of the repentant sinner: "I grew fond of her Company, and being
at this time under no Religious Restraints, and presuming on my
Importance to her, I attempted Familiarities (another Erratum) which

she repuls'd with a proper Resentment, and acquainted him [Ralph] with my Behavior" (BF 99). However, the voice of the moralist is soon overruled by the voice of the pragmatic businessman. Franklin does not deal with the ethical implications of his erratum but duly notes its effect on his fortunes. On learning of Franklin's conduct, Ralph declares himself free of all obligations to him. This, Franklin deduces, refers to financial obligations. "I was never to expect his Repaying me what I lent to him or advanc'd for him" (BF 99). But there are unexpected indirect gains from the erratum. "In the Loss of his Friendship I found myself reliev'd from a Burthen. I now began to think of getting a little Money beforehand; and expecting better Work, I left Palmer's to work at Watts's" (BF 99).

It is clear that Franklin found that a major threat to the new capitalist ideology would come from those who could repudiate the workings of this hegemonic order by attempting to live outside the workings of the culture of individualism and success. Franklin attempts to deal with the voices of these Others by disallowing them to participate fully in the text. An example of this authorial control is the translation of monasticism into economics. To demonstrate how an individual's way to success is dependent upon frugality, Franklin tallies the gains that resulted from his thrifty measures during his stay in England. His temperance lowers his living costs, and his good habits become a good bargaining power, enabling him to persuade his landlady to decrease his rent. As if merely multiplying the illustration, Franklin continues with an account of the manner in which a pious Catholic woman lives. Having resolved to lead the life of a nun, this lady donates all her estate to charity, lives on twelve pounds a year, remains confined to her room, and confesses daily to a priest. Franklin describes her living quarters thus: "The Room was clean, but had no other Furniture than a Mattress, a Table with a Crucifix and Book, a Stool…and a Picture over the Chimney of St. Veronica, displaying her Handkerchief with the miraculous Figure of Christ's bleeding Face on it, which she explain'd to me with great Seriousness" (BF 103). Such an existence was, in fact, a challenge to the ethic of individualism, work, and success that Franklin was propounding. But by rhetorical address to the reader Franklin converts this instance into a Poor Richard tale about the merits of parsimonious living and frugality necessary for a citizen aspiring to business success. "I give it," says Franklin, "as another Instance on how small an Income Life and Health may be supported" (BF 103).

At other times the authorial voice defuses the challenge of these religious voices by using the garb of Enlightenment reason and rationality. The itinerant preacher Rev. George Whitfield, who drew his auditors by "his common Abuse of them, by assuring them they were naturally *half Beasts and half Devils*," must surely have been a threat to the liberal Franklin, who assured every person his freedom and showed him the way to success in the social-material world (BF 175). Franklin himself confesses to being moved by the Reverend's appeals for charity and finds himself making a donation when he had resolved otherwise. However, the manner of narration here ensures that the voice of the itinerant preacher does not really question the power of the authorial voice. Describing his experience of being at one of Whitfield's sermons, Franklin turns Whitfield's sermon into his own experiment in reason and calculation. "I had the Curiosity to learn how far he could be heard…. Imagining then a Semi-Circle, of which my Distance should be the Radius, and that it were fill'd with Auditors, to each of whom I allow'd two square feet, I computed that he might well be heard by more than Thirty-Thousand. This reconcil'd me to the Newspaper Accounts of his having preach'd to 25000 People in the Fields, and to the antient Histories of Generals haranguing whole Armies, of which I had sometimes doubted" (BF 179).

In the above instances the author controls other ideological voices by means of what we have called the *instructive episode*. Another frequently used method of introducing heterogenous voices in the *Autobiography* is that of the *contrastive fable*. Here the array of ideologies and voices that Franklin seeks to control are dramatized. The pessimist, the aspiring poet, the aspiring actor, the speculative philosopher—all of whom challenge the creed of work, success, and ownership—are put to test on the business streets of Philadelphia. The contrastive fable operates by first associating these "types" with both public and private loss and then by giving contrasting examples of the felicitous actions of the industrious hero. Franklin's manner of introducing these adversarial voices into the narrative is one that is often used by other liberal writers of the personal-political narrative. Despite his parody of Franklin, Thoreau would also use typified characters who would serve as the butt of his satire. Here is how Franklin introduces the "Croaker": "There are Croakers in every Country always boding its Ruin. Such a one lived in Philadelphia…an elderly Man, with a wise Look, and very grave Manner of speaking. His Name was Samuel Mickle" (BF 116). Because the creed of industry and success assumed that success for the individual was always possible and because the liberal consensus demanded a faith in the workings of capitalism, pessimism about the future of business was early associated with a lack of patriotism and a pernicious disruption of the social order. Franklin thus uses the example of Samuel Mickle to demonstrate the inevitable business failure of all such pessimists. Mickle advises Franklin not to buy a printing house "because it was an expensive Undertaking and the Expence would be lost; for Philadelphia was a sinking Place, the People already half Bankrupts or near being so; all Appearances of the contrary, such as new Buildings and the Rise of Rents being to his certain Knowledge fallacious.... And he gave me such a Detail of Misfortunes, now existing or that were seen to exist, that he left me half-Melancholy" (BF 116). Because of his lack of faith in business enterprise, Mickle refuses to invest in property till he is finally forced to spend five times the amount years later. Franklin, in contrast, invests in the printing house and prospers in his business.

But perhaps more than croakers and religious enthusiasts Franklin had to control the voices of those whose activities were seemingly nonutilitarian. Although a writer himself, in the *Autobiography* Franklin supported the view that the arts did not constitute work or productive activity. Ironically, Franklin assented to the separation between the material and ideal that proponents of aesthetic ideology would subscribe to a generation later. Franklin distinguishes between prose, a utilitarian tool, and poetry, mere fancy and verbal play. His own experiments with poetry are short-lived because his father wisely discourages him from wasting his time by telling him that "Verse-makers were generally Beggars." "So I escap'd being a Poet, most probably a very bad one. But...Prose Writing has been of great Use to me in the course of my Life" (BF 60). As an adult Franklin himself echoes his father's opinions about poetry: "I approv'd the amusing one's self with Poetry now and then, so far as to improve one's Language, but no farther" (BF 90). Again, the use of the word *amusing* to describe poetic activity reinforces the separation between productive work and nonproductive play and art.

Because Franklin was offering the *Autobiography* as a guide to young people who aspired to bourgeois ownership, and to the world at large to show how in America every poor person could aspire to be a capitalist, he could not endorse the lifestyles of poets and scholars. Like Plato's madmen, they had to be exiled. Poets and scholars are thus figures of contempt, and Franklin takes care to introduce only poor practitioners of the craft in the *Autobiography*. Translated to the ideology of work and ownership, verse making would beget idleness, which would further abet reckless habits. It is through this kind of semantic trick of appropriation that Franklin sequentially connects poets, dandies, idlers, and drunkards. In the *Autobiography* most of the characters given to too much "learning" or art await inevitable ruin. George Webb, the itinerant actor and poet, James Ralph, the aspiring poet, and Collins, the student of mathematics and philosophy, all have dismal futures. So much does Franklin reinforce the connection that images of the versifier or actor become icons of foppery.

The most interesting example of the scholar-turned-degenerate is that of Franklin's childhood friend, Collins. Collins is a "Bookish Lad" who wins arguments with Franklin more by his eloquence and fluency than by reason. His collection of books constitutes a "pretty Collection of Mathematics and Natural Philosophy" (BF 82–83). Collins devotes more time to reading than Franklin, develops his skills in mathematics, and is respected by the clergy for his learning. Within the exemplary and instructive intent of the *Autobiography* the inclusion of such a character would have served no rhetorical purpose. The voice of the reasonably learned scholar served neither instructive nor contrastive purpose and threatened to undermine the singular devotion to industry and frugality that the stately and patriarchal author was recommending to the young. Franklin himself read and debated, but, as he was always careful to point out, did so in moderation and used these abilities to further his business. But because Collins did not use his learning in a similar fashion, he had to be used as an example of the dangers of pure learning alone. "While I liv'd in Boston most of my Hours of Leisure for Conversation were spent with him, and he continu'd a sober as well as an industrious Lad...; but during my Absence he had acquir'd a Habit of Sotting with Brandy; and...he had been drunk every day since his Arrival at New York.... He had gam'd too and lost his Money" (BF 84). The omission of any reasons given for Collins's falling into bad ways here is rhetorically effective. The implication clearly is that pure learning is inherently degenerative to the moral fiber of a person.

Ralph, the poet, presents a similar contrastive example. It is appropriate that Ralph, a genteel, eloquent, pretty talker, aspires at first to be an eminent poet and then an actor. Not surprisingly, Ralph also assumes a false identity and falls into debt. Franklin, in contrast, works industriously at the printing house, acquires a degree of influence among his co-workers, and achieves recognition from his employer. After the misfortunes of Ralph and Collins, the decline of George Webb from Oxford scholar to bought servant occasions no surprise. Webb, after all, had fallen prey to acting and writing verse, the consequences of which were all too well known.

The instructional intent of the aforementioned examples becomes clearer if we see, in contrast, the manner in which Franklin describes several of his own accomplishments. Franklin does not present his scientific experiments or inventions as actions to be imitated because they could serve an instructional purpose. Knowing full well that he was creating a manifesto for a cohesive new world citizenry, Franklin was careful to deemphasize his learning and ingenuity. While creating a consensual, individualistic society, it was imperative to denounce and mock ambitions that were not directly associated with use value. The image of the frivolous man of letters served this purpose.

Franklin was not the first statesman or writer of the personal-political narrative to use these instructive and contrastive methods for consolidating power and creating ideological hegemony. Many Puritan legislators used similar rhetorical strategies in their personal-political narratives as well. But because these legislators understood well that they were exercising precarious power over a populace ill-inclined to think of their immigration as spiritual, they had to forcefully denounce all "evil" elements. This meant, in a sense, acknowledging their arbitrary power and justifying their means of governance. In his *Of Plymouth Plantation*, for example, William Bradford included exemplary biographies of men like Brewster and the contrasting villainies of people like Thomas Morton, whose bacchanalian excesses were in opposition to the mission of the spirituals. But Bradford could not dismiss these miscreant voices as outside of and powerless before the body politic; he recognized that these voices were potent enough to challenge the power structure of the colonies, and therefore he repeatedly justified the mission of the city on the hill. With the liberal temper, on the other hand, there was no need to justify the culture of ownership and individualism because it could be shown to appeal to the desires and interests of all. Other voices could pose only a limited challenge to the ideology of liberal capitalism and did not therefore cause ruptures in the narrative or question the power of the authorial voice.

The structure of the *Autobiography* also provides an early insight into the relationship between liberal individualism and community. In the middle of Part III Franklin shifts the discourse to deal with the public projects that occupied him during the later years of his life. The bulk of Part III is taken up with Franklin's efforts to develop an indigenous means of fortifying the colonies. The remainder describes the various public projects that Franklin initiated: public libraries, street paving, cleaning, street lighting, and so forth. This shift in subject matter does not, however, constitute a change in the conception of subjectivity and individualism presented so far.[20] The human subject is still conceived of as autonomous and whole, dependent only on herself or himself, and individualism still forms the basis of society. The public projects signify a nationalism and social pride by no means at odds with the notion of solitary individualism. As Tocqueville had discovered, in the culture of nascent capitalism, conceptions of community were paradoxically based on "self interest rightly understood," the principle that the personal advantage of each individual is furthered by doing good for all.[21] Within the culture of liberal individualism, the concept of community is thus distanced from changes in subjectivity and identity. Robert Shulman points out that Franklin, like other Lockeans, saw "the world in general as separate and distinct from the individual self." "Ideologically, Franklin's view of society minimized close ties and cohesiveness."[22] In fact, because the individual and social realms were essentially separate for him, Franklin could divide the narrative of his life into his own, personal, individual activities and the activities in which he acted as a "public" person.

Franklin's *Autobiography* reveals both the radical and hegemonic roots of liberal discourse as they are developed within personal-political narratives over the next two centuries. Through a great deal of rhetorical sophistication Franklin manages to dialogically question and subvert the hierarchies of class and traditional family structure and also to control the voices of those that threaten the culture of liberal capitalism. Despite the various voices he adopts, he speaks through a language of power and control and advocates the ideology of autonomous individualism that remains, in different forms, in future liberal personal-political narratives. The *Autobiography* also raises issues of continued importance in later personal-political narratives: the relationship between the authorial voice and political agenda and the working out of a politics through an interaction of voices.

3

Carnival Rhetoric, Aestheticism, and Transcendence in *Walden*

By the mid-nineteenth century Franklin's success myth of the self-made man had captured the imagination of the nation; indeed, it had become part of the national character and no longer possessed the subversive implications it had in the revolutionary period. Success manuals for young men now proliferated in the market and were consumed eagerly by ambitious youth.[1] Bolstered by a growing urban population and increasing private enterprises, the Lockean imperative to ownership and property became a business goal for all.[2] The historian Bray Hammond vividly describes the money-grabbing fever of the period: "People were led as they had not been before by visions of money-making. Liberty became transformed into *laissez faire*. A violent, aggressive, economic individualism became established."[3] The eighteen-thirties were the period of a speculative boom. A writer describing the boom said, "A young man who went to any of our large cities penniless was considered a blockhead if he did not report himself worth one or two hundred thousand dollars in a few years."[4]

New England transcendentalists took it as their agenda to attack this culture of ownership, success, and possessive individualism. Whitman questioned the very roots of capitalism by undermining the concept of a singular and autonomous subject. The speaker of "Song of Myself" is a filter through which different social voices pass. He can become in turns the hounded slave, the bridegroom, the mashed fireman with broken breastbone, and he delights to merge himself with whatever he sees. Instead of creating a defined, individualized self, Whitman revels in making the boundary between self and Other highly problematic. Emerson and Thoreau, on the other hand, critique the business culture not by questioning the concept of individualism but by resorting to a different kind of individualism—one of radical nonconformism. Emerson dismisses society as a "joint-stock company in which the members agree, for the better securing of his bread to each shareholder, to surrender the liberty and culture of the eater."[5] Emerson's individualism went so far as to advocate nonconformism from all associations, including the abolitionists. Thoreau similarly celebrated an individualized and privatized self as a source of value and tried the Walden experiment partly to prove the material possibility of living outside of, and in opposition to, the dictates of the business culture.

The radical liberalism of Emerson and Thoreau was partly an attack against aspects of Lockean liberalism that Franklin had not questioned. Emerson and Thoreau questioned the idea that the right to property was the motivating factor for human action; instead of a society built on the principle of ownership, they advocated a mode of living that did not bind individuals in any set way. Human beings were all autonomous and different. But at the same time Emerson and Thoreau's individualism relied on a problematic separation of life and art that tempered its radicalism. Raymond Williams has noted that, with the emergence of market society in the nineteenth century, culture became "the court of appeal in which real values were determined, usually in opposition to the 'factitious' values thrown up by the market and similar operations of society."[6] If market society caused the alienation of art from society, the desire to maintain and perpetuate these separations led to a problematic aestheticism, an endorsement of a spiritual and mystical unity beyond and above all social differences.[7] *Walden* clearly exemplifies the energies and dilemmas of radical individualism and aesthetic ideology.

Walden is foremost a text of social and political criticism. It is clear that Thoreau wished to write polemically and saw literature as a forum for subverting existing institutions. His vision of the author was that of a "Cincinnatus in literature" who attempt[ed] to make his readers "dangerous to existing institutions."[8] On the other hand, he was aware that his radical individualism and nonconformism were at odds with the demands of the public. Recording in his journal his afterthoughts about public lecturing, Thoreau wrote of his audience thus: "I feel that the public demand an average man,—average thought and manners,—not originality nor even absolute excellence. You cannot interest them except as you are like them and sympathize with them."[9] Whereas in the *Autobiography* Franklin attempted to ensure that his readers would not hanker after difference and diversity, and that they would idolize him as the embodiment of a national archetype, the self-made man, to Thoreau the possibility of being thus regarded by the public (and being popular) was dangerous. Like many liberals of his day, such as Josiah Warren, Ezra Heywood, and William B. Greene, Thoreau despised averages and aggregates.[10] Thoreau writes about a fear of "cheapening" himself by attempting to interest the public and avows not to do so.[11] We can obviously see here Thoreau's attempt to rationalize the actual unpopularity he had met with in the lecture circuit; but Thoreau also saw his attainment of obscurity as his resistance to mass society. In *Walden* he similarly urged his readers to follow the bents of their own wills, to imbibe difference as a principle. Early in *Walden* he declares, "I desire that there may be as many different persons in the world as possible; but I would have each one be very careful to find out and pursue *his own* way and not his father's or his mother's or his neighbor's instead."[12] Like Emerson in the "Divinity School Address," Thoreau urges his readers to dismantle the altars of imitation; most importantly, he urges them not to believe in the omnipresent ideology of business profit and success.

Thoreau's move to Walden gave him a position from which to critique and reinterpret the marketplace, to mimic, parody, and undermine its conventions. From the very first paragraph of *Walden* Thoreau makes us aware of his challenge to the business culture. Under a chapter titled "Economy" Thoreau tells us how he, like the self-made man Franklin praised, "earned [his] living by the labor of [his] hands only" (W 3). But the rest of the narrative details his deliberate experiments in loafing, lazing, disorder, and nonprofitability. The rhetoric of *Walden* replicates this kind of parodic appropriation and dialogic questioning of liberal capitalism. Thoreau assails the business-oriented ideologies of his readers by using their expressions, momentarily adopting their views, and then exposing these views through a parodic counterlogic and counterlanguage. Reinterpreting the lexicon of his culture was crucial to Thoreau for his polemical stance. In the final chapter of *Walden* Thoreau assesses the nature of his linguistic experiments:

> I fear chiefly lest my expression may not be *extra-vagant* enough, may not wander far enough beyond the narrow limits of my daily experience, so as to be adequate to the truth of which I have been convinced. *Extravagance!* it depends on how you are yarded.... I desire to speak somewhere *without* bounds...; for I am convinced that I cannot exaggerate enough even to lay the foundation of a true expression. Who that has heard a strain of music feared then lest he should speak extravagantly any more forever? (W 324)

The key issues of *Walden* are raised here: the nature of the language, the role of the authorial voice, and the character of the reader. Language for Thoreau is never mere stylistics. He is aware of the ideological implications of language and of the inseparability of form and content. He is anxious to demonstrate the limits of the language of his culture and to transgress these limits. Thoreau's separation of the word *extravagant* emphasizes both its Latin origins: *extra* (outside) and *vagari* (to wander). He wants to use a language that will wander outside the bounds of socially acceptable ways of thought. Wandering, rambling, and walking are metaphors Thoreau uses to suggest the freedom of thought from socially defined limits and conventions. But Thoreau is also aware that part of the polemical force of his language derives from its oppositional value, the presence of a limiting social context, or, as Thoreau puts it, extravagance depends upon how one is yarded. We also note how in the above passage Thoreau illustrates the concept of extravagance by recontextualizing the word itself; the word *extravagant* acquires its multiple, "extra" connotations because of the different ways in which it is used. Thoreau's effort throughout *Walden* is similarly to question the ideological limits of language by freeing it from singular signification.

We might think of Thoreau's linguistic experiments as "carnivalistic." For Mikhail Bakhtin the carnival world is democratic, permeated with a laughter that destroys all forms of authority and breaks social codes. Carnivalistic life is "life turned inside out." "The laws, prohibitions, and restrictions that determine the structure and order of ordinary, that is, noncarnival, life are suspended during carnival."[13] Although the carnival is, by its very nature, a temporary ritual which appeases the have-nots for the moment only, the rituals themselves are ideologically significant. Acts like crowning and mock crowning make us aware of the relativity of power structures. In *Walden* Thoreau carnivalizes language in order to invite his readers to participate in the subversion of the cultural consensus.[14] The fictional readers that Thoreau incorporates into his narrative are ones who belong to the business culture; Thoreau strives to demonstrate the falsity of the conformist and commercial ideologies which these readers hold. In order to do so, however, he knows that he must speak to and use the very language of his readers. The epigraph to the book, "I do not propose to write an ode to dejection, but to brag as lustily as chanticleer in the morning, standing on his roost, if only to wake my neighbors up," is an assertion of his endeavor both to speak to his readers from within their worlds and to jolt them to an unexpected awareness of its limitations. The most apparent technique Thoreau uses to this end is to create reader-characters who subscribe to the ethos of competition and success and then to parody these views.

A general picture of the readers Thoreau later admonishes emerges from his direct characterizations of them in "Economy." These characterizations are preceded by verbal cues indicating direct address: "I speak to," "To those who would," "Some of you," and so forth. His readers include New Englanders convinced that their conditions cannot improve (W 4), the asphyxiated poor "gasping for breath" (W 6), those leading "mean and sneaking lives" (W 6), the "mass of men who are discontented" (W 16), those in "moderate circumstances" blindly following convention (W 35), those "who would not know what to do with more leisure than they now enjoy" (W 70), and the "class of unbelievers" who cannot imagine how one can live as simply as Thoreau (W 64). The definition of his readers through a material calculus is appropriate to the language of economy. Washington Irving had characterized America as the "Land of the Almighty Dollar." Thoreau records the moral deterioration consequent upon adopting such a self-definition and records his own liberal dissent from this definition. Whether rich, poor, or middling, Thoreau's readers form a mass motivated by discontent and hunger for more consumption of goods.

These value systems are reflected in the typified characters that Thoreau mocks. In fact, they are less characters as conventionally conceived than ideologues of what Thoreau perceives is a debased society.[15] As Joseph J. Moldenhauer notes, "Thoreau creates individual characters who express attitudes to be refuted by the narrator and who serve as foils for his wit".[16] Thoreau's wit or extra-vagance involves stretching the implications of established conventions to their illogical conclusions until they appear ludicrous and the authorial voice's indictment of them necessary. Contrasting what he lives for with what his neighbors live for, for example, Thoreau depicts the regular and monotonous existence of the newsmonger thus:

> Hardly a man takes a half hour's nap after dinner, but when he wakes up he holds up his head and asks, "What's the news?" as if the rest of mankind had stood his sentinels. Some give directions to be waked every half hour, doubtless for no other purpose; and then to pay for it, they tell what they have dreamed. After a night's sleep the news is as indispensable as the breakfast. "Pray tell me any thing new that has happened to a man any where on this globe,"—and he reads it over his coffee and rolls, that a man had his eyes gouged out this morning on the Wachito River; never dreaming the while that he lives in the dark unfathomed mammoth cave of this world, and has but the rudiment of an eye himself." (W 93–94)

At a very fundamental level we see how Thoreau mocks those habitu-
ated to reading the news by exaggerating their actions or surrounding
these actions by extravagant contexts. The news-hungry reader is a
comic character continually distraught, ill, and agitated in his anxiety
to know current news items. The carnivalization here proceeds by a
continual pattern of reader characterization followed by a commentary by the authorial voice. The picture of the reader waking up from
the postdinner nap, for example, is followed by the authorial voice's
acerbic questioning of the importance of the news ("as if the rest of
mankind had stood his sentinels"); the reader's interest in the sensa-
tional (a man having his eyes gouged out) is similarly trivialized by
the suggestion that the reader is himself gouged of his inner vision
and of original insight. At a more socially conscious level this carnivalization calls attention to the alienation of human beings within
bourgeois society. Within such a society people relate to each other
only as producers or consumers of commodities and begin to perceive
each other only in relation to commodities. The reader in the above
passage is a compulsive consumer and lives and acts only in relation
to the "news," which to him is a commodity to be consumed. This is
not to suggest that Thoreau anticipated Marx, even though critics
have found pre-Marxist tendencies in Thoreau.[17] Thoreau, like most of
the liberal writers discussed here, is sensitive to the social costs of
capitalism and the ideology of ownership. His critique of ownership
and possessive individualism, in fact, makes him a close cousin to the
literary compatriot who seems most unlike him—Henry James. But
the problem with Thoreau's attack on capitalistic ideology, as we will
see later, lies in his inability to find a viable stance, distanced enough
from capitalism, from which to voice his critique. However, the
method of the critique itself and the carnivalization of capitalist ideology introduces a double voicing that questions the hegemony of a singular culture. The creation of antagonistic, typified reader-characters
is one way of questioning this hegemony.

It is important to emphasize that this reader characterization, the
attacks on social conformity by the authorial voice, and the consequent
subversion of the capitalist center are integral parts of *Walden*. Just as
Franklin created rhetorical strategies to contain the difference of ideologies inimical to the culture of possession and ownership, Thoreau
maintains an attack on the ideologies that make this culture cohere.
This polemic is not limited to merely the first few chapters of *Walden*.
Even in "The Ponds," the chapter that most formalist critics have
viewed as the central one, Thoreau assaults the voices of monetary
value and ownership that characterize the Concordian farmer. Thore-

au castigates the farmer for whom "everything has its price; who would carry the landscape, who would carry his God to market, if he could get anything for him" (W 196). He assails the crude ownership of the landlord who names a pond "Flint's pond" after himself and to whom "the reflecting surface of a dollar" is more endearing than the surface of the pond (W 195). In fact, nearly every chapter introduces character-ideologues whose voices Thoreau carnivalizes. There are readers who question Thoreau's solitary life ("Solitude"), the hosts of restless visitors who demand "hospitalality" ("Visitors"), the labor-loving farmers incapable of "studying" beans ("The Bean-Field"), the John Fields who love servitude ("Baker Farm"), and so on.[18]

Overt characterization of the voices of antagonist readers, however, is only the most apparent method of carnivalization. *Walden* is shot through with voices and countervoices, questions and responses. Lawrence Buell's identification of the sources of transcendentalist writing in conversation and the sermon is particularly relevant here.[19] In *Walden*, as with many of the personal-political narratives, we see the emphasis on the spoken voice, on dialogue and argumentation, as well as on the authoritative polemic of the pulpit tradition. As Molden-hauer suggests, it is in the context of "debate, of challenge and rejoinder, of provocation and rebuttal and exhortation, that the language of *Walden* must be understood."[20] At times the authorial voice introduces obviously rhetorical questions: "Have not men improved somewhat in punctuality since the railroad was invented? Do they not talk and think faster in the depot than they did in the stage-office?" (W 118). At other times the authorial voice and the voice of the conventional reader are not separated by grammatical markers but coexist to create a clear double voicing within the narrative. An example of this technique is Thoreau's dramatization of his conviction that "society is commonly too cheap." Although Thoreau avoids direct question and response, the internal structure is so balanced by the parallelisms that the passage might easily be written in the form of an argumentation between the prototypical reader Thoreau fictionalizes—one bound by the rules and conventions of bourgeois society—and the anarchist Thoreau:

"We meet at very short intervals."
"Not having had time to acquire any new value for each other."
"We meet at meals three times a day."
"And give each other a new taste of that old musty cheese that we are."
"We have to agree on a certain set of rules, called etiquette and politeness."

"To make this frequent meeting tolerable and that we need not come to open war." (W 136)

The authorial voice often throws out challenges to its readers in an effort to wake them from their complacency. Questioning the self-evident value of institutions, he asks, "Should the world be confined to one Paris or one Oxford forever?" "Cannot students be boarded here and get a liberal education under the skies of Concord? Can we not hire some Abelard to lecture to us?" (W 109). The rhetorical questions, the reiterations, the rejoinders, devices common to the homiletic style, all combine to question social conventions.

By far Thoreau's most persistent way of undermining what he sees as the omnipresent ideology of competition and success in *Walden* is through intricate language games. It is as if Thoreau is aware that established ideologies can only be destabilized by a deconstruction of the language of their slogans, by an exposure of the caveats in their ideo-logical processes. To this end, Thoreau tries to destroy commonplace expressions, expressions in which ideology is masked and mystified by becoming part of everyday lexicon, by using the language and logic of consensual culture in such a manner as to finally invalidate it. While describing the sounds of birds during his early morning ramble, for instance, Thoreau interjects the following: "Who would not be early to rise, and rise earlier and earlier, every successive day of his life, till he became unspeakably healthy, wealthy and wise?" (W 127). In "The Way to Wealth" Franklin had advised, "He that riseth late must trot all Day.... Early to Bed, and early to rise, makes a Man healthy, wealthy and wise."[21] Thoreau mocks the economic functionality of this work ethic dictum both by exaggerating its literal content and by deliberately misplacing it in a description of the pleasures of loafing, a nonproductive activity. Similarly, Thoreau ridicules the truth status of proverbs by subjecting their figurative expressions to literal rebuttal so that they lose their metaphoric value. He questions the ethic of industry in the proverb "Man should earn his living by the sweat of his brow," for example, by ridiculing the value placed on work: "It is not necessary that a man should earn his living by the sweat of his brow, unless he sweats easier than I do" (W 71). In like manner, Thoreau debunks other maxims designed to consolidate the machinery of profit and loss: "Men say that a stitch in time saves nine, and so they take a thousand stitches to-day to save nine to-morrow" (W 93); "If you have built castles in the air, your work need not be lost; that is where they should be. Now put foundations under them" (W 324). In each case the authorial voice reveals the arbitrariness of commonplace truths by demonstrating that the language structure that supports them, that structure that is invested with unquestionable authority, collapses when the ideological base of the language is questioned and the hidden agenda, designed to maintain the central ideology, is revealed. Language assumes an institutionalized "truth" form only when it assumes certain ideologies (such as the intrinsic value of laboring and earning) that are hidden from the surface of the original statement and are never questioned. These maxims are contingent upon the presumed ideologies. The way to destabilize these statements is therefore to reinterpret their ideologies and restate them on the basis of a new interpretation.

A similar strategy is at work in the numerous wordplays with which *Walden* is rife. The subversive potential of wordplays is, of course, well known. Derrida has shown how devices such as homonyms and puns introduce "frivolity" into language by creating breaches in it, by exposing the gap of the signifier.[22] The different wordplays in *Walden* operate in a like manner. Their effect is to wrench language from its traditional cultural significations and to demonstrate the arbitrary nature of socially accepted signifier-signified associations. Contrasting truly lived experience with the mere appearance of it, for instance, Thoreau distinguishes between "philosophers" and "professors of philosophy." "There are nowadays professors of philosophy, but not philosophers. Yet it is admirable to profess because it was once admirable to live" (W 14). The word *professor* is deprived of its status and reduced to merely *professing*. To take another case, consider Thoreau's denunciation of the intellectual mediocrity with which his townsmen are content. "Instead of noblemen," he urges, "let us have noble villages of men" (W 110). The effect of this reexperiencing of language is a liberation of the reader. "The endless computations of words in *Walden*," says Stanley Cavell, "are part of its rescue of language; its return of it to us."[23]

In addition to using linguistic subversions, Thoreau carnivalizes capitalist ideology by overtly adopting the similitude of the industrious businessman but covertly destabilizing the ethics of competition and success. In a sense, "Economy," with its emphasis on the necessities of life, is a manual on acquisition and prudence as much as Franklin's "Poor Richard" essays were. But in *Walden*, instead of being shown the way to wealth, the readers are shown that poverty lies less in a scarcity of goods than in an undue emphasis on them. Thoreau's own activities at Walden similarly mimic the actions of the prudent, hardworking Lockean male. The author of *Walden* builds his cabin with a thrift Franklin would have commended. He begins his "enterprise" by borrowing an axe, paying $4.25 for a shanty, and finishing the cabin at a cost of $28. But Thoreau makes this enterprise serve distinctly unbusinesslike ends. He proudly confesses: "I made no haste in my work, but rather made the most of it" (W 42). Unlike Franklin, who wanted his life to exemplify the fact that wealth and ownership were within the reaches of all, Thoreau questions the value of possession itself. Instead of raising capital to buy a farm, he proudly boasts that he "never got [his] fingers burned by actual possession" (W 82); and looking at a person moving his possessions, he states, "I could never tell from inspecting such a load [furniture] whether it belonged to a so called rich man or a poor one; the owner always seemed poverty-stricken. Indeed the more you have of such things the poorer you are" (W 65–66).

For Thoreau, any labor done for profit, whether agrarian or industrial, was part of the capitalistic system. That is why hardworking farmers do not escape censure in *Walden*. Thoreau himself takes on the garb of the industrious farmer in order to subvert the values of the work ethic. "The Bean-Field" is probably the best example of this appropriation and subversion of the work ethic. Here Thoreau temporarily adopts the mercantile ideology of the prudent farmer and gives detailed accounts of his income and expenses. He follows this up with meticulous instructions to farmers on planting beans: "Plant the common small white bush bean about the first of June, in rows three feet by eighteen inches apart, being careful to select round and unmixed seed" (W 163). But the voice of the busy farmer, adopted by Thoreau, is soon succeeded by another voice concerned less with planting beans and corns than "such seeds...as sincerity, truth, simplicity, faith, innocence and the like" (W 164). Planting here is translated and transformed into the ideology of self-culture rather than the cultivation of beans as commodities for consumption and exchange. The conflicting voices are resolved a little later when the authorial voice subverts the language of the farmer used earlier. "Why should not the New Englander try new adventures," asks Thoreau, "and not lay so much stress on his grain, his potato and grass crop, and his orchards,—raise other crops than these? Why concern ourselves so much about beans for seed, and not be concerned about a new generation of men?" (W 164).

Taken together, these carnivalizations of the business culture allow Thoreau to deauthorize what he sees as the established rhetoric of market society. The language of bourgeois society, deprived of its socio-ideological significations, becomes powerless as a cohesive tool.

Having dispersed its significations, Thoreau can redefine language so as to deemphasize business culture. After describing his early morning activities, for instance, the author can conclude, "Morning is when there is dawn in me. Moral reform is the effort to throw off sleep" (W 90). Common sense becomes for Thoreau "the sense of men asleep, which they express by snoring" (W 325). Or, there is his Tocquevillean redefinition of liberty in America. Liberty is not the false freedom of having the ability to purchase goods but the "liberty to pursue such a mode of life as may enable you to do without these" (W 205). The liberty which compels people to desire commodities, Thoreau shows, is a form of tyranny reinforced by social definitions of liberty.

Thoreau's questioning of the "Americanism" which by the mid-nineteenth century was synonymous with laissez-faire capitalism was a powerful indictment of the cultural values of his age. This was, after all, the generation that would be followed by a resurrection of Franklin's Poor Richard as Horatio Alger. The social theories of William Graham Sumner, popularized as social Darwinism, would provide proof of the ethics and inevitability of capitalism as the "natural" system of society. Thoreau's polemic and carnivalizations question the very idea of a single theory being used to explain the workings of society; under his calls for a radical individualism is a belief in the necessity of social and ideological differences. But at the same time Thoreau participated, to an extent, in the intellectual movement that questioned materialism and exalted a universal Reason. Thinkers like Brownson, Emerson, and Channing criticized Locke not so much for his emphasis on labor, acquisition, and ownership as for his belief in knowledge as something derived from the outside, from the physical and material world. Transcendentalists believed in values beyond society and history, and the political cost of maintaining such beliefs was high. Emerson's theories, for instance, proved inadequate in dealing with the problem of slavery. Margaret Fuller, on the other hand, brought her awareness of the injustices faced by women in the everyday world into full participation with her version of transcendental philosophy and produced a radical political and aesthetic manifesto in *Woman in the Nineteenth Century*. In "Civil Disobedience," Thoreau, like Fuller, combined transcendentalist reason with the particularized problem of the individual's fidelity to the laws of the government. But in *Walden*, despite the polemical critique of capitalist culture, Thoreau was ambivalently bound to an idealism that circumscribed and undermined his radical political critique.

This separation of a realm of ideas beyond society and history was the transcendentalist version of the nineteenth century split between culture and the market analyzed by Raymond Williams. The problem with this split was that it really did not empower literature and culture; if the separation meant that literature could remain uncontaminated by the marketplace, it also meant that the marketplace could essentially be immune to ideas from literature and culture. Benjamin Franklin, the astute businessman of Philadelphia, had long recognized the efficacy of such a separation. We have seen how in his *Autobiography* Franklin dismissed poets as dandies and idlers so as to maintain a cohesive capitalist structure for the emergent country. The transcendentalist separation of the aesthetic from the material and the market ironically reinforces the split.

In *Walden*, Thoreau constantly invokes distinctions between the material, earthly, commercial life on the one hand and the ideal, divine, spiritual life on the other. Some of these separations polemically critique the market for not nurturing the inner, spiritual being. "Talk of a divinity in man," Thoreau writes. "Look at the teamster on the highway, wending to market by day or night; does any divinity stir within him? His highest duty to fodder and water his horses! What is his destiny to him compared with his shipping interests?... How godlike, how immortal, is he? See how he cowers and sneaks...not being immortal nor divine" (W 4). Thoreau's picture of the teamster dramatizes the brutalization of human beings through the environment of work and competition; it also posits a realm of the divine and spiritual beyond society from which values can be formulated. Thoreau's aesthetics and ideology depend upon a clear distinction between the outer (material) and inner (spiritual) life. At times this distinction is dramatized as one between the daily material life and True values. "When we are unhurried and wise," Thoreau writes, "we perceive that only great and worthy things have any permanent and absolute existence,—that petty fears and petty pleasures are but the shadow of reality.... By closing the eyes and slumbering, and consenting to be deceived by shows, men establish and confirm their daily life of routine and habit" (W 95–96). At other times the distinction is one between the inner-worthy and outer-irrelevant lives. Toward the end of his narrative Thoreau urges his readers: "Be a Columbus to whole new continents and worlds within you, opening new channels, not of trade, but of thought. Every man is the lord of a realm beside which the earthly empire of the Czar is but a petty state" (W 321).

The creation of an area of imagination, Truth, and value apart from society obviously undermines political effectiveness because it assumes that behaviors and values are independent of social conditions. Thoreau cannot really critique the historically rooted phenomenon of nineteenth century capitalism from an ahistorical and asocial perspective. This belief in ahistorical values also has important implications for individuality and subjectivity. If subjectivity is seen to be affected by society in any way, it means that individual consciousness will be dialogically constituted by differences and contradictions. But if subjectivity transcends the social-material world, it can be perceived as unified and whole. And despite his critique of social unanimity, Thoreau's impulse is also to gain access to a state of unity or noncontradiction above and beyond the social and material world, a state where values are universal and absolute.

The importance of the material-ideal, inner-outer separation can be seen in "Higher Laws," where the status of these separations becomes the subject of the chapter. Here the authorial voice is pulled between the attractions of wildness and spirituality. This chapter is a central one in dramatizing Thoreau's confrontations with the hierarchies of Western dualistic thinking, which work as a set of moral and cultural oppositions. The soul (Truth), for instance, has been associated with spirituality, purity, cleanliness, and order, whereas the body (untruth, Woman) has been associated with physicality, degradation, uncleanliness, and disorder. Nietzsche's correlation of Woman and Truth was a powerful indictment of this dualism.[24] Nietzsche recognized the political ramifications of dualistic hierarchies where the Other was always associated with evil and untruth and fought these binaries all his life. Thoreau also realizes the importance of the oppositions he is confronting, and although he is aware of the need to deconstruct them, he is also compelled to reinscribe these oppositions and maintain their dualistic hierarchy.

He begins his meditations by subverting the hierarchies: "I found in myself, and still find, an instinct toward a higher, or, as it is named, spiritual life, as do most men, and another toward a primitive rank and savage one, and I reverence them both. I love the wild not less than the good" (W 210). But he goes on to maintain the strict opposition and hierarchy. The "animal," "sensual," and "appetitive" are associated with impurity, uncleanliness, sin, and Nature (Thoreau always treats Nature with a capital *N* as feminine); the higher nature is associated with chastity, purity, virtue, and spirituality.[25] Although he confesses to his own sensual instincts, he longs for a monologic, Aristotelian state of unity where the sensual has been transformed into the spiritual. "He is blessed who is assured that the animal is dying out in him day by day, and the divine being established" (W 220). For Thoreau, the aesthetic, moral, and imaginative were all connected, separate from and above the market, above the social-material world. "Higher Laws" ends with a parable which illustrates the possibility of the working man "transcending" his workaday environment and cultivating his "higher" nature. "The notes of the flute came home to his ears out of a different sphere from that he worked in, and suggested work for certain faculties which slumbered in him. They gently did away with the street, and the village, and the state in which he lived" (W 148).

The separate sphere of aesthetics and imagination that Thoreau postulates has important ideological and formal implications. Speaking as an aesthete, a spiritual being, means giving voice to a set of moral and ethical operatives that deny ideological multiplicity. It is no wonder that one of the characteristic languages of *Walden* is the language of aphorisms. Obviously the identification of aphoristic statements in a text is subject to interpretation. It might be possible to detect aphorisms through stylistic qualities such as parallelism, parataxis, and antithesis, but because our concern here is with forms of authorization it is more pertinent to locate them according to the way they function in the text.[26] For Emerson, proverbs possessed an unquestionable authority. They were "the statements of an absolute truth without qualification."[27] Now this capability of language to function as absolute truth is workable when one's own language is conceived as free as possible from interaction with other languages, other contextual voices. Such a situation denies intertextuality and the inherently dialogic nature of language. As Bakhtin points out, separate thoughts or formulations such as maxims derive their monologic force from the fact that "when removed from their context and detached from their voice" they "retain their semantic meaning in an impersonal form."[28] *Walden* is replete with attempts to create such aphoristic formulations that can function as absolute truth. A few examples of such aphorisms are "The mass of men lead lives of quiet desperation," "The swiftest traveller is he that goes afoot," "To be awake is to be alive," and "If a man does not keep pace with his companions, perhaps it is because he hears a different drummer." Often, these maxims follow each other in quick succession, as in "Higher Laws": "We speak conformably to the rumor we have heard. From exertion come wisdom and purity; from sloth ignorance and sensuality" (W 147). "Conclusion" is similarly composed of numerous maxims linked together: "Cultivate poverty like a garden herb, a sage.... Things do not change; we change. Sell your clothes and keep your thoughts" (W 328).

Thoreau's separation of the aesthetic and spiritual from the everyday world (and his conviction that this spiritual world is a source of True values) obviously facilitates and perpetuates the abstract language of aphorisms and creates the conditions for a prophetic authorial voice. The conception in transcendentalist aesthetics of the artist as an "inspired demi-god" or poet-priest derives from the idea of this privileged spiritual sphere.[29] The authorial voice in *Walden* often speaks in the imperative, and toward the end, in "Conclusion," it assumes the abstract, imperative language of command. "However mean your life is, meet it and live it. Do not shun it and call it hard names. It is not as bad as you are. It looks poorest when you are richest.... Love your life, poor as it is" (W 328).

In the context of the aphoristic, universalist language used in *Walden*, it is important to examine the role of the numerous quotations from Eastern texts. Every reader of *Walden* is bound to be struck by its rich texture of allusions. In one sense allusions create textual multivoicing because they bring in different contexts and voices; their very presence implies that no text is unified and autonomous and that what we have are texts echoing and refracting each other. But allusions can also be used less dispersively to reinforce a central point and to contain other voices. The Eastern references and quotations in *Walden* are used for the latter purpose. These references do not bring in diverse social contexts because Thoreau's purpose in including them was to transcend context altogether. The East for Thoreau was merely a topography through which he could reinforce his spiritualism, not a concrete, historical, and geographical area that in the mid-nineteenth century was undergoing a massive colonization by various European powers. Thus Thoreau's quotations from Indian texts, for example, are all abstract ethical statements taken from scripture: "There are none happy in the world but beings who enjoy freely a vast horizon" (W 88); "The house-holder is to remain at eventide in his court yard as long as it takes to milk a cow" (W 270). Such quotations do not enter the text as voices that bring in different social perspectives or voices that question the authorial voice, but rather, like Benjamin Vaughan's letter in Franklin's *Autobiography*, like a group of assenting voices.

Thoreau's retreat from the world of commerce, the marketplace where commodities are exchanged, to an inner, spiritual world was symptomatic of the movement of culture and of the particular Anglo-American romanticism in which he could not help but participate. But the plays with institutionalized language and the carnivalizations of business culture were Thoreau's own unique contributions to the tradition of liberal questioning and endorsement of cultural difference that would increasingly occupy writers of personal-political narratives after the mid-nineteenth century. In different ways the separation of culture from the "everyday" world also continues as a problematic stance for other critics of the liberal consensus. In his veneration of culture and civilization as aspects of intellectual growth far removed from the vulgarity of American capitalist democracy, Henry James has more in common with the philosopher from Concord than seems apparent. Henry Adams manages to write a narrative of social and cultural difference only by adopting the pose of detached philosopher, and Addams continually ponders on the separation between Hull-House culture and inner-city life. In antebellum America poised on the brink of total industrialization, Thoreau's voice sounds a dissentful note but an individualistic one, divorced from a concrete social philosophy and necessarily at odds with the concept of community.

4

Democratic Capitalism and the Role of Culture: The Identity of Multiple Observers in *The American Scene*

The America that Henry James returned to in 1904 after an absence of nearly twenty years was vastly different from Thoreau's Concord. During the Gilded Age, the period of prosperity following the Civil War, huge fortunes were amassed and an American plutocracy of the rich and powerful flourished. By the end of the nineteenth century, the Horatio Alger success story of the lone, penniless individual conquering the business world was hardly a possibility, but people still continued to believe in it. Wealth and power were concentrated in the hands of big trusts and corporations. In 1913 Woodrow Wilson would declare that "the masters of the government of the United States [were] the combined capitalists and manufacturers."[1] Businessmen were the real powerbrokers. No wonder, then, that James was struck everywhere by the face of the ubiquitous businessman.

In another sense the American scene was not too different from the one Thoreau had viewed from Walden Pond. The structure and organization of businesses had changed, but the value attached to the business world had not. Like Thoreau, James felt that American democratic capitalism had created a consensual culture intolerant of individual difference or social diversity. Thoreau had responded to this culture by carnivalizing its conventions and languages, on the one hand, and by seeking refuge in a spiritualism and aestheticism that transcended the social and material world, on the other. James could not use the romantic prerogative of transcending the social and material world because he was foremost a novelist with a novelist's commitment to a densely textured social world. He was the practitioner of a craft which was least susceptible to mysticism and the most immured in a social context.[2] Of course, it is not as if James did not attempt a certain kind of transcendence and separation from the world of commerce, even the world of labor and earning. His indifference to the sources of income in his novels has been noted by many critics.[3] But such omissions indicate a desire not so much to transcend the social-material world as to mystify the realities of power and dominance within class society. Thus in *The American Scene* James critiques the homogeneity of American democratic capitalism and valorizes instead a realm of high culture based on entrenched class hierarchies. James associates culture with history, art, and taste, and views it as a dialogizing force sensitive to variations and differences and which questions a standardized Americanism.

But the paradox about the America James returned to was that although the vast democratic-capitalist machine obviously overpowered the social scene, the fabric of American society was undergoing dramatic changes. Immigrants were coming in numbers as never before. Between the turn of the century and the beginning of World War I, 13 million immigrants arrived in the United States.[4] Most of these immigrants were not, as formerly, from northern Europe but were Slavs, Jews from eastern Europe, Sicilians, and Greeks.[5] James was sensitive to the social changes generated by these new immigrants and honest enough to voice his fears about the threat that they posed to the concept of a singular American identity. *The American Scene* is a narrative of James's conflictual liberalism—highly critical of mass society but uneasy about racial difference and egalitarianism. The rhetorical structure of the text, particularly the interactions between the authorial voice (the voice of culture) and the various voices of the American scene, reflects this conflictual politics.

James obviously recognized that his concept of culture was a political one. In a sketch in Chester in *English Hours* he declared, "Conservatism has here [in England] all the charm and leaves dissent and democracy and other vulgar variations nothing but their bald logic.... Conservatism has the cathedrals, the colleges, the castles...the traditions, the associations, the fine names, the better manners, the poetry."[6] Conservatism, as used here, is synonymous with culture. Like his spiritual mentor, Hawthorne, James asserts the necessity of traditions and cultural "associations" for art. But what is more interesting here is the manner in which the concept of culture is politicized. Democracy in its subversive aspect as a community of difference is deradicalized by its association with "bald logic," a set method of interpretation; conservatism or culture is energized by its diverse associations—religious, academic, political, and aesthetic. James also rewrites his politics in the lexicon of taste so as to provide an aesthetic overcoding for his ideological narrative. He classifies dissent and democracy merely as "vulgar" and dismisses them so that they cannot pose a dispersive threat to the realm of culture, which he associates honorifically with cathedrals, colleges, and castles.

In *The American Scene* James associates democracy less with dissent than with mass society, but he places the same value on culture as he does in *English Hours*. Indeed, we can say that in *The American Scene* James speaks as the voice of culture. This concept of culture, associated as it is with traditional class-structured societies, is subject to questioning and accommodation, but it is valorized nonetheless.[7] James writes that in the cities of Europe, unlike in America, "good taste is present, for reference and comparison, in a hundred embodied and consecrated forms."[8] Europe has acquired these consecrated forms through a process of cultural evolution. As James explains, "It takes an endless amount of history to make even a little tradition, and an endless amount of tradition to make even a little taste, and an endless amount of taste, by the same token, to make a little tranquility" (AS 169). Clearly, James does not create a mythical, untainted, ahistorical past as a total repository of moral value. Rather, it is the forward movement of civilization, its continual change, that is most important. But it is also clear, here, how historical processes are good only insofar as they are evidence of a continuous, teleologically governed and ideologically compatible evolution. "Civilization," in these terms, has to be a slow movement from "history," to "tradition," to "taste," and to "tranquility." Bypassing any of these stages is a violation of the process. That America has attempted a shortcut to civilization is one of James's major criticisms of the country. What is inimical to this process are abrupt changes that lead to irregular and discontinuous evolution. That is why tranquility is at the apex of James's view of civilization.

It is necessary to emphasize that such pronouncements on social growth are not merely "aesthetic." The historian Robert Wiebe characterizes the end of the nineteenth century as a "search for order," a time when the established were anxious to quell mob disorder and base a society on known and accepted social, economic, and political privileges.[9] James's explanations of cultural evolution are anxious expressions of this search for order. As it was, twentieth century America had severed his connection with a stable past. James's horror at finding a former childhood home razed to the ground within a month of his visiting it is an expression of the anxiety of disconnection and a wish for more stability that was not his alone. Many writers of the Gilded Age believed in the importance of ordered and regular evolution. Although Howells, for example, mocked the pretensions of the upper-class Coreys in *The Rise of Silas Lapham*, he could not destabilize the current social structure by allowing Silas entry into refined Boston society. Similarly, although James's newly rich Christopher Newman of *The American* is endowed with exemplary moral virtues in the midst of a decadent aristocracy, James prefers to keep class lines intact. Lest Newman marry the titled Madame de Cintre and rupture traditional class boundaries, James whisks her off to a nunnery. The necessity of "progressive" cultural growth is the subject of many of James's novels. But although critics have examined the political implications of *The American Scene*, many of them (curiously paralleling the market-culture split) have maintained an untenable separation between the ideas in the book and its art.[10] One critic, for instance, finds James's conception of the historical process in *The American Scene* simplistic but "from an artistic point of view" an invaluable unifying force.[11] Another critic concedes that the book can be seen as an account of James's "cultural biases" but points out, as if in contrast, that it is also a "work of art."[12] Such bifurcations, by assuming that *art* (a seemingly neutral term) can be devoid of *ideas* and vice versa, do injustice to both.

In *The American Scene* the play of voices and the ideology are so interdependent that neither can be seen in isolation. Given James's views of the historical process, "tranquility," for instance, is not merely an aesthetic quality but also a stable social order free of radical class upheaval and restructuring. Culture, for James, meant both social density and variety and a means of preserving order and stability. Just as the mysticism of Anglo-American romantics was a means of reaching truths through the East (spirit) when the ideas of the West (mind) no longer sufficed, culture was, for James, a realm of value in a world which he felt lacked stable values.[13] Thus "taste," in the above passage, is an aesthetic preference, but it also refers to the acquisition of abilities by those who adhere to certain beliefs or "traditions." Throughout *The American Scene* these important cultural values are contained in a cluster of analogous venerated terms which consolidate what we might call a "politics of taste." History is associated with other value-laden terms like *antiquity, old,* and *past; tradition* is associated with *continuity* and *preservation;* taste is linked to *weight, charm,* and *character;* and tranquility is related to *felicity, serenity,* and *presence.* There is no doubt that the special value given to the old over the new, the traditional over the radical or innovative, in effect endorses the established status quo of social classes. James is agonizingly conscious of the class-bound nature of his concept of culture. As he puts it, "'Society,' as we loosely use the word, is made up of the fortunate few" (AS 453). Thus although James's ideology necessarily endorses a "civilized" leisure class and its status quo, he is well aware of its political exclusivity. Yet he is also bound to his concept of culture because it seems to be the only refuge of difference from the monotonizing force of American democratic capitalism. James's veneration of culture is thus at once a call for social difference and an anxious expression of the need for social stability. In the interactions between the voice of culture that James adopts and the voices of the American scene, we see the workings of these contradictory political implications. James is able to use the concept of culture to effectively critique the consensual aspect of American democracy, but he finds the concept limited in dealing with egalitarianism and ethnic difference.

The two aspects James finds most persistent in America are its social homogeneity and its empowerment of the business culture. Both, for James, are a result of American democracy. Like Tocqueville, James used the term *democracy* synonymously with *standardization* and *consensus*. *Democracy* as used in *The American Scene* to signify consensus, really means democratic capitalism.[14] James characterizes American (capitalist) democracy as a "huge…broom that has made the clearance and that one seems to see branded in the empty sky" (AS 55). It is a broom that erases all differences and monotonizes the social fabric, or, to cite one of James's frequently used metaphors for American society, a canvas covered with gray paint. Although he often disavows the ideological implications of his assessment, claiming a disinterest in the political, civic, and economic view of democratic institutions, James's interpretations of the democratic system are necessarily politicized. Analyzing the causes that contribute to the monotony of American society, for instance, James writes that "the usual, in our vast crude democracy of trade, is the new, the simple, the cheap, the common, the commercial, the immediate, and, all too often, the ugly" (AS 67). James associates democracy with a political emphasis on equality that sanctions the simple, common, immediate, and vulgar and with an economic emphasis on functionality that prizes the new, the cheap, and the marketable. And along with the political and economic interpretation we have the aesthetic interpretation of democracy as ugly. Speaking as cultured observer, James shows how American democracy is unchanging and sterile and has no potential for dialogic interaction.

The most significant feature of James's inquiry into the American scene is that he does not so much describe its aspects as have them describe themselves to him. The representative artifacts of America—the skyscrapers, the villages, the Pullman cars—literally speak to and taunt the authorial voice. This clearly demarcated dia-

logue does not, of course, indicate a dialogic openness of meaning in
the text but rather serves to further James's argument about the lack
of dialogic potential offered by the conditions of democratic capitalism. Indeed, no matter what form they take, these voices of various
artifacts signify themselves only as capital investments. At times self-
congratulatory, these voices directly confess to their monetary functions. The houses of the newly rich New Yorkers, for example, seem
to James to exult, "We are only installments, symbols, stop-gaps....
Expensive as we are, we have nothing to do with continuity, responsibility, transmission, and don't in the least care what becomes of us
after we have served our present purpose" (AS 11). Similarly, the shop
windows in Boston, proudly exhibiting their commodities, tell the
author, "Oh come; don't look among us for what you won't, for what
you shan't find, the best quality attainable; but only...the best value
we allow you" (AS 235). At other times these voices merely assert
their merit and worth. The numerous "good" New England houses,
for instance, claim, "We are good, yes—we are excellent" (AS 42). The
continuous rumble of the Pullman cars seems forever to be saying,
"See what I'm making of all this—see what I'm making, what I'm
making" (AS 463). Collectively, these voices testify to a commercial
spirit that chants its lore of buying and selling: "See how ready we
are...ready to buy, to pay, to promise; ready to place, to honour our
purchase. We have everything, don't you see?" (AS 184).

This device of characterizing voices opposed to the authorial
voice, that the authorial voice responds to, is a polemical strategy
used by many writers of the personal-political narrative. We have
seen how Franklin used this strategy to demonstrate the ineptitude of
idlers, scholars, and poets. In a manner closer to James's, Thoreau created typified readers whose conventional ideas he could parody.
What is novel in James's technique is that his strategy of characterization is in itself a critique of what he perceives is a sterile democratic-
capitalist ideology. The very fact that objects seem to possess voices of
their own which glorify them and proclaim their right to exist independent of their relationship to people dramatizes the inevitable
alienation of the human being from the self-sufficient world of commodities. As Georg Lukacs points out from the other end of the ideological spectrum, capitalist society creates a process of "reification"
whereby commodities become mysterious, autonomous entities, confronting man "as invisible forces that generate their own power."[15]
Human beings are reduced to merely being observers of this spectacle. James was obviously no Marxist, but, like Thoreau, his liberal dis-
like of capitalist uniformity made him a sensitive analyst of alienation

and reification. In fact, the commodification of human relationships is also the subject of James's later novels—*The Ambassadors*, *The Wings of the Dove*, and *The Golden Bowl*. But although James could address the phenomenon of reification and could show how the rich were imprisoned in a world of commodities and could relate to each other only through commodities, he could not bring himself to question the fact of ownership itself. He dramatized the alienation of human beings in a capitalistic world but also repeated the alienation in his texts by dissociating his characters completely from the world of labor.

James was, however, sensitive to the human cost of capitalism, and like Tocqueville he realized how the world of consumerism was inimical to human relationships. New York City, for James, embodies this isolation of individuals: "The whole costly up-town demonstration was a record, in the last analysis, of individual loneliness; whence came, precisely, its insistent testimony to waste" (AS 159). James also records the alienation of people from the world of commodities. He believes that "objects and places, coherently grouped, *disposed for human use and addressed to it*, must have a sense of their own, a mystic meaning proper to themselves to give out...*to the participant*" (AS 273, italics mine). But the reified artifacts in the American scene, according to James, are rarely addressed to human use. Instead of having a meaning and use that would connect them to the human being, they signify only their exchange value.

For James, this sense of reification further manifests itself in the majority of Americans who seem to place no worth on their actions other than that of exchange value. To a large extent, James holds this economic motivation responsible for the "pettifogging consistency" of American society. *Sister Carrie* was Dreiser's depiction of the tragedy of innocence corrupted by the lure of commodities. In James's version of commodification in *The American Scene* there are few innocents because consumerism is endemic. The insidious swarms of businessmen that James observes early on the New Jersey shore subsequently appear in various versions. There are churchwardens, for example, who care little about religion and sanction the razing of churches to accommodate the more lucrative skyscrapers (AS 83); there are aristocracies defined less through social distinctions and a social context than their high "material pitch" (AS 163); and there are "summer people" who create phantom towns of seasonally discarded homes (AS 37). It is not surprising, then, that most people are not interested in the social implications of their actions. The phenomenon of reification exists by virtue of a lack of connection with a socio-historical context. As James observes, "The American scale of gain" demands "the individual's participation in it, that of his being more or less punctually and more or less effectually 'squared.' To make so much money that you won't, that you don't 'mind' anything—that is absolutely the main American formula" (AS 237).

By the time James was writing, Lockean liberalism had spawned the culture of democratic capitalism, and it is in contrast to the homogeneity of this culture that James in 1905 projects himself just as Thoreau had done a generation earlier. James speaks as the voice of culture and uses narrative strategies that suggest that his concept of culture is not a fixed ideology or an a priori standard. Thus James gives this voice features that suggest its variety and multiplicity. The voice of culture, as opposed to the voices of American democracy, is presented as an unmerged plurality of voices. The illustration of the multiplicity of this authorial voice takes two potentially dialogic strategies. The first is the use of what we might call different "author-characters." We see the author (often the "I") parading as a host of characters. He appears as the "restless analyst," the "story seeker," the "returning absentee," the "waiting observer," the "earnest observer," the "fond critic," the "student of manners," the "unappeased visitor," the "picture maker," and so on. The guises are numerous and nondevelopmental; that is, James does not present these author-characters in a successive series. Rather, they appear, reappear, and replace each other in a role of development and change instead of reinforcement. But James uses this method as a means of working out his doubts and conflictual politics. While he speaks through seemingly different voices, thus using rhetorical strategies that signify ideological dispersion, he simultaneously deprives these voices of all semantic difference so that, in effect, the concept of culture remains a stabilizing one.

Thus although James ostensibly employs different author-characters, he does not put this device to dispersive use, and the difference between the voices remains only a verbal one. It is perhaps for this reason that, except for calling attention to the complexity of narrator-voices and assuming that these generate ideological multiplicity, most critics have preferred not to deal with this strategy.[16] The few attempts by critics to identify really divergent voices among the author-characters seem forced. The suggestions that these voices undercut the self-absorption of the authorial voice because the author refers to himself at one point as "the ancient contemplative observer" and at another as "the mooning observer" and that the narrators are appropriately different for the opposed conditions of New York and rural New England are both unworkable.[17] James, in fact, uses different voices for describing very similar scenes of rural America. The narrator appears in rural New England, for example, as "restless analyst" and "indiscreet listener." The two are equated as the narrator notes the monotony of New England villages: "the scene is everywhere the same whereby tribute is always ready and easy, and you are spared all shocks of surprise" (AS 39). Continuing the sojourn, now as "story seeker curious of manners," the narrator gets this response from a Midwest resident when he asks him about the conditions of life in his hometown: "The conditions of life? Why, the same conditions as everywhere else" (AS 42). Surely the observations of the "restless analyst," "indiscreet listener," and "story seeker" show little ideological variation. But these narrator-observers also serve an important purpose. They allow James to endorse an aesthetic of difference and variation at the same time that they enable him to maintain a fairly fixed interpretation of the American scene. It is also significant that the names of the different author-characters reflect only postures of observation and alienation. Whether as "lone observer," "unappeased visitor," or "picture maker," James presents himself as an observer rather than as a participant in the American scene.

James wanted his voice to question the homogeneity of American capitalist democracy and to reveal it as vacuous. A rhetorically effective method of accomplishing this criticism was to give his voice a stance different from the merely definitional or descriptive. Thus when James speaks as the voice of culture, he does not merely record his impressions and judgments. He always appears as bewildered—questioning, inquiring, probing beneath the surface of American society. The dialogic possibilities of this voice lie in its propensity to continually question other social voices. The contrast between this voice and the democratic-capitalist voices is made clear. Whereas the democratic-capitalist voices proclaim their wholeness and presence, the voice of culture, by virtue of its bewilderment, seems to question its own presence; whereas these monologic voices are content with outer signification, the voice of culture searches for what these voices really signify.

This interrogative stance of the authorial voice is a polemical strategy of redundancy; through a series of rhetorical questions James reinforces his interpretation of American society as morally and culturally decrepit. Confronting the newly rich New Yorkers, for instance, the bewildered observer wonders, "What had it been their idea to *do*, the good people...do exactly, *for* their manners, their habits...their general advantage and justification? Do that is in affirming their wealth...and yet not at the same time affirming anything else" (AS 10–11). The answer—that the newly rich care little about what they affirm—is evident in the question. Or again, when the bewildered observer notes the relentless expansion of commercial, urban America and wonders if it can be checked, the negative response is implicit in the questions: "Thin and clear and colourless, what would it ever say 'no' to? or what would it ever paint thick, indeed, with sympathy and sanction?" (AS 54). Similarly, the authorial voice is able to reinforce the interpretation of New England villages as culturally vacuous by asking: "*Were* there any secrets at all, or had the outward blankness, the quality of blankness, the quality of absence, as it were, in the air, its inward equivalent as well?" (AS 43).

Between the rhetorical questions of the bewildered observer and the democratic-capitalist voices exulting in themselves, James suggests that there can be no dialogue. The authorial voice is, in a sense, forced to repeat the same questions because it is faced with continuously identical voices. By dramatizing his fruitless encounter with these voices, James illustrates the alienation and lack of communication created by the uniform conditions of democratic capitalism and associates his concept of culture with the missing conscience of the American scene. While American democracy destroys the past and sanctions a consumer society, James, the observer, insists on the need for conscious social growth, for social differences, and aesthetic sources of value. The inability of American society to appeal to anything but commodity value reinforces the need for a separate area of value, that of culture, and even justifies the class hierarchies that this culture depends upon. For instance, James shows how in comparison with the complete "abolition of *forms*" (except for the "wage standard," which James dismisses as insignificant) and the lack of "reference to...their past, present or future possibilities" in New England villages, the religious hierarchy of the squire and parson society of England is desirable (AS 23–25). It is in moments like this that James appears not as a critic of the liberal consensus but as a proponent of a more conservative order. He seems to want and value not only ideological differences and social variety but also a traditional class hierarchy that most liberalism rejects.

Whereas James's concept of culture works effectively to question and undermine the homogeneity created by democratic capitalism, it becomes problematic when the author is confronted with the more diverse aspects of American society. When James is faced with voices that cannot be absorbed by the same "democratic broom," he attempts to either delegitimize these voices as "un-American" and therefore "Others" he does not have to understand or to remove the difference and threat they represent by continuing to interpret them as part of democratic uniformity. In this complex process of confrontation and interaction, James's self-doubts and conservatism come to the surface.

The newly arrived immigrant, the Jew, and to an extent the southern black appear to James as the diverse voices that challenge his concept of culture and his separateness from the American scene.[18] Unlike the voices of democratic capitalism from which the author was alienated, which invited no dialogic interaction, and from which he could remain separate as inquiring observer or proponent of culture, these voices challenge the authorial voice and demand response. James's very first encounter with the immigrant sets into motion a dislodging of the status of culture. The sight of aliens entering Ellis Island initially seems to him to represent another facet of the uniform democratic machinery, the need of the capitalist system to absorb all differences. As "earnest observer" he is aghast at the methodical, mechanical procedure by which these immigrants are assimilated. They are "marshalled, herded, divided, subdivided" in an almost "'scientific' feeding of the mill" (AS 84). Here James speaks as a proponent of social difference and variation decrying this assimilative process. However, James soon realizes that he can celebrate social differences only as long as they are static and do not have the potential of destabilizing the social structure. James was probably appalled by the diverse types of new immigrants in America at the turn of the century. He responded, as F. O. Matthiessen put it, by drifting "dangerously close to the doctrine of racism" on the immigrant question (AS 110).

James obviously did not want to endorse a hegemonic, consensual America, nor did he buy into the patriotic Americanism that Tocqueville had found so irritating. But the new group of immigrants forced James to live up to, and confront, his most cherished belief—that society, in order to be worth anything, had to be complex and varied. The new immigrant stood out as a most visible sign of difference, but he also challenged the existing social hierarchy and culture. The alien made it painfully obvious to the author that he had an investment in a particularly "American" culture that he wished to protect. James realized his own participation in the democratic-capitalist system even though he was its critic. Thus when the immigrants strike James not as people undergoing crude homogenization but as socially disruptive voices, he speaks as a conservative American unwilling to accept differences. The immigrants resist familiar modes of description, the power of the definitional gaze, and by so doing subvert the concept of a unified culture. James's perplexed query, "What are you then?" to a youth he is unable to classify as French, Canadian, or Italian is indicative of the social differences brought in by immigrants (AS 119). James is shocked by the realization that he has to "share the sanctity of his American consciousness, the intimacy of his American patriotism, with the inconceivable alien" (AS 85). The possibility that the entry of the alien might create social readjustment horrifies him: "We, not they, must make the surrender and accept the orientation. We must go *more* than half-way to meet them; which is all the difference for us, between possession and dispossession" (AS 86). We note how clearly James has given up his position of the voice of culture, the observer distanced from the scene, and taken up instead an identification with a Euro-American nationalist self.

James tries to maintain a separation between a unified American selfhood and the amorphous groups of aliens even as he knows that the separation is becoming untenable. He tries to recreate, by definition and binary opposition, an ethnic selfhood in a society where these binaries keep breaking. This is a crucial moment in the text, not, as some critics have asserted, because James identifies with the immigrants, but because the modes of definition and parameters of political expression employed so far do not work now.[19] We also note James's ironic reliance on capitalist values like possession. James cannot simply remain as a distanced observer decrying the absence of heterogeneity in American society; he is now involved in what he sees and is forced to question himself. He even finds himself defining his voice as an "American" voice, grounded in a sense of community with other native voices that are similarly threatened by difference.[20] In response to the immigrant threat the identity of the authorial voice becomes highly ambiguous. The voice of the alien continues thereafter to challenge the author. After his experience at Ellis Island, James is compelled to retreat from the threat of the alien voice. He seeks, as he puts it, an "escape from the ubiquitous alien" that only a memory of the past can provide (AS 87). He finds Philadelphia a tranquil refuge partly because of the "elimination of the foreign element" in it (AS 282); and he is continually disquieted by the aliens' presumptuous possession of the American scene.

This interaction with dispersive voices continues in James's encounters with Jews and blacks. Like the immigrants, the Jews and the blacks also constitute the diversity of American society. In the Jewish quarter of New York, James is once again dismayed at the "Hebrew conquest of New York" and the tenacity with which this alien voice has established itself (AS 132). Here, for James, "Jewry...[has] burst all bounds" (AS 131). Jews not only presume their claims to America but insist on maintaining their own culture. James notes with horror, not unlike many of his fellow citizens who set up private Americanization programs, that the Jews resist integration into a unified melting pot. The fact that Jews have created their own social scene addressed to "New Jerusalem wants" within America seems to undermine the author's sense of a unified American identity. Unlike the newly arrived immigrant and the Jew, James sees the black not as a present threat but as the alien force that caused the moral turpitude of the South. The burden of the Southerner, James suggests, was to have been born into living with the continuous presence of the black. "Their condition was to have waked up from far back to this thumping legacy of the intimate presence of the negro.... The haunting consciousness thus produced is the prison of the Southern spirit" (AS 375). And although James is critical of the presumption of white Southerners trying to keep blacks in semislavery, he is nonetheless disquieted at the ease with which, it seems to him, blacks move in Washington. While waiting for his luggage in Washington, James watches "while a group of tatterdemalion darkies lounged and sunned themselves within range.... they represented the Southern black as we knew him not.... And to see him there...'in possession of his rights as a man,' was to be not a little discomposed, was to be in fact very much admonished" (AS 375). James is clearly double-voiced in his response to the blacks. He speaks both as a guilty liberal, conscious and aware of his problematic discomfiture at seeing blacks in possession of the scene, and as a conservative believer in a singular American identity who needs to marginalize all Others by restrictively defining them.

These interactions between the authorial voice and the dispersive voices of Others, I suggest, are not anomalies that can be isolated from the rest of the text. Many critics, however, rely on a separation of aesthetics and ideology and treat these moments in the text as aberrations that can be dismissed for purposes of critical appreciation. Their procedure is to acknowledge the existence of some politically problematic stances and then to minimize the implications of these stances.[21] There is, for example, the argument that although James's response to immigration might be part of a white fear of race mixture, there is little anti-Semitism because James's hostility to Jews is that of a "literary man" concerned about "the fate of the English language in Jewish New York."[22] Such a view obviously overlooks the fact that concerns for linguistic purity and the desire to maintain the jargon of the dominant culture are far from apolitical. We need only look at the calls for the institution of a standard English and the "English only" movements in the United States today to realize that linguistic agenda is highly political. Besides, James's comments on the Jewish quarter of New york are

not merely "literary." James describes the inhabitants of these tene-
ments as animals in a zoo, but merry like squirrels and monkeys. The
Jewish masses are to him "ant-like" in their numbers and similar to
"snakes or worms" in that they carry their race intensity even when
divided (AS 132,134). Other critics concede James's problems regarding aliens but point out that these attitudes are balanced by James's
sympathy for the aliens' subjection to the artificial process of immigration.[23] The problem with such apologetic strategies is that they undermine points of conflict in the text and totally ignore its racial politics.

James is able to maintain the polemical stance of being an
observer committed to social variation and heterogeneity only as long
as he is dealing with the homogeneity of democratic capitalism. It is
when he is faced with dispersive voices that he must interact with,
and cannot keep his distance from, that James is forced to question
the concept of culture. Instead of presuming a position of assumed
moral and aesthetic worth and speaking as the voice of culture and
difference, he adopts a singular American identity and makes overt
efforts to keep this identity inviolate. Between the endorsement of
social differences and the prospect of a society without unanimity and
constituted by differences was a chasm that James's liberalism could
not overcome. James's problem was one that all the liberal writers discussed so far had faced. They responded in various ways by attempting to circumvent the idea of a community of difference—Franklin by
containing the voices of Others that denied the value of competition,
Thoreau by transcending the social-material world, and James by
endorsing a more conserving and unified social order.

In this connection it is useful to consider briefly the role of
women in James's depiction of American society. In *The American
Scene* James continually singles out women as the exceptions to his
social generalizations. James is accosted everywhere by the same
businessman, but "the women, over the land...appear to be of a
markedly finer texture than the men, and...one of the liveliest signs of
this difference is precisely in their less narrowly specialized, their less
commercialized...physiognomic character" (AS 65). Yet if women are
free of the commercial spirit, James notes that their voices carry little
power. "American life may...fall upon the earnest view as a society of
women 'located' in a world of men...; the men supplying, as it were,
all the canvas, and the women all the embroidery" (AS 66). There is a
crucial difference between James's response to women and his
response to aliens, Jews, and blacks. James recognizes the marginality
of women to the world of business but does not see the voices of
women as challenges of difference and Otherness to the voice of cul-

ture. Women, in fact, maintain and perpetuate the role of culture that James venerates.[24]

But there are other dispersive aspects of American society that cannot be contained within the concept of culture. American democracy challenges the class divisions upon which James's concept of culture implicitly depends. James's response to this aspect of American society is similar to his reaction to racial and ethnic Others. It was not as if James actually found a radical social and economic equality in America. Democratic capitalism, as I have pointed out earlier, was premised on huge disparities. But the myth of capitalistic opportunity and Algerlike advancement created a visible cultural emphasis on egalitarianism that James found threatening. Throughout *The American Scene* James is conscious of the politically egalitarian force of democracy. He finds the immigrants' presumption of equality disquieting. It asserts its disregard for social privilege and insists on its right to generate changes in the social fabric. James recognizes the subversive potential of this voice and his own hesitations in accepting its ideology. As he observes, in the United States "every one is, for the lubrication of the general machinery, practically in everything, whereas in Europe, mostly, it is only certain people who are in anything" (AS 103). It is this expansive potential of democratic ideology that challenges the hierarchies implicit in the concept of culture.

Because egalitarianism threatens all forms of enclosure, James searches for and eulogizes the few social institutions that resist it. In fact, images of closure form an important ideological subtext in *The American Scene*, although closure is coded so as to seem aesthetically and ethically (rather than politically) necessary. Universities "glow the humblest of them, to the imagination—the imagination that fixes the surrounding scene as a huge Rappaccini garden, rank with money-passion" (AS 57). James appeals to the imagination and suggests that the outside represents commodification (money-passion) and evil (Rappaccini's garden), whereas the inside, in contrast, represents creativity. But the image of Rappaccini's garden to represent the outside world also reveals a fear of temptation, a need to mark this world as Other so as to justify the need for enclosure. Thus, like Thoreau at Walden reclaiming a higher nature, James idealizes the closure of Harvard as a reclamation of higher, spiritual values. Harvard is "the place inaccessible…to the shout of the newspaper…the place to think, apart from the crowd" (AS 57–58). The signs of the enclosure of Harvard, the gates around the college yard, are of value because, in the land of the "open door," they limit entry to other voices. For James, this "especial drawing of the belt" reinforces his belief that the "formal enclosure of objects at all interesting immediately refines upon their interest, immediately establishes values" (AS 62). Harvard provides James with a social context where he can affirm his concept of culture, and the hierarchies it depends upon, without interference from the disruptive aspect of egalitarianism which questions closure.

Throughout *The American Scene* James venerates other social institutions and localities that signify stability. The charm of Philadelphia, for instance, lies in its apparent resistance to change. It seems to have an air of "serenity" for James because as a society it is a "thoroughly confirmed and settled one" (AS 277). James prefers the city of the founding fathers as opposed to the newer metropolitan areas like New York and Chicago because unlike these cities, which are subject to "alteration, extension, development," Philadelphia has the charm of being a "fixed quantity" (AS 278). More importantly, in the high-culture equation of time and moral value, it has earned its right to consecration. As James confesses, "One is so uncertain of the value one would attach to her [Philadelphia], if she hadn't been so by prescription and for a couple of centuries" (AS 280). That Philadelphia's appeal for the author lies in its apparently hermetic social order is made evident in James's description of Philadelphia society. It seems not only to represent an "old order," an *"ancien* regime," but also a "closed circle that would find itself happy enough if only it could remain closed enough" (AS 286).

By idealizing Harvard and Philadelphia James is able to give his concept of culture a privileged position. Terms like *antiquity, fixity,* and *closure,* which operate out of a stable political structure, begin to operate as transcendent terms, that is, as values in themselves. Just as Thoreau had created a realm of Truth which transcended the social-material world, James creates a realm of culture which transcends not only the business world of democratic-capitalism but also the everyday world of twentieth century America. But even while James exalts Harvard and Philadelphia as repositories of conserving values, he makes clear that he is aware of treating these values as norms by making them function in isolation from other social voices. He relies on hierarchies at the same time that he puts them under question. The value of the past at Harvard, James confesses, was made possible by his instinct "not to press, not to push on, till forced, through any half-open door of the real. The real was there, certainly enough…but there was standing-ground more immediately for a brief idyll" (AS 59). The "real" here constitutes the world outside the enclosure drawn by James, a world he deliberately ignores. Metaphorically, this image suggests the hesitancy of the Jamesian subject to be immersed in the plurality of the social world and a need to maintain a unified and autonomous subjectivity.

But James recognizes the political and social implications of the ideology of closure, and by questioning and valorizing it at the same time he, in a sense, puts this ideology under question. A vivid illustration of James's ambivalent valorization of high culture, and the idea of closure that goes along with it, is his description of the tomb of General Grant. Many critics have seen James's description of Grant's tomb as evidence of his final understanding and acceptance of American culture, his willingness to be less European.[25] But although James asserts at the end of the description that he distinctly likes the tomb, he does not eulogize it as he does, for example, Harvard or Philadelphia. What is important about this encounter is that although James finds that he cannot dismiss the egalitarian aspects of democracy (the concept of public privilege) as vulgar variations, he still wishes to assert the ascendancy of the voice of culture. In doing so, however, he reveals the ideological problems of a transcendent concept of culture. James's commitment to the voice of culture is clear from the outset. Though the tomb presents features that deny spatial or temporal enclosure and presents a "rupture with old consecrating forms," James is determined to find in it "a new kind and degree of solemnity" (AS 145). In other words, even if the individual aspects of the tomb do not invite to be consecrated, James will still attempt to find a consecration in the sum of its aspects. That this consecration of the tomb is a covert means of attempting to evade the dispersive threat of democratic egalitarianism is evident in James's description of the tomb: "The tabernacle of Grant's ashes stands there by the pleasure drive, unguarded and unenclosed...*the property of the people*, as open as an hotel or a railway station...and as *dedicated to the public use* as builded things in America...only can be" (AS 145, italics mine). The slogans of egalitarianism—"the property of the people" and "dedicated to public use"—are here subjected to criticism through a strategic rhetorical misplacement. James questions the ideology of these slogans, not by providing different ones or by analyzing their ideological flaws, but by equating them with artifacts of mass culture that he has already demonstrated his abhorrence to—hotels and railway stations. This equation works polemically to make a causal connection between two political aspects that are not necessarily linked—egalitarianism and mass culture.

James's problem in dealing with the ideological bases of egalitarianism poses a dilemma. He cannot find a "solemnity" in the monument without confronting his own equivocal attitude toward social difference. The dilemma posed by the democratic-egalitarian voice forces the author to finally impose a conserving interpretation on the scene without apparently skirting the ideological issues. The tomb is evidence, James decides, that in some cases "publicity, familiarity, immediacy," because sincere, "may stalk in and out of the shrine with their hands in their pockets and their hats on their heads, and yet not dispel the Presence" (AS 146). Despite the fact that the tomb is a public monument that invites people in the spirit of equality rather than hero worship, James treats its egalitarian aspects (publicity, familiarity, and immediacy) as forces that the monument might be surrounded with, but which it finally resists. However, the attempt to find some kind of consecrating "Presence" in the monument is clearly a forced effort to overcome the power of the egalitarian ideology embodied in the tomb.

James realized the political problems involved in dismissing egalitarianism as mass culture and knew that his class allegiances were at stake. The Boston Public Library raises questions similar to those raised by his encounter with General Grant's tomb. In the library James deliberately searches for "some part that should be sufficiently *within,*" "sufficiently withdrawn and consecrated not to constitute a thoroughfare." He is shocked to find art treasures "hanging over mere chambers of familiarity," but also finds that "one had no good reason for defending them against such freedoms" (AS 251).

James's self-consciousness about espousing a class-based cultural politics points to a fundamental ambivalence in *The American Scene* and also helps explain the role of such deauthoritative strategies such as the creation of different narrators and the use of the bewildered observer. Just as James is committed to difference, both socially and philosophically, at the same time that he cannot give up the notion of a stable American identity, he needs to speak through multiple voices at the same time that he needs to deprive these voices of all semantic difference. By using numerous voices to address aspects of mass culture, James questions the consensus of democratic capitalism and points to the need for marginal perspectives on the world of big business. The fact that his receptiveness to difference is hampered by his own need to protect a unified identity and to find absolute value in a concept of culture is related to both the modernist period to which James belonged and to his conservatism. Much before the modernist response to mass culture would be exemplified in T. S. Eliot's *The Waste Land,* James had already suggested that the answer to the waste of the modern world lay in a culture that would "save" us all. The politically limited nature of a perspective that assumes the ability of an unchanging culture to save everyone is obvious. James's ambivalent politics also made it difficult for him to deal with the threat of difference posed by the voices of aliens and Jews and created a double bind for him. Liberalism has always had difficulty dealing with racial otherness because, although its theories apparently apply to different types of people, it restrictively assumes that all individuals have the same needs and social goals. Liberalism cannot, therefore, conceive of a decentered society. James was limited not only by this aspect of liberalism that he was committed to but also by his more conserving commitment to the concept of culture which had difficulty, even in principle, accepting the similitude of egalitarianism that American society offered.

Within the personal-political narratives discussed so far, *The American Scene* also marks a change of rhetorical strategies. Unlike Franklin and Thoreau, who polemically spoke as cultural spokespersons, Franklin as national patriarch and Thoreau as the prophetic voice of conscience, James speaks as the voice of culture but constantly puts this voice under question by dramatizing its inability to deal with the voices of different Others. A recognition of the relativity of his own ideological voice/s becomes the starting point for Henry Adams. That a unified self and cultural coherence are constructs imposed on sociopolitical diversity in order to exclude Other different voices becomes the subject of discourse in *The Education of Henry Adams*.

5

The Artifice of Boundaries: Language Intersection in *The Education of Henry Adams*

In the preface to the narrative of his life, Henry Adams wrote, "The twentieth century finds few recent guides to avoid, or to follow. American literature offers scarcely one working model for high education. The student must go back, beyond Jean Jacques, to Benjamin Franklin, to find a model even of self-teaching." Such praise for the entrepreneurial Franklin, coming from an avowed opponent of State Street, seems curious and ironic. But just as Franklin thought that young men in revolutionary America could learn from the way he had risen to wealth and prominence, Adams thought that the youth of the early twentieth century could learn from his methods of acquiring an education. Of course, between Franklin's patriarchal voice guiding youth to business success and Adams's radically undefined sense of self, liberal thought within personal-political narratives had undergone many changes. Franklin spoke from within the business culture, whereas later writers like Thoreau and James questioned the predominance of this culture and the very ideal of cultural consensus. Henry James questioned the unanimity created by the conditions of democratic capitalism but found his liberalism challenged by the new immigrants that were changing the ethnic makeup of New England.

Like James, Henry Adams saw little ethical value in the world of democratic capitalism. His own family had begun its quarrel with State Street, as Adams puts it, when John Adams had parted ways with Alexander Hamilton.[1] With the emergence of new capitalists, Adams, like James, knew that the power of the traditional elite was a relic of a bygone era. But whereas James still attempted to derive moral values from a traditional concept of culture, and took the concepts of culture and tradition seriously, Adams could look at this culture as if from the outside and see its excesses and comic flaws, even though he sympathized with it. He admired Harvard College, for example, but he saw comedy in the spectacle of joining Harvard in order to gain respectability; and he satirized endlessly the education of those like him who had to be gentlemen. So when Adams criticized all types of cultural consensus in America he did so with a consciousness that his own position was no less flawed, that it could only be a position of radical instability and relativity. In the *Education* Adams questions mass culture by demonstrating the unfeasibility of consensus in all spheres—social, political, economic, scientific—and uses a dialogic authorial voice that recognizes its own temporality and contextuality. Of all the liberal thinkers discussed so far, Adams is the first to relativize and destabilize his own position and thus question the universalism that Franklin, Thoreau, and, to an extent, James believed in.

Adams had always found forms of cultural consensus problematic. His essay "The New York Gold Conspiracy" was a searing indictment of the business culture. As a historian he found no easy interpretations or answers. He wrote nine volumes of the *History* of the Jefferson and Madison administrations and concluded not with answers but "with a series of ponderous and perhaps unanswerable questions."[2] In the *Education* Adams offers a similar resistance to consensus, unity, and ideological fixity. The pedagogical method Adams wished to introduce in the Harvard curriculum is an apt description of Adams's narrative of his education. In order to create "conflicts of thought" in his students, Adams "would have seated a rival assistant professor opposite him, whose business would be strictly limited to expressing opposite views" (E 303–4). The *Education* expresses Adams's conviction of the necessity of a heterogeneous community. Adams is aware that at any moment within the ideological horizon different voices act upon, refract, and interanimate each other. He also recognizes that insofar as any proposition is treated as an absolute belief system—Darwinism as used by proponents of capitalism, for example—its claims to a transcendent truth status depend upon an artificial drawing of boundaries, a suppression of its relationships to other ideologies and voices.

In *The American Scene* James had valorized a fairly stable concept of culture while opposing the uniformity of democratic capitalism. But while James attached ethical value to this concept of culture, he also put its ideals under question. Adams takes the process of ideological self-consciousness a step further. He makes the undermining and questioning of his own desires for a unified history and tradition a starting point for his narrative and proceeds to write a cultural history of multiple ideological perspectives. Adams often appropriates a unified and autonomous voice that answers to a "higher truth." As a believer in "unity," as the lone successor of colonial New England reformers, and the son of founding fathers, he is uniquely destined to "fail" (and hence triumph morally) in the twentieth century. But just as Adams establishes this unified voice, he aggressively sets into motion a dispersive process that decenters this voice and reveals the ideology of unity to be not something affirmed as faith but to be treated as something posited. Through this rhetorical process, Adams questions the concept of the autonomous and self-sufficient subject so important to liberal capitalism and initiates a line of more radical liberal alternatives to capitalist notions of subjectivity.

The *Education* is a sustained demonstration of the impossibility of any language, ideology, or subjectivity being independent of all others or beyond history and context. And this awareness of the open nature of every utterance, ideology, and discipline is for Adams a creative insight. It enables him to show that technology and religion, for instance, are not separate realms of value. More importantly, the *Education* as a whole is itself a compendium of diverse languages. In the *Education* evolution, physics, politics, economics, history, and religion are not autonomous modes of inquiry followed by the author but voices that are made by Adams to dialogically interact, intersect, interpret, and thus modify each other.

The *Education* relies on and yet questions the assumptions of the works we have discussed so far. Like the previous writers of the personal-political narrative, Adams often depicts himself as the missing conscience of the age. Just as Thoreau and James, for example, repudiated conventional "success" and laid claims to a higher truth, Adams emphasizes his failure to achieve social prominence and suggests that he is the true interpreter of his age.[3] Like Thoreau, he will interpret in order to teach his readers. But unlike these previous liberal critics, Adams operates from the beginning with the awareness that his own interpretational paradigms are not innocent. Again, although Adams uses the polemical strategies of the personal-political narrative to deliver an indictment on the twentieth century as materialistic, technological, fast-paced, and expedient, he, unlike Thoreau, refuses to reduce these diverse characteristics to a singular identity whereby they can easily be dismissed or repudiated. That is why the *Education* resists being seen simply as a critique of "the gilded age" or "the age of technology." For Adams, any age is too complex to be defined by a single totalizing label. Therefore, even when Adams opposes certain ideologies he does not maintain a stability and autonomy for his voice. He is

aware that his voice is modified by these ideologies, even if by antagonistic relation. In many ways, Adams's method is the opposite of
Thoreau's. Whereas Thoreau insists on the necessity of ideological
diversity, he attempts to transcend interaction with other social voices.
Adams continually professes a need for a single belief system but
develops a narrative of ideological proliferation and undermines the
assumptions of all stable and unified ideologies.[4] The *Education*
demonstrates both the suppression inherent in all unitary languages
and ideologies and the reality of the diverse voices in any utterance.

In the preface to the *Education*, Adams describes how he will figure as the subject of his narrative. He will be a "manikin" (rather than
an "Ego") that will have value only as "any other geometrical figure of
three or more dimensions, which is used for the study of relation." By
comparing himself to a manikin and a geometrical figure, Adams suggests that as the subject of the *Education* he will be a mere device (a
geometrical figure) and will lack volition (a manikin). As if in the same
self-effacing vein, Adams continues his description of this subject: "It
is the only measure of motion, of proportion, of human condition" (E
xxiv). Although Adams's reference to the manikin as the "only measure of motion" might indicate a tragic acceptance of functional and
performative (as opposed to "true") interpretation in an age of multiplicity, it also suggests that for Adams the manikin is a stable referent
and true interpreter. The sole means of measure, it is not itself a part of
motion. Insofar as it is a measure of the human condition, it has a universal human applicability and is an exegete of the human condition.
Indeed, despite his self-deprecation, Adams implies that his teachings
will be for the twentieth century what Franklin's were for eighteenth
century America—models for "high education," even if they teach by
default (E xxiii). It is against this paradoxical Emersonian self definition—"I am nothing; I see all"—that Adams in the *Education* formulates his unified voice.

Throughout the *Education*, this unified voice rests upon the two
aspects of the Emersonian formula. Adams pursues a unique "education" that will provide him with a formula to explicate American history, contemporary science, politics, and indeed Western history. It is
his burden to see all. On the other hand, because of (and in spite of)
his efforts to see all, he is uniquely qualified to be a "failure," to be
nothing. Failure is thus a necessary result of engaging in the bold project of seeing all. In the course of the *Education*, the reiterated cry of
failure becomes a mark of Adams's success in pursuing an education
higher than anyone else's and therefore inevitably failing to meet his
own standards of learning. As private secretary in Washington, for

instance, Adams finds himself "among the most ignorant and help-less." But he is also aware that "the knowledge possessed by every-body about him was hardly greater than his own" (E 99). In fact, Adams suggests that his failure is inevitable because he alone is seek-ing "education" in a world that is "both unwise and ignorant" (E 100). As Ernest Samuels points out, the "Socratic pose of ignorance" is repeated for "rhetorical emphasis" and is an ignorance that is "always less than that of other persons."[5] This mode of elevating self-depreca-tion becomes a validating base for what Adams claims is his search for a unified cultural formula.

Early in the book, Adams delineates the purpose of his educa-tion (and indeed of all true education). The task of education, says Adams, is always that of "running order through chaos, direction through space, discipline through freedom, unity through multiplici-ty" (E 12). The method of thinking in polarities is a key strategy in the *Education* just as it was in *Mont Saint Michel and Chartres*. Through these polarities Adams overtly creates a hierarchy of values. Here, by valorizing the first terms in the hierarchy—*order, direction, discipline*, and *unity*—Adams endorses cultural stability, a nostalgia for a lost aristocracy that seems to be similar to Thoreau's realm of spirituality and James's concept of culture. But it is also clear that Adams does not see order or unity in culture as somehow natural but rather as constructs that are posited. They are systematic artifices imposed on "chaos" and "freedom" in order to provide education with a stable center. In fact, by linking the idea of freedom to chaos, Adams recog-nizes what many liberal thinkers choose to ignore—that the freedom to affirm social difference is not an easy or comfortable one because it involves willingness to accept a certain amount of social "chaos" which inevitably results from the coexistence of irreconcilable social ideologies. By presenting his polarities in this manner, Adams puts his valorized terms into question from the moment of their inception, thereby opening them to the possibility of dialogue. Nevertheless, throughout the *Education* Adams exalts the first terms. These terms, *direction, order*, and *discipline*, are often collapsed into a higher "Unity" which is proclaimed as a normative entity and which becomes the quest of the author's education. Just as the insistent emphasis on fail-ure elevates Adams's quest for an education, the perceived existence of "chaos" and "multiplicity" serves to valorize the search for unity and epistemological certitudes.

This search for unity becomes an important part of the *Educa-tion*. Whereas Thoreau saw his age as uniform and standardized, Adams sees his lifetime as a series of tumultuous events. The crisis of the Civil War, Britain's questionable advances toward the Confederacy, the ponderous inertia of Russia, the scientific movements in evolution, chemistry, and physics which continually challenge current definitions of the universe, all seem to demand a coherent formula for explanation. The *Education* abounds with Adams's attestations to a faith in a unified system and his unswerving search for it. Beginning his study of Darwinism, Adams is confident that the ideas of evolution will lead to "some great generalization which would finish one's clamor to be educated" (E 224). Even when faced with doubts, Adams tells us he "insisted on maintaining his absolute standards, on aiming at ultimate Unity" (E 232). If the unity asserted by the church no longer suffices, the "motives for agreeing on some new assumption of Unity, broader and deeper than that of the Church" have redoubled (E 430). His belief in a progressivist history convinces him that "history had no use for multiplicity; it needed unity; it could study only motion, direction, attraction, relation. Everything must be made to move together" (E 377–78). The reiteration of these and other assertions serves to define Adams as a believer in a stable, consensual, if precapitalist culture. It marks the authorial voice as separate from the relativity and multiplicity of other voices, a modernist voice, able to find universal truths in a world where traditional religious sanctions are no longer operative. Indeed, this nostalgia for a world of perfect harmony suggests that Adams seems to want in the philosophical sphere what James sometimes wishes to conserve in the social: order, coherence, and above all, stability.

Adams ironically also seems to legitimize the cultural consensus endemic to liberal capitalism by presenting an autonomous selfhood. He insists that the search for an education is necessarily *his* unique burden. True, Adams often reminds the reader of his unexceptional nature. His need for a unified system, he suggests, is a necessary consequence of the radical upheavals that have destabilized his whole generation. All have been reared unprepared for the twentieth century, and in this sense "between 1850 and 1900 nearly every one's existence [is] exceptional" (E 38). As with his peers, his conventional education denies him proficiency in mathematics, French, German, and Spanish, four tools needed for success. He, again like his peers, has witnessed the convulsions of the Civil war, the assassinations of three American presidents, the use of the ocean steamer, the electric telegraph, and finally the introduction of new forces by the discovery of radium. To such men only the past offers a modicum of stability.

To an extent, then, Adams speaks as part of his society, warning young university men whose education might be similarly handicapped. But just as often the rhetoric of the *Education* suggests that Adams's attempts to divest himself of any extraordinary propensities are often forced.[6] Indeed, Adams (especially in the early chapters of the *Education*) belabors the point that he is particularly well suited for the task of pursuing a unified education. If all in his generation are ill-fitted for the twentieth century, he is a virtual anachronism because of his special circumstances. From the moment of his birth, Adams tells us, he was branded into an inheritance that would handicap his twentieth century education. "Whatever was peculiar to him was education, not character, and came to him, directly and indirectly, as the result of that eighteenth century inheritance which he took with his name" (E 7). In part, this inheritance comprises a moral certitude to distinguish between good and evil and thus to undertake the removal of evil as a righteous duty. More importantly, for Adams, it is an inheritance of the ideology of the founding fathers. Adams often sees the early republican era as one of undefiled origins, of inviolate political morality in comparison to which his own age signifies only the collapse of moral law. Describing the political quagmire of Grant's administration, for instance, Adams concludes, "The system of 1789 had broken down, and with it the eighteenth century fabric of a priori, or moral principles" (E 280–81). Adams's observations here reflect not merely an aversion to Grant's moral debilitation, but also his valorization of the ideological certitudes he believes the eighteenth century possessed. Adams is born into a world that is an extension of these certainties and principles. A belief in a priori, moral principles, which permeate his boyhood home, promises an ultimate certitude. "Viewed from Mount Vernon Street," says Adams, "politics offered no difficulties, for the moral law was a sure guide. Social perfection was also sure because human nature worked for Good.... *Education* was divine, and man needed only a correct knowledge of facts to reach perfection" (E 33). Having been indoctrinated in tenets inapplicable to his own age, Adams emerges as one burdened from the start with disadvantages greater than any of his peers. Because it is his solitary fate to be so marked, it is his task alone to seek an education that will provide a formula for his own age. Adams, the unity seeker, thus speaks as a representative of his age but also as a special one, destined to experience the maximum of its handicaps and therefore to be its legitimate prophetic spokesperson.

These repeated assertions about the necessity of finding a unified system and the eulogies to a pristine eighteenth century past seem suspiciously like nostalgic attempts to retain, intellectually, the patrician status and power that the Adams family had, in reality, lost.

Moreover, as unity seeker, Adams reiterates his opposition to the diverse and changing forms of knowledge he encounters. No matter where his education leads him, Adams maintains that he continues to abide by a faith in unity. Indeed, so vehement is Adams in his protestations that many critics have seen the *Education* simply as a treatise on finding order and unity, Adams's "supreme no to chaos and disorder."[7] But although Adams claims to adhere to ideological hegemony and unitary languages, his educational process vigorously repudiates all unity or stability. It is important to emphasize here that, despite his assertions on finding Unity, Adams is determined to *discover* cultural differences and contradictions. This is a dimension not adequately stressed by most critics. John Carlos Rowe points out that Adams seeks order and coherence in systems like evolution and history but actually finds contradiction. What this suggests to Rowe is a "tentative pluralism" in the *Education.* [8] But Adams had moved from an easy liberal affirmation of pluralism to an active participation in difference. Adams begins his philosophical inquiries with a skepticism about Unity, indeed, a desire to locate disunities. In fact, Adams's description of the book as "a study of Twentieth-Century Multiplicity" is particularly appropriate because in the *Education* Adams not only records "multiplicity" as a phenomenon but uses it as a cognitive tool.[9] The process of Adams's education involves a radical and continuous search for caveats within each ideological system he explores.

Perhaps the most obvious of his inquiries into multiplicity is his study of evolution. In Adams's age evolutionary theories had enormous socio-political significance and were used in the most dogmatic manner to bolster the individualist business culture. Thus when Adams refused to accept Darwinian evolution as an uncomplicated theory (even though he acknowledged its attractions), he attacked an important scientific basis of the proponents of capitalism. Adams states at the outset his skepticism of Sir Charles Lyell's theories of uniformity. He sees "unbroken Evolution under uniform conditions" at best as a "substitute for religion; a safe, conservative, practical, thoroughly Common-Law deity" (E 225). Nevertheless, he maintains the necessity of such theories because, as he puts it, "Life depended on it." "Unity and Uniformity were the whole motive of philosophy" (E 226).

But clearly, unity and uniformity do not motivate Adams in his study of evolution. As a substitute for a biblical system, the principles of natural selection, unbroken evolution, and survival of the fittest had provided many nineteenth century thinkers with what they perceived were immutable foundations for their social theories. William Graham Sumner, the most well known social Darwinist, applied concepts of evolution almost directly to social questions. In *What Social Classes Owe to Each Other* he ridiculed the idea of welfare organizations for the needy, for example, by arguing that hardships were "part of the struggle with Nature for existence."[10] For many others, evolution seemed less a substitute than a complement to religion. To Asa Gray natural selection seemed inevitably a part of God's plan, and he urged Darwin to postulate a deity in his grand design.[11] As Richard Hofstadter points out, by the 1880s "evolution had been translated into divine purpose" and religion was bolstered by "the infusion of an authoritative idea from the field of science."[12]

If Adams had found in evolution an all-explanatory system, he would not have been alone. But consistent with his practice in the *Education* of questioning the authority of any system, Adams chose not to do so. What interests him most in evolution are the ruptures within the theory. For Adams, the existence of a few deviant forms like the *Terebratula*, which have stayed virtually stable, and the *Pteraspis*, for which no preceding forms have been found, is enough to invalidate the theories of evolution. Natural selection and uniform evolution become, for Adams, merely convenient concepts, "precisely like the inference of Paley, that, if one found a watch, one inferred a watchmaker" (E 230). The lack of evolution illustrated by these freakish forms preoccupies Adams so much that when years later he finds that Charles Walcott has discovered an ancestry for the *Pteraspis* he sees in it no cause for hope in finding uniform evolution substantiated. In fact, he is "almost aggrieved" to find Walcott researching the ancestry of the *Pteraspis*. Adams continues instead to stress the breaks that invalidate evolutionary theory: "Evolution finished before it began—minute changes that refused to change anything during the whole geological record—survival of the highest order in a fauna which had no origin...to an honest-meaning though ignorant student who needed to prove Natural Selection and not assume it, such sequence brought no peace" (E 399). Again, it is obvious here that although Adams claims to be looking for an absolute theory that will bring him "peace," his own focus on the breaks in it suggests otherwise. Throughout the *Education* Adams focuses on similar ruptures. Although Adams sees Rome as a civilization that had given "heart and unity" to the Western world, he is aware that it was also a "bewildering complex of ideas, experiments, ambitions and energies" (E 93). It is the disjunctions in Roman history that interest Adams. "No law of progress applied to it [Rome]," says Adams. "The Forum no more led to the Vatican than the Vatican to the Forum. Rienzi, Garibaldi, Tiberius, Gracchus, Aurelian might be mixed up in any relation of time, and never lead to a sequence" (E 91). Here, by creating a narrative of assassinations, Adams suggests his resistance to more consensual and integrative methods of historical thinking and undermines the possibility of any historical sequence. In fact, the unity of Rome preoccupies him less than the eternal "Why?" of its fall. Similarly, current events signal to Adams ruptures and disjunctions in American history. Roosevelt's policy of strict neutrality toward the Boer War suggests to Adams that the very principles of freedom drawn up for the country in 1776 might be suspect and have to be redefended. Indeed, in "Dilettantism," he becomes a sort of detective of disunity, insistent on gathering evidence about the lack of consensus among art experts about the authenticity of a Rafael drawing. Finally, in his dynamic theory of history, Adams concentrates less on progress than on the problems of explaining sequence and on the sudden changes brought about by the discovery of gunpowder, the compass, and radium. Adams, it seems, is determined to amass evidence that questions the very notions of cultural stability and coherence.

Whereas Adams's clear emphasis on ruptures (in the process of purportedly seeking an education that promises unity) repudiates the ideal of cultural consensus, the continual demonstration of the artificiality of all autonomous ideologies and languages questions this consensus even more. Adams questions both individualistic notions of self and concepts of universalism. He is aware, as Mailer is later in The Armies of the Night, that no language system is ideologically neutral or self-contained. It can pose as such, and with absolutist pretentions, only by arbitrarily separating itself as unconditional truth from its intertextual ideological base. Historians seem to Adams to be particularly prone to seeing their language as innocent: "Historians undertake to arrange sequences—called stories, or histories—assuming in silence a relation of cause and effect." "These assumptions," he continues, "have been astounding, but commonly unconscious and childlike; so much so that if any captious critic were to drag them to light, historians would probably reply...that they had never supposed themselves required to know what they were talking about" (E 382). Adams's professional difficulty as a historian arises precisely because he recognizes and foregrounds these silent assumptions of cause and effect. He requires himself to know what his stories mean and ideologically imply. Adams's theory of history is "post-realist" and relativistic.[13] That is why as a teacher of history at Harvard he is unable to teach a historical method that assumes a beginning or progression. For him, every beginning is arbitrary because no point can be established as an origin. Adams's criticism of the well-made narrative is also a criticism of the well-made world of positivistic humanism.[14] As he puts it, one cannot begin at the beginning because "complexity precedes evolution. The *Pteraspis* grins horribly from the closed entrance" (E 302). Similarly, insofar as history can either affirm or deny progression, it cannot be ideologically innocent. In either case, says Adams, the historian "falls into the burning faggots of the pit. He makes of his scholars either priests or atheists, plutocrats or socialists, judges or anarchists, almost in spite of himself" (E 300–1). History, in other words, cannot dissociate itself from religious, political, ethical, and economical spheres because it relies on their substructures (by reaching ethical and political conclusions) even if it claims otherwise.

By continually showing how all social theories are contrived rather than True, and thus suggesting that social truths are highly variable, Adams creates a dynamic and multiple social vision. We have seen how Franklin was able to consolidate an individualistic culture of ownership and success by attempting to read diverse voices through the culture of Lockean liberalism. On the other hand, Thoreau destabilized the maxims of commercial culture by questioning their ideological bases; James undermined the consensual business culture of democratic capitalism by contrasting it to his own changing voices. Adams's enquiries into different theories and language systems also work toward dialogizing them and thus questioning their privileged Truth status. The above enquiry into historical language, for instance, reveals the diverse social languages operating within history: economics, politics, religion, and ethics. The supposedly innocent language of conventional historians begins to be seen as a power construct that works by keeping from view the political and ethical judgments it makes.

In a similar manner, Adams also deconstructs his own nostalgia for an older, more coherent culture and his attempts at seeking a philosophical unity. Although he wishes, belatedly, for the cultural coherence of a pre-Darwinian world, Adams is aware that unity is a posited construct imposed on historical multiplicity because, "except as reflected in himself, man has no reason for *assuming* unity in the universe, or an ultimate substance, or a prime motor" (E 484, italics mine). Yet unity is repeatedly invoked for false comfort. Scientists, perplexed by sudden changes, "imitate the church, and invoke a 'larger synthesis' to unify the anarchy again." However, Adams realizes that "a point must always be soon reached where larger synthesis is suicide" (E 402). Throughout the *Education*, by simultaneously insisting on the necessity of cultural unity while examining the motives for maintaining it and by analyzing its manifestations throughout Western history, Adams destroys the very idea of cultural coherence and undermines the validity of his own nostalgic desires for unity. Adams radically decenters his voice in a manner that James did in *The American Scene*, almost in spite of himself. Faced with radical egalitarianism and the dispersive voices of immigrants, James was forced to see the ideological motives behind maintaining his concept of culture and thus to question the autonomy of his own voice. But James continues to hold on to his concept of culture, and the sanctity of an American identity, for him, simply exists. But for Adams no unconditional truths simply exist; they are constructed for expedience. Thus Adams recognizes, for example, that George Washington can stand for absolute moral good, an "ultimate relation like the Pole Star," only if one ignores the visible presence of slavery even in Washington's home state (E 47).[15]

Adams was sensitive to social heterogeneity and the fact that society was always constituted by differences. As private secretary to his father in England, he noted the fictiveness of an exclusive or fixed idea of society. English society was a heteroglot mixture of different social groups none of which absolutely defined it. There were "groups of nebulous societies" such as the legal groups, the clergy, "the medical and surgical professions; city people; artists; county families; the Scotch; and indefinite other subdivisions" (E 197). Adams does not merely take account of divisions constituted by a single factor like class or race but considers the interactions of a number of them so that he creates diverse ideological contexts and effectively challenges his own affirmations of cultural coherence.

Adams not only demonstrates cultural heterogeneity but also shows the artificiality of the traditional boundaries that separate different areas of knowledge. The cultural consensus created by capitalism sanctions the isolation of knowledge into different compartments so that the ideological structures of each can remain unquestioned and interrelatedness can be denied. Capitalism survives by this isolation because the separation of different ideologies from each other ensures that society will not be constituted by ideological difference but by a liberal acceptance of the reasonableness of all ideologies. Adams questions this legitimized isolation of knowledge. In the *Education* the languages of religion, science, politics, philosophy, and art intersect and implicate each other. Even national languages are not self-contained. In order to fit the *Education* into a "cultural" schemata, many critics have viewed it in terms of some American "tradition." Sacvan Bercovitch, for instance, sees the *Education* as an "antijeremiad" that is "not so much a rejection of the culture as it is a variation

on a central cultural theme." Like other antijeremiads, the *Education*
confirms "the cosmic import of the American way." For Bercovitch,
Adams becomes "a prophet reading the fate of humanity, and the universe at large, in the tragic course of American history."[16] Bercovitch's
analysis shows a hegemonic national mythos that extended through
the centuries since the first foundations. The *Education*, however,
breaks that hegemony. Although Adams acclaims pure beginnings
and founding fathers, the *Education* works, as I have shown, to
demonstrate the posited nature of this voice and the arbitrariness of
all beginnings. And if eighteenth century America remains a locus of
value for Adams, it is obviously not the only one. It certainly pales
before Adams's valorization of the twelfth century. More importantly,
Adams does not see American history as a paradigm for all history
because for him American history does not exist as an autonomous
entity. No national histories or myths do.

Even a cursory look at the *Education* reveals that for Adams
American history cannot be separated from the general course of
Western history, the discourses of science and philosophy, or the
influence of various social and scientific "forces" that determine
action. Early in the *Education* Adams connects the Boston of his childhood to the forces moving all of Europe. The economic and social
forces which would change the world of the upper-class bourgeoisie
would also change the Paris of Louis Phillipe and the London of J. S.
Mill (E 33). Later, in "A Dynamic Theory of History," Adams sees the
Puritan emigration as the continued expression in Western history of
a faith in the *Civitas Dei* , a faith that dates back to Bishop Augustine's
treatise bearing that title. Adams suggests that this same faith also
impelled Gutenberg and Fust to print the first Bible. This does not
mean that Puritan intellectual history is a replication of the ideas of
the fifth and fifteenth centuries. What it does suggest is that American
history cannot be wholly unique and therefore autonomous. A
national mythos ("the American way") always assumes a fiction of
oneness which actually suppresses the diverse forces which constitute
it. This is the knowledge Franklin uses to create a capitalist ethos and
to contain the difference of Others who question this ethos; Henry
James discovers that the concept of a singular American identity
clearly ignores the presence of diverse ethnic and racial Others.
Adams is aware of the fictiveness of singular conceptions of national
character and therefore refuses to create a unifying national mythology. The beginnings of the American republic include the morality of
the founding fathers *and* the fact of slavery. Adams describes the eighteenth century atmosphere in which he is reared as "Colonial, revolu-

tionary, almost Cromwellian" (E 7). That Adams cannot describe eighteenth century America simply in national terms is both linguistically and ideologically inevitable. A "new" language can be formulated only by using the existent terms in a different context. Conversely, even if overtly "new" terms are formulated, they arise from and reflect different contexts.

In addition to questioning the unity and self-sufficiency of national myths, Adams demonstrates the interrelatedness of all languages and forms of knowledge by dramatizing the interplays between different languages. Often he uses these languages deliberately in startling combinations. The discovery of deviant forms that defy evolution, for instance, provides Adams with a key for examining social, political, and technological systems. In the chapter "President Grant," the languages of political and evolutionary theory (to isolate only two) are so interlinked that it is difficult to say which one serves and thus helps to prove the other. The double voicing is evident from the beginning. The reason Grant was elected was simple. "Grant represented order. He was a great soldier, and the soldier always represented order" (E 260). Ostensibly *order* is used here as a socio-political term. But the term *order* also suggests its meaning as an orderly sequence in evolutionary theory and more so because the second sentence is introduced to qualify the semantic boundaries of the first ("Grant represented order"). The possibility that the languages of both politics and evolution are being used here is made stronger as Adams continues to muse on the efficacy of President Grant. Had Grant been a congressman, Adams confesses that he would have expected less of him, for Adams had been forewarned, "You can't use tact with a Congressman! A Congressman is a hog! You must take a stick and hit him on the snout!" (E 261). While this unflattering description of a congressman as a hog is obviously a statement on political greed and mindlessness, the animal analogy employed here reflects the idea of nonevolution or perhaps reversion. The dialogic use of the languages of politics and evolution is made explicit later in the chapter. For Adams, Grant is one of those aberrations whose actions, for example, the choice of his cabinet, reflect little thought. His own meeting with Grant merely confirms Badeau's observation that one could not follow "a mental process" in the president's thought. As a totally preintellectual type, "Grant fretted and irritated him, like the *Terebratula,* as a defiance of first principles. He had no right to exist. He should have been extinct for ages" (E 266). Obviously the equation of Grant with the *Terebratula* is hyperbolic. More importantly, the existence of forms like the *Terebratula* enables Adams to account for aberrations like Grant. Conversely, the political retrogression implied by Grant's accession confirms the ruptures in evolutionary theory. "The progress of evolution from President Washington to President Grant," he concludes, "was alone evidence enough to upset Darwin" (E 266). By interpreting evolution through politics and vice versa, Adams generates a double-voiced language that denies the self-contained nature of both the languages and shatters the hegemony of a singular language of cultural coherence.

A similar interaction of languages is evident in Adams's other social observations. Pondering on the assassinations of Presidents Lincoln, Garfield, and McKinley, Adams reflects as follows:

> America has always taken tragedy lightly. Too busy to stop the activity of their twenty-million-horse-power-society, Americans ignore tragic motives that would have overshadowed the Middle Ages; and the world learns to regard assassination as a form of hysteria, and death as a neurosis, to be treated by a rest-cure. (E 416)

The fact of political assassination cannot be explained within the confines of a single language. Here Adams suggests that the acceptance of political assassinations cannot be separated from the frenetic social pace engendered by present economic and technological conditions. The apparent acceptance of these assassinations is also linked to the quasi-scientific (and therefore apparently acceptable) categorizations provided by psychoanalysis. Through psychoanalysis, ethical deviances like political assassination can be translated into explanatory and less morally offensive terms like *hysteria*. And Adams's own interpretation of the assassinations cannot be dissociated from his conceptions of what constitutes tragedy (a historical and aesthetic criterion).

Even when Adams claims to be searching for a unified formula, he does so by breaking traditional disciplinary boundaries. When he states that he would like to see the "political and social and scientific values of the twelfth and twentieth centuries...correlated in some relation of movement that could be expressed in mathematics," his desire for a single, unified formula is only apparent (E 376). We note how Adams is always aware of different types of values—political, social, scientific—and the need to interrelate them.

Given Adams's distrust of all forms of consensual thinking and a belief in diverse socio-ideological formulations, it is no wonder that the *Education* refuses, in its voices and languages, to be a jeremiad or a treatise on lost unity. To be sure, the last few chapters of the *Education* reflect Adams's misgivings about, and his fear of, the implications of twentieth century science. Science not only denies any claims of offering complete explanations, but it revels in proceeding from difference. Scientific theories are legitimated not by proving the consensus of experts but by emphasizing the different opinions among them. Even in the most elementary textbooks of science Adams finds phrases such as "The cause of this phenomenon is not understood," "Science no longer ventures to explain causes," "Opinions are very much divided," and "Science gets on only by adopting different theories, sometimes contradictory." Amazed by the rejection of consensus in the process of learning, Adams concludes, "Evidently the new American would need to think in contradictions, and instead of Kant's famous four antinomies, the new universe would know no law that could not be proved by its anti-law" (E 497–98). His protestations notwithstanding, I suggest that Adams was himself partly this new American. He could hardly help being one once he had opened himself up to new scientific theories. His own method of searching for an education, as I have shown, is itself motivated by contradiction rather than by a search for consensus or final solutions.

Consequently, the *Education* cannot be seen as merely an acceptance or rejection of science. In fact, one of the principal achievements of the *Education* is that it narrativizes scientific language and makes it function as part of the several languages in the text. One of the distinguishing features of scientific knowledge, according to Jean Francois Lyotard, is that it is dependent on denotation alone. "A statement's truth-value is the criterion determining its acceptability."[17] Scientific discourse, in other words, closes itself from criteria like justice and beauty. In this way, Lyotard continues, scientific knowledge is "set apart from the language games that combine to form the social bond.... The relation between [scientific] knowledge and society becomes one of mutual exteriority."[18] Scientific language is thus separate from other social languages because of its ostensible disengagement from aesthetic, social, and ethical concerns. Adams clearly recognizes this exteriorized, disparate nature of science. But instead of accepting it as such and therefore discarding it as alien, Adams opens up the hermetic nature of scientific language by making it function as something more than pure and narrow denotation, that is, as a socio-cultural language. In its nondenotative aspect, it opens itself up to the nexus of textual languages, enters into dialogic relationships with other languages, permeates the cultural narrative, and therefore refuses to be a separate entity that can either be accepted or rejected. To "risk translating rays into faith" is to risk transforming the nature of both (E 383).

The chapter "The Dynamo and the Virgin" is perhaps the best illustration of this simultaneous transformation. The very title of the chapter indicates Adams's determination to open up (even if by juxtaposition) the languages of science and religion to each other. Reflecting on the predicament of artists to whom the inventions of science always remain alien, Adams writes, "They all felt a railway train as power; yet they…constantly complained that the power embodied in a railway train could never be embodied in art. All the steam in the world could not, like the Virgin, build Chartres" (E 388). Science has remained exteriorized and outside cultural concerns, Adams suggests, because it has remained within the denotative paradigm. Christianity, on the other hand, is a powerful social force partly because it has been repeatedly embodied in narrative. Adams attempts to narrativize scientific language by taking it out of the denotative paradigm and making it the referent of ethical criteria. The contrast between the denotative (exclusive) and nondenotative (cultural) use of science is dramatized early in the chapter. To the scientist Langley, the dynamo merely spells a residuum of inert facts. "To him," Adams writes, "the dynamo itself was but an ingenious channel for conveying somewhere the heat latent in a few tons of poor coal hidden in a dirty engine-house carefully kept out of sight." But for Adams it becomes "a symbol of infinity," a "moral force" like the cross. "Before the end, one began to pray to it; inherited instinct taught the natural expression of man before silent and infinite force" (E 380). Adams's prayer to the dynamo, I suggest, is not a mock gesture that involves a parody of the culture and a serious point made about science.[19] The cultural exaltation of the dynamo is an expression of Adams's refusal to let scientific language be disparate. He demands that scientific language be nondenotative, that it open itself up to ethical criteria. In the process of making these demands, he makes the dynamo more than a machine for converting coal into energy. It becomes a representative of the forces of science from which human beings cannot remain immune and embodies a language of science implicated in other languages.

It is this interplay between the scientific and ethical that is reflected in Adams's description of his project at the end of the chapter. For him, the Virgin had always functioned as a felt force in the Western world. Clearly, the knowledge of the Virgin is not exteriorized like scientific knowledge, but Adams proposes to treat it as such. His business as a historian was, says Adams, "to follow the track of energy; to find where it came from and where it went to…; its values, equivalents, conversions. It could scarcely be more complex than radium" (E 389). The use of scientific jargon—*energy, values, equivalents, conversions,*—is obvious here. To study religious force through apparently scientific methods in the medium of scientific language is to destroy it, but only in the logocentric sense. Adams is not interested in the monolithic aspects of Christianity. He opposes the new energies unleashed by the dynamo not to a singular Law or God but to the Virgin, who resists and questions the singular and divine Law. The Virgin represents what is outside the Law and what challenges Law. Adams's apotheosis of the Virgin is a striking contrast to Thoreau's attempts to repress femininity and James's attempts to appropriate woman as an exemplification of his concept of culture. For Adams, femininity, multiplicity, and cultural difference are interrelated, and he celebrates them all. In *Mont Saint Michel and Chartres* Adams saw the Virgin as representing "whatever was not Unity; whatever was irregular, exceptional, outlawed."[20] In the *Education* the Virgin similarly represents sexuality, fecundity, mystery, Woman. It is for this reason, Adams surmises, that Woman as force has been suppressed in Puritan America: "Any one brought up among the Puritans knew that sex was sin" (E 384). The Virgin and the dynamo are set up in the chapter as polar opposites, but neither term suggests a stability. It is probably the lack of a stable center that critics lament when they label Adams as "pessimistic" or "nihilistic." Tracing the decline of tradition and authority in religion, Paul Elmer More wrote: "By a gradual elimination of its positive content the faith of the people had passed from Calvinism to Unitarianism, and from this to free thinking, until the days of our Adams there was little left to the intellect but a great denial."[21] The *Education* does constitute a "denial" of religion and all other belief systems insofar as they are conceived of as autonomous and fully explanatory. Such belief systems build up a consensual culture intolerant of change and dissension.

In the *Education* the languages of science and religion are not absolute and separate. The attempts to analyze scientifically the Virgin's force and to gauge the moral value of the dynamo in "The Dynamo and the Virgin" are enactments of Adams's belief in the interrelatedness of science and religion. For Adams all social languages are connected in complex dialogic relationships which keep them from being fixed or defined. It is a similar kind of mixture of languages that animates chapters like "A Dynamic Theory of History" and "A Law of Acceleration." These chapters, and indeed the *Education* as a whole, evade and question labels like *philosophy, history,* or *science,* because the voices of the philosopher, the historian, and the scientist (among many others) are themselves interlinked rather than discrete, and they continually interact with each other.

Yet it is also clear that, although Adams questions all universalizing ideologies, he does not joyously substitute a play of different
voices for a singular and stable voice. The very equation of "multiplicity" and "diversity" with "anarchy" and "chaos" suggests a hesi-
tant acceptance of both cultural destabilization and the breakdown of
the unified subject. But if Adams does not begin with a novelistic presumption of what Bakhtin calls "a verbal and semantic decentering of
the ideological world," neither does he begin either by presuming an
ideological center.[22] As John Carlos Rowe points out, even by the time
Adams wrote *Mont Saint Michel and Chartres*, he "recognized that language intends its own violation and revision. The constant transformations built into language...seem to deny the idea of a fixed and
final center for human signification."[23] That is why, although Adams
in the *Education* might assert the need for a coherent social formula,
his use of multiple discourses repudiates the very idea of social coherence. He laments his failure to find an absolute truth while he simultaneously exposes the ruptures of all systems that make truth claims.
He locates cultural unities but shows how these unities are inherently
oppressive.

The *Education* thus presents a cultural vision in which no ideology is empowered to be dominant because each is context bound,
interdependent, and interrelated to all others. Adams goes beyond
liberal pluralism by questioning the ideological investments and
interrelatedness of all social theories and thus denying them autonomy and universality even as he retains an old-world nostalgia for the
stability and order of his patrician inheritance. As a teacher wanting
to equip his young readers for any emergency, Adams invites students who will question all totalizing systems, who will dialogically
react to rather than simply accept his pronouncements.[24] As author, he
retains the privilege of speaking as the sole conscience of his age, but
he denies the cultural coherence and authority that speaking through
such a voice might imply.

6

Class and Gender: The Divided Voices of *Twenty Years at Hull-House*

The social, cultural, and technological changes at the turn of the century were disorienting for both Henry James and Henry Adams. While Henry James maintained the position of equivocal liberal, both condemning the unanimity of democratic capitalism and fearing the breakdown of a unified American culture, Henry Adams celebrated, albeit reluctantly, the heterogeneity of different social theories and maintained a posture of relativity that challenged the unity of New England culture. For Jane Addams democratic capitalism posed problems of a different order. Capitalism had always promoted the creed of a self-sufficient individualism which denied the relevance of social responsibility and social conceptions of selfhood. But this myth of an inherently egalitarian society in which upward mobility was available to all was nowhere more in question than in the heart of capitalist America—in the slums of big cities. Here, there was a challenge not only to the myth of opportunity but also to the morality of individualism which was central to liberal thought. Jane Addams questioned the ideologies of autonomous individualism and social consensus by turning to a materialistic interpretation of culture and by emphasizing class as an important factor in the determination of social values. Like Henry Adams, but for very different reasons, Jane Addams was able to question the concept of universal values that previous writers of the personal-political narrative were unable to.

It was not as if Jane Addams was the first social theorist or writer to recognize the existence of poverty in America. Franklin, as we know, constantly wrote about Poor Richard, and in his own *Autobiography* paid great attention to dramatizing pictures of his days as a poor youth. But this kind of Horatio Alger mythologizing of poverty as an early hardship which merely had to be overcome in order to build character was really a means of denying the importance of class difference (and the existence of poverty itself) and reinforcing the ide-

ology of competition.[1] The industrialist Andrew Carnegie, for example, lectured about the advantages of poverty in early life.[2] Jane
Addams, however, saw the urban poor as voices of difference that
could not be repressed behind the ideology of competitive individualism. When she established Hull-House in Chicago in January 1889, it
was with the understanding that the underclass of industrial America
had its own special and different needs.

In *Twenty Years at Hull-House* Addams speaks as a progressivist
reformer seeking to arouse the conscience of the nation and forcing it
to recognize its underclass, but she does not do so by creating an
essentialized poor that can be easily defined or by offering a transcendent social theory to replace that of competitive individualism. Such
definitional moves, as theorists of subversion have noted, only participate in the very power structures that they attempt to subvert. Kristeva points out, for instance, how any group which has not given up
the belief in "its own identity" "can be recuperated by that power
[which it opposes] and by a spirituality that may be laicized or openly
religious."[3] If capitalist ideology defines the economically disadvantaged by their lack of enterprise and thus denies the threat of difference that they pose, an easy idealization of "the poor" no less simplifies the complex cultural determinants of these people. James Agee,
the documentary writer of the Depression a generation later, would
recognize the complexity of his tenant farmers but still choose to idealize them as holy. Addams, on the other hand, speaks for the urban
poor, not by idealizing them or their contexts, but by problematizing
the distinctions between high and low culture and by complicating
the notion of oppression itself. Instead of following a particular social
theory as a basis for her reform activities, she voices the problems and
contradictions she confronts as she attempts to find an appropriate
theory. Thus even though she, at times, longs like Henry Adams and
her socialist contemporary, Tolstoy, to find a single theory to believe,
she undermines the authority of absolute and transcendent theories
by emphasizing the social and historical conditions that contribute to
their creation. Like Henry Adams, she recognizes the contextuality of
all theories. Similarly, Addams also makes clear that her voice is not
autonomous and self-sufficient, but rather influenced by the particularities of class and gender. It is a voice that recognizes its historically
contingent and circumscribed role. In fact, class and gender play an
important role in determining the nature of Addams's criticism of the
American liberal-capitalist consensus. While Addams often seems to
speak from within her upper-class inheritance, like Henry James
bestowing the difference of culture on the homogenized masses, she

is also genuinely interested in dialogically questioning the supposedly innate moral value of high culture. She speaks as a woman both disempowered by patriarchy and emboldened to voice herself in opposition to it, and also as a tempered radical unwilling to completely separate herself from the capitalist, patriarchal culture.

Jane Addams's social position was anomalous, to say the least. Like Henry Adams, she belonged to a patrician family, her father being a wealthy state senator and mill owner. But even more than Adams she experienced the powerlessness of the only social position available to her—that of a "lady." Yet lady she did become, and like many of her class traveled to Europe in search of culture and education.[4] But behind this mask of gentility lay the nervousness, anxiety, and depression that had plagued her incipiently throughout her adolescence and which surfaced with the death of her father. I will discuss later the particular conjunctures between Addams's reformist politics and her writing as a woman. Here, it is important to mention that Addams's representation of her girlhood doubts, anxieties, and fears in *Twenty Years* creates another voice for the text, one that Gilbert and Gubar describe as the voice of the author's double. "Through the violence of the double…the female author enacts her own raging desire to escape male houses and male texts, while at the same time it is through the double's violence that this anxious author articulates for herself the costly destructiveness of anger repressed until it can no longer be contained."[5] Addams enacted the patriarchal role of ladyhood even as she exposed its repressions. She maintained a lifelong commitment to culture and the arts while living within the inner-city slums of Chicago. She developed a popular image as a saint, but by 1919 she was targeted by the U.S. government as the most dangerous woman in America.[6]

Addams's particular vision of community and her subversion of the beneficiary-recipient relationship between the upper and lower classes in *Twenty Years* derives from these peculiarities of her social position. Addams begins her narrative by denying and discrediting the modernist claims to objectivity and authorial distance that are characteristic of the bourgeois concept of authorship. "No effort is made in the recital to separate my own history from that of Hull-House during the years when I was 'launched deep into the stormy intercourse of human life' for, so far as the mind is pliant under the pressure of events and experiences, it becomes hard to detach it."[7] The authorial voice in *Twenty Years* is not presented as singular, original, and beyond the social contexts in which it participates. Addams, unlike Thoreau and James, was uneasy with the idea of championing universal values across cultures. Her political visions depend upon her positioning in both the upper class and the working poor. In an extended argument about the need for social settlements like Hull-House, Addams formulates her belief in the social nature of self and subjectivity:

> These [educated] young men and women, longing to socialize their democracy, are animated by certain hopes...; that if in a democratic country nothing can be permanently achieved save through the masses of people, it will be impossible to establish a higher political life than the people themselves crave; that it is difficult to see how the notion of a higher civic life can be fostered save through common intercourse; that the blessings which we associate with a life of refinement and cultivation can be made universal and must be made universal if they are to be permanent.... You may remember the forlorn feeling which occasionally seizes you when you arrive early in the morning a stranger in a great city: the stream of laboring people goes past you as you gaze through the plate-glass window of your hotel.... You turn helplessly to the waiter and feel that it would be almost grotesque to claim from him the sympathy you crave because civilization has placed you apart, but you resent your position with a sudden sense of snobbery. (TY 116–17)

I quote this passage at length because it illustrates the varied contexts within which Addams's voice operates, contexts which make her commitment to a social sense of self highly complex. She speaks as a reformer decrying the class-bound concept of high culture, as an empathizer of the leisure class and its ennui, and as part of an alienated bourgeoisie. The passage reiterates the necessity of a social self, but the rhetoric of the passage reinforces the traditional separations between public and private by dramatizing the opposed voices of the detached public reformer and the private, emotional person. We can also detect a separation between the bourgeois self and the working Others in the classic protosocialist sentimentalization of the laborers even as they appear only as objects of the narrator's gaze. But Addams brings in this class separation not in order to save the bourgeois self (indeed, nothing could be farther from her intentions) but to acknowledge the differences of class.

   Addams's alternative social vision is one of social intercourse where the hierarchical distinctions between the "higher" political and civic life and the "common" will become only lateral distinctions. The need for intersubjective space, in which no voice is autonomous or separate, is poignantly expressed in the unspoken dialogue between the waiter and the hotel guest. But this notion of intersubjectivity, based as it is on the notion of a dialogic self, where the boundaries between self and Other are erased, cannot be an absolute one. Indeed, visions of community, whether Bakhtininan or feminist, risk becoming overly sentimental when community is viewed as a complete absence of conflict.[8] But intersubjective space is not a neutral or monologic construct but a space constituted by differences. Addams recognizes these differences as a vital part of community and formulates a social vision that transvaluates these differences.

In *Twenty Years*, Addams's settlement is both the practical organization that is the object of discussion and the pervasive metaphor for borderland culture. Hull-House is strategically located within the inner-city slums of Chicago; it is a refuge to children of working-class mothers, to the elderly poor, and to malnourished workers. But Addams conceives of Hull-House as more than a physical welfare organization. Hull-House is, more importantly, a sanctuary of culture. Members organize poetry readings, put up Shakespeare performances, host art exhibits, and hold piano recitals. The multiple functions, social intercourse, and location of Hull-House raise interesting questions. If Hull-House symbolizes culture, where does the demarcation between high and low culture, the refined and the masses, begin? Because the essence of the settlement is that it is open to, and a vital part of, the community, can the "inside" of Hull-House be separated from the urban slums "outside"? The question of social boundaries has always been a crucial one for promoters of culture and the arts. Faced with the cultural instability of immigrant America on the one hand and the homogeneity of capitalist democracy on the other, James had struggled to maintain a separation between culture and the masses. He saw the gates around the college yard at Harvard as valuable symbols of cultural enclosure in the land of the open door. Addams, on the other hand, sees culture and the arts as means of communication across class barriers. Hull-House, Addams feels, should "promote a culture which will not set its possessor aside in a class with others like himself, but which will, on the contrary, connect him with all sorts of people" (TY 436). Addams does not suggest that there is no cultural difference between Hull-House and the slums surrounding it, because, in that case, there would be no need for Hull-House. But Hull-House and the slums redefine each other. The factory workers who become craftsmen and the tired working women who become artists within Hull-House demonstrate both the cultural potential of the urban working masses and the ability of Hull-House to nurture this potential.

Addams's use of Hull-House to literally and symbolically break down oppositions between high culture and the masses is a means of democratizing her own voice. Addams's own role as benefactress, sympathizer, and neighbor of the poor was a profoundly ambivalent one. It was too often easy for Addams to speak of the urban poor as simply a category or group that needed certain types of cures or remedies. On the other hand, her more socialist inclinations compelled her to think of them as potential equals, hindered only by being an economic underclass.[9] In *Twenty Years at Hull-House* Addams's authorial position in relation to the urban poor maintains this same kind of ambivalence. Most of the inner-city poor that Addams talks about are new immigrants, and Addams describes them in all their variety and differences. The Italian, German, and Russian immigrants bring in their own music and handicrafts, their own cultural difference into the streets of Chicago, and Addams wishes to help the immigrants retain their differences and creatively nurture them. The Italians, particularly those from the South, bring their knowledge of agriculture; the Germans contribute to evenings of folksongs and poetry; the Russians show their facility with spinning machines.

Addams's rhetorical strategies similarly reflect a desire to let the immigrants appear in all their differences as commanding narrative presences that she is compelled to write about. "Addams refused, in her writings as in her life, to reduce the immigrants to blocs and averages.... She buil[t] her arguments out of concrete examples—persons, conversations, actions."[10] *Twenty Years* abounds with such examples. There is, for instance, the ninety-year-old woman who is rehabilitated by Hull-House from her destructive pastime of picking plaster off her apartment walls. Hull-House workers redirect her energies toward making large, decorative paper chains, which she is content to make all day. But this immigrant woman, like many others, also has unexpected talents. "In course of time it was discovered that the old woman could speak Gaelic, and when one or two grave professors came to see her, the neighborhood was filled with pride that such a wonder lived in their midst" (TY 107). The poorest quarters of the inner-city produce Amazon women who not only raise children and support the family in the place of dissolute fathers but who also maintain the fiction of the responsible father for the children to revere (TY 170–71). Instances such as these, of strong and proud women, question theories of urban degradation and divest the authorial voice of the powers of definition and categorization which constitute the hierarchical prerogatives of the polemical social critic.

On the other hand, Addams's polemical attempt to make the larger public aware of urban degradation inevitably involves a cataloging of the vices and problems of inner-city immigrants. The purpose of the chapter "Public Activities and Investigations," for example, is to reveal the unhealthy sanitation facilities of tenement houses and the problem of garbage in the inner city. But the overflowing sewers and garbage-strewn streets also become signs of an undesirable immigrant lifestyle. Garbage decomposes in the streets because rustic immigrants sweep dirt outside their houses just as they did in the rural areas of their home countries (TY 283); diseases break out because Greeks slaughter sheep in basements and Italian women sort rags collected from the city dump, all inside the inner city (TY 294). Indeed, southern Italian peasants seem particularly unreceptive to using sanitary amenities, even when supplied with them, and seem to revel in their dirty surroundings. An old Italian ex-resident of an unsanitary tenement house which had to be demolished for health reasons nostalgically recalls his former dwelling, saying that "he had never succeeded so well anywhere else nor found a place that 'seemed so much like Italy'" (TY 291). In instances such as these, where Addams separates her voice from the voices of the immigrants and speaks about them from a fixed and defined class-based distance, she unwittingly comes close to supporting the xenophobia and immigrant hysteria that had gripped the nation at the turn of the century and to which even a sensibility like Henry James's was not immune.

But Addams's relationship with the immigrant poor in *Twenty Years* is complicated by more various factors than those that affected Henry James. James approached the immigrants in various ways—as American, as aesthete, as social critic—but always as a private person. Addams, on the other hand, had the public roles of custodian of culture, benefactress, and social worker, all of which reinforced hierarchical class separations.[11] In the process of attempting social amelioration it was easy to view the immigrant poor as Others who were in some way aberrant. Such a problematic authorial position, it must be stressed, is not only a factor of cross-cultural politics, the fact that Addams is faced with immigrants from other cultures just as Henry James was. Booker T. Washington, the benefactor of poor black youths, was all too prone to viewing blacks as dirty and uncivilized. In *Up From Slavery* he focused almost obsessively on teaching hygiene and cleanliness to the students of Tuskegee as a means of "lifting up" the race. The position of benefactor, material or otherwise, is always one of power, and it is, in part, this kind of prerogative of power that James Agee, the documentary writer reporting on tenant farmers, attempts problematically to resist. Addams is also aware of the hierarchical imperatives of her position, and although her descriptions categorize and thus demarcate the urban poor, she also insists on the necessity of breaking the demarcations between her voice and subjectivity and that of the working Others. The chapter "Activities and Investigations" closes with such an invocation to intersubjectivity. Addams responds to criticism about people living "where they did not naturally belong," saying, "that was exactly what we wanted—to be swallowed and digested, to disappear into the bulk of the people" (TY 309).

It is important to recognize that such statements reflect a radical element in Addams's thought that goes beyond the liberal notion of pluralism. The denial of an autonomous subjectivity means not only that many ideological positions are possible (the classic liberal position) but also that each ideological position is so implicated in, and dependent upon, diverse social contexts that no position can be universally valid. Thus, independence and objectivity are both impossible and undesirable. Henry Adams arrived at the questioning of objectivity through his researches into science and philosophy, whereas Jane Addams arrives at this position through her involvement with social projects. But for both thinkers all social theories are ultimately tentative and none final and absolute. Like Henry Adams, Jane Addams expresses the need for "a definite social creed, which should afford at one and the same time an explanation of the social chaos and the logical steps towards its better ordering" but finds no creed adequate and explanatory. Socialism explains certain socio-economic relations but poses problems for Addams in its insistence on the strict materialism of ideas (TY 186). Tolstoyism, with its concepts of 'back to the land' and 'bread labor', seems to provide solutions to poverty and to enable one to translate social theory into practical action, but Addams's meeting with Tolstoy and her visit to an experimental Tolstoyan community demonstrate to her the contingencies of Tolstoy's theories.

The chapter "Tolstoyism" illustrates Addams's refusal both to succumb to absolute theories and to use an authoritative authorial voice. Addams does not approach social analysis with the authority of a reformer with a well-defined critical and ideological methodology. Her analysis is openly subjective and emphasizes the doubts and internal inconclusions of the authorial voice. Addams begins the chapter by emphasizing the fact that her social observations are intimately linked with her personal feelings, doubts, and hesitancies.

While Henry Adams looked at the exhibits of the World's Fair in Chicago and was bewildered by the scientific exhibits of the Exposition, Jane Addams looked outside the windows of the fair and saw the poor huddled outside in the cold. During the winter following the World's Fair, relief organizations struggled with a lack of funds, and Addams, speaking as social worker, found her efforts "inadequate to the situation" (TY 259). But soon Addams also reveals that her misgivings about relief efforts are also rooted in her guilt about her own class privilege. "I was constantly shadowed by a certain sense of shame that I should be comfortable in the midst of such distress. This resulted at times in a curious reaction against all the educational and philanthropic activities in which I had been engaged. In the face of the desperate hunger and need, these could not but seem futile and superficial" (259). The anxiety about leisure-class alienation, on the one hand, and the need to find a viable social theory, on the other, culminate in the physical breakdown caused by typhoid fever, during which the author ruminates about her readings of Tolstoy.

In *Newer Ideals of Peace* Addams had criticized Tolstoy for "reducing all life to personal experience."[12] But for Addams personal experience and theory were never far apart because she did not view theories as transcendent. In describing her meeting with Tolstoy, Addams chooses incidents that emphasize her own guilt about class status. She describes in detail how Tolstoy ridicules her for following the fashion of wearing monstrously long sleeves and reprimands her on the waste. Addams responds by criticizing Tolstoy's strict morality but in the process also reveals how her voice is necessarily implicated in her upper-class status and her consciousness of hierarchical cultural distinctions. "I tried to say that monstrous as my sleeves were they did not compare in size with those of the working girls in Chicago...; even if I had wished to imitate him and 'dress as a peasant,' it would have been hard to choose which peasant among the thirty-six nationalities we had recently counted in our ward" (TY 268). Whereas Tolstoy bases his theories on a singular notion of class that cuts across differences of race and nationality, Addams is concerned with these differences. But Addams does not offer a more coherent or complete theory in the place of Tolstoy's imperfect work ethic. Her meeting with Tolstoy leaves her with unresolved questions and no answers. "Was Tolstoy more logical than life warrants? Could the wrongs of life be reduced to the terms of unrequited labor?... Was it not always easy to put up a strong case if one took the naturalistic view of life? But what about the historic view, the inevitable shadings and modifications which life itself brings to its own interpretation?" (TY 274).

The chapter on Tolstoyism is a synecdoche of the narrative method of *Twenty Years*. It is an analysis of Tolstoy's theories *and* a dramatization of Addams's personal conflicts. Similarly, *Twenty Years* as a whole is also split into two major sections, the first in which Addams speaks as a woman describing her alienation from patriarchy, and the second in which Addams speaks as a social analyst and reformer looking for solutions to the problems of urban poverty. This kind of dual narrative structure is by no means uncommon for writers we have discussed so far. Henry Adams begins his narrative by linking his childhood experiences with the gradual weakening of power of the New England aristocracy and ends by discussing theories of uncertainty. However, Adams maintains some kind of unity in the narrative by continuing to use the voice of the perplexed education seeker throughout. It is an indication of the generic similarity of these personal-political narratives that *Twenty Years* is, despite all other differences, most structurally similar to Franklin's *Autobiography*. In the first part of his autobiography Franklin describes incidents involving his family and friends, and in the second part he explains the different social projects he undertakes as a public figure. But Franklin treats his early experiences as exemplary, as means by which erring youth can learn how to succeed. Addams, on the other hand, stresses the traumas of growing up in a patriarchal culture and does not offer her experiences as fit to be imitated.

There is also a political difference between Addams's authorial voice here and those of the male critics of democratic capitalism. Even counterculture figures such as Thoreau and seemingly alienated persons like Henry Adams can attempt to speak to the culture at large, without claiming undue privilege, in a way that is problematic for women because women begin by writing under some sort of sign of difference. This does not mean that, for women, writing is always implicated in their own otherness. As Helene Cixous warns us, "To be signed with a woman's name doesn't necessarily make a piece of writing feminine."[13] Feminine writing, as Cixous calls it, does not involve a notion of an inherent woman's psyche or biological difference but an awareness of the constraints and limitations felt by women as a result of the cultural constitution of gender and the phallocentric organization of society.[14] "One is not born a woman," Simone de Beauvoir recognized, "one becomes one." Feminine writing thus reflects the oppression felt by women as they are forced to go through this process of acculturation. And this oppression can cut through differences of class. "Marxists think that there is contempt for women at every level of society. It's not by accident that bourgeois women become the first feminists: they are slaves in gilded cages."[15] Addams's Hull-House project is, in part, an attempt to break out of the cage of bourgeois womanhood.

Twenty Years may also express a sense of marginalization because of the particular mode in which it is written: personal narrative. Women's personal narratives are often accounts of social disempowerment.[16] Personal narratives emphasize a sense of self and voice, both of which, within patriarchy, have been defined as male. Thus even when women do not overtly thematize this marginalization, or seem to speak to the culture at large as Addams does, they recognize this voicing as a prerogative that they have had to appropriate. American literature offers many examples of such narratives where speaking "slant," in the manner of Emily Dickinson, seems to be the only appropriate mode. Gertrude Stein is able to write with assurance as an arbiter of culture but only in a highly mediated manner through the persona of Alice B. Toklas. *Woman in the Nineteenth Century* is highly polemical, radical, and hortatory, but Margaret Fuller still feels compelled to fictionalize herself as Miranda when she uses her own life as an example of how women can be nurtured into intellectual study and independence by their parents.

Addams had certainly experienced conventional success and begun to speak on behalf of women by the time she published *Twenty Years at Hull-House*. Already in *Democracy and Social Ethics* (1902) she had advocated a social feminism in which women could become caretakers "of the well-being and morality not just of their families but of society at large."[17] *Newer Ideals of Peace* was published in 1907, and *The Spirit of Youth and the City Streets* in 1909. *Twenty Years* was her summation of settlement activities and was directed to the society at large. But when Addams turned to her own life in order to recount the influences in her childhood and adolescence, her overwhelming memories were those of insecurity, nervousness, and lack of confidence. *Twenty Years* reflects the sense of aberrant difference experienced even by upperclass women under an oppressive patriarchy. The most imposing figure of Addams's childhood is her father. Addams attributes his dominant influence in her early years to her lack of a female role model. "I centered upon him all that careful imitation which a little girl ordinarily gives to her mother's ways and habits. My mother had died when I was a baby and my father's second marriage did not occur until my eighth year" (TY 11). But Addams's relationship with her father is not one of identification but of gendered separation.

The young Addams constantly engages in self-abasement. She tosses in bed at night because of her wickedness in having told a lie and cannot rest till she has confessed to her strict Quaker father. In comparison to her father, who presents an imposing sight as he teaches Bible class, Addams thinks of herself as deformed and inconsequential. "I imagined that the strangers were filled with admiration for this dignified person, and I prayed...that the ugly, pigeon-toed little girl, whose crooked back obliged her to walk with her head held very much upon one side, would never be pointed out to these visitors as the daughter of this fine man" (TY 7). To the young Addams her father appears as an embodiment of perfection who can only be degraded and tainted by contact with her. After church the young girl contrives to walk with her uncle rather than with her father so that strangers should not know that "my handsome father owned this homely little girl" (TY 8). The young Addams's feelings of shame in relation to her father are metaphors for the degradation and inadequacies experienced by women who internalize the norms and values of patriarchy and who consequently think of themselves as aberrant. The process of negative self-definition is experienced as much (though differently) by the patrician Addams as it will later be by Maxine Hong Kingston, the first-generation Chinese-American who in *The Woman Warrior* will attempt to question and subvert the pathologizing of Asian women as passive and unchanging. Simone de Beauvoir explains this cultural marginalization of women through a series of dichotomies: "She is defined and differentiated with reference to man and not he with reference to her; she is the incidental, the inessential as opposed to the essential. He is the Subject, he is the Absolute—she is the Other."[18]

It is important to emphasize that speaking as an Other is a question of positionality rather than definition. Just as every marginalized group is categorized (particularly by those not belonging to it) according to what it does not have relative to a dominant group, women are conceived of as aberrant or marginal in relation to dominant patriarchal values. Kristeva's attempts to view femininity as marginality and Wittig's insistence on separating the mythical "woman" from "women" are both motivated by a need to question the notion of an inherent femaleness and to socialize the concept of femininity.[19] The purpose of the early chapters of *Twenty Years* is to situate the authorial voice in a gendered otherness. But this otherness is not absolute and all-explanatory. Experience teaches the young Addams that the notion of inherent gender qualities is a problematic one. As the representative of Rockford Seminary in an oratorial contest, Addams loses to William Jennings Bryan, who speaks with a "moral earnestness which [she] had assumed would be the unique possession of the feminine orator" (TY 55). Moreover, as Jane Addams realizes, the marginalization of women takes different forms across class lines. If middle-class women are weighted by the drudgery of housework, upper-class women are weighted by social pressures. The bourgeois woman is "cultivated" for society and "smothered and sickened with advantages" but is allowed no goals (TY 73).

But, as *Twenty Years* demonstrates, speaking from the position of the Other is not simply restrictive but also potentially subversive. The very marginalized position of women can be paradoxically productive because women can both challenge the consensus of the dominant culture and acclaim the difference that other marginalized groups represent. Addams recognizes that her marginalization is both a result of oppression and a position from which the dominant culture can be questioned. The girl who is rewarded with a quarter by her father for intelligently reporting on every one of Plutarch's male heroes goes on to celebrate the female heroes of Rockford Seminary: the missionary wife who founds a school in Japan; the medical missionary in Korea who successfully treats the queen; and the teacher of the blind (TY 48). It is precisely because of her repressions and forced inactivity that the voice of the bourgeois woman breaks through the individualism endemic to capitalism and seeks a connection to a community of women and to the urban poor. "The bitter poverty and the social maladjustment which is all about her...peers at her in the form of heavy-laden laborers, gibing her with a sense of her uselessness" (TY 73). At Rockford Seminary, where the daughters of upper-class families are sent in order to become cultivated, the women take the traditional symbology of femininity but radicalize its intents. "We took for a class motto the early Saxon word for lady, translated into breadgivers, and we took for our class color the poppy, because poppies grew among the wheat, as if Nature knew that wherever there was hunger that needed food there would be pain that needed relief" (TY 48). The evolution of the class motto of Rockford Seminary reflects Addams's own attempts to translate bourgeois femininity— being cultivated as a "lady"—into social feminism. If women have traditionally been viewed as nurturers of the family, the college women use this concept in order to change the social order and extend the influence of women outside the home.[20]

Addams thus makes it clear in the early chapters of *Twenty Years* that she speaks from the position of a marginalized other. The voice of the child who can only see herself as degraded and aberrant in relation to her perfect father, the voice of the college woman who begins to question the status given to women, and the voice of the bourgeois woman repressed into ladyhood all dramatize the stiflement women endure in patriarchy. Addams's marginalized position itself ruptures the capitalistic consensus about equality and liberal universalism by introducing the difference of gender. But the major thrust of Addams's polemic, like that of previous writers of the personal-political narrative, is directed against the ideology of democratic capitalism. However, unlike the critics of capitalism discussed so far, Addams emphasizes the particularities of her own speaking position. The reformer in the latter part of the book is linked to the marginalized woman of the earlier sections in that she is concerned about the different voices of others who are similarly oppressed—the urban poor.[21] It is this simultaneous positioning within otherness and the liberal advocacy of otherness that Addams brings to the critique of the consensus of democratic capitalism. Thoreau's dissociation from the commercial, capitalistic culture of Concord and his retreat to a better culture of Nature were acts of choice. His rejection of Concord culture was an act of will that empowered him in his role as counterculture figure. James experienced an alienation from American society in both its capitalistic and overly egalitarian aspects, but it was an alienation that reinforced his sense of cultural difference and which he therefore viewed as a somewhat valued possession. Only Henry Adams clearly felt branded by his patrician heritage, but he chose not to emphasize this position and to turn instead to an exploration of difference within scientific and philosophical fields.

Although Jane Addams does not thematize the connection between her own sense of difference and her attempts at making the voices of others heard, the connection is structurally clear. Addams hints at the complicity between patriarchy and capitalism if only obversely by suggesting the ability of women to foster a community based on nurturance rather than competitive individualism. But although she questions the capitalist consensus about individualism and opportunity which maintains the hierarchy of classes and the patriarchal imperatives that define women as aberrant, her social views often reflect a compromise between embracing a dialogic community which includes the differences of the urban poor and women and envisioning a society supported by consensual "human" values. Part of her hesitancy is caused by her complete involvement in current social reforms and her pragmatic awareness that immediate gains are more possible if they do not completely upset the social status quo. There is a difference in the text between the sceptical Addams who cannot accept any theory as transcendent and the practical Addams who is willing to accept a working social model which still maintains consensual, patriarchal values.

An example of Addams's tempering of radical politics with humanist and patriarchal values is her effort to obtain the municipal franchise for women in Chicago. Addams strengthens the case for women's suffrage by demonstrating how the concerns of women cut across class and religion lines; she also strategically breaks the distinction between the domestic world and the larger political world that is often invoked to deny political rights to women. The women demanding franchise have concerns as varied as better sanitation, clean milk, property rights, and university curricula. But just as Addams has established herself as a suffragette speaking for women who demand political expression, she adopts a liberal voice hostile to women's activism. Instead of demonstrating the common concerns and solidarity of women regarding the issue of political choice, Addams now perpetuates the familiar distinction between the irresponsible activists and the sensible women who limit themselves to a few reasonable demands. "There was a complete absence of the traditional women's rights clamor, but much impressive testimony from the busy and useful women that they had reached the place where they needed the franchise in order to carry on their own affairs.... It was all so human.... None of these busy women wished to take the place of men nor to influence them in the direction of men's affairs, but they did seek to cooperate directly in civic life through the use of the ballot" (TY 340). Here Addams speaks as a liberal humanist invoking a hierarchical distinction between common "human" concerns and the overly special (aberrant) needs of women activists.

Addams's simultaneous endorsement of a society constituted by differences and her allegiance to a common humanism stem from the peculiarities of her divided voice within the politics of liberal discourse. As a woman living within a patriarchal culture, she speaks to a community of women who can understand her experience of marginalization; but as a reformer trying to awaken the awareness of her readers about the differences represented by women and the urban poor, Addams attempts to speak to the culture at large, a culture that is formulated by the values of patriarchy and capitalism. And as she speaks to this larger culture, she wants to speak both out of her own sense of gendered and economic difference and as a practical reformer claiming a common human affinity with the dominant culture. The key to claiming that affinity is retaining the universalism so important to liberal thought. That is why even when she deals with women's issues in the latter part of *Hull-House* she uses the rhetorical strategies appropriate to the "objective" (read: universal) social scientist rather than interjecting her particular gendered voice into the narrative. Subsequent liberal writers of personal narratives are faced with similar problems. Agee attempts to give the rural poor—the tenant farmers—a voice, a purpose that conflicts with his moves toward authority and consensual religious transcendence. Mailer is, in a sense, the political beneficiary of Addams's progressivist version of a politics of difference. Mailer uses the personal-political narrative to deny the autonomy and authority of his voice and to celebrate a politics of continual decentering that questions the liberal-capitalist consensus.

7

Language and Ideology:
Linguistic Depoliticization in
Let Us Now Praise Famous Men

To many intellectuals in the American Left in the generation after Jane Addams, there appeared to be a scarcity of alternatives to the uniformity of consumer society. The horror of the Stalinist purges and the subsequent disillusionment with radical utopian thinking left many intellectuals suspicious of political doctrines, even social theories. It was a generation that felt, in Daniel Bell's terms, the end of ideology altogether.[1] These disaffected intellectuals were prime candidates for affirming the liberalism or "Americanism" which, in the context of the Depression, meant a continued faith in the autonomy and self-reliance of the individual. The New Deal hardly affirmed classic Lockean liberalism, and indeed questioned individualism and free enterprise, but it was not presented as a new social theory. Roosevelt presented New Deal programs as pragmatic "American" experiments rather than the results of new ways of thinking about social relations.[2] Intellectuals unwilling to read any radicalism in the New Deal could therefore continue, despite a changed context, to believe in actions and ideas divorced from ideology.

James Agee, a young reporter and a former communist who broke allegiance with the party, was one of these disaffected intellectuals. Agee represents an extreme and exacerbated case of the tensions experienced by the writers of the personal-political narrative who are inclined both to question the liberal consensus and yet are very much part of it. Rhetorically and thematically, *Let Us Now Praise Famous Men* reflects the tensions of the writer who chose to deal with the politically sensitive subject of tenantry but tried to be apolitical, who believed at once in social differentiation and in transcendent visions. Agee is also the only writer of the personal-political narrative who theorizes on the possibility of a discourse outside of social influences or ideology altogether.

This belief in the apolitical nature of language is, of course, a stance of traditional humanism. Humanism argues that at the end of all theorizing we are left with an essential humanity, a metaphysical identity which it is the purpose of literature to affirm. Feminists and poststructuralists have, for good reason, challenged these assumptions of objectivity and universality. But Agee's criticism of ideology is particularly ironic given the fact that he is engaged in a most political project in *Famous Men:* to document for the world the lives of three tenant families in rural Alabama during the Great Depression. Yet Agee forcefully denounces ideology as false consciousness and "bias," views all interpretation as something imposed on Truth, and criticizes all ideology in writing. The writer with a clear "agenda," in other words, perceives language as a transparent, idea-free medium.

The political implications of Agee's paradoxical use and denial of ideology can be seen in his theorizations about his project early in the text. Agee explains to his readers that they will find his treatment of tenant life complicated because he and Walker Evans are "trying to deal with it not as journalists, sociologists, politicians, entertainers, humanitarians, priests, or artists, but seriously."[3] Agee does not want to subject the tenants to journalistic, sociological, or political analysis because he feels that, by viewing the tenants only as objects of reform and restrictively defining them as improvident and victimized, these analyses have ignored the complexity of tenant life. His own attempt will be to question the validity of these narrow definitions, to reinterpret them, and to emphasize the diversity of each aspect of tenant life. Like Jane Addams, who was determined to subvert restrictive stereotypes about the inner-city poor, Agee is determined to do the same for the tenant farmers. Rhetorically, his efforts seem similar to those of Henry Adams, the believer in a multiple universe, who could not operate within a unitary language. Writing about the tenants seems to be a series of analytical articulations that can be initiated but not completed. But Agee's explanation of his project also reveals a different aspect. There is an obvious grammatical, taxonomical, and logical asymmetry in the series between "journalists, sociologists, politicians," and "seriously." The former terms describe individuals in their professional roles in a social context, whereas *seriously* is an abstract evaluative term. The attempt, here, to place his voice outside a social context is part of Agee's endeavor throughout *Famous Men* to deny the socialization of language and to present the tenants, as he puts it, "in their actuality," that is, beyond society and ideology. This purist attempt does lead to an agonizing self-consciousness in the narrative as Agee realizes his position of power as an outside reporter; but, on the other hand, it also leads to efforts on Agee's part to transcend social contexts altogether through spiritual or mystical visions. *Famous Men* is thus almost an inversion of the workings of Adams's *Education*. Whereas Adams voices his need for a unified system but sets up a narrative of ideological proliferation, Agee continually professes his allegiance to a relativistic epistemology but proceeds to establish a monologic truth about the essential holiness of the tenants. Not only is such a mythologizing of poverty socially problematic, but it also makes of the tenants voiceless Others. Like the transcendental poet-priest of *Walden*, Agee invokes a "spiritual" context in which the tenants can function symbolically at best. Socially and culturally decontextualized, and thus disempowered, they are deprived of their own voices.

Thus while Agee's belief in a relativistic epistemology prompts him to undertake a democratic decentering of all ideologies and languages, his conviction that language can ultimately be idea free, a "pure" medium beyond society and ideology, leads him to privilege a "spiritual" Truth that renders the tenants voiceless. We will see how the attempt to depict the multiplicity of the tenants' lives is subsumed by an aesthetics that desocializes them and denies them legitimate voices.

Even a cursory reading of *Famous Men* reveals that Agee intends his work to be aesthetically and politically subversive. Agee constantly attacks not only the conventions of journalism but also the assumptions associated with art and writing in general. He challenges the motives of reformers dealing with tenant life, the vested interests of critics, booksellers, and publishers deriving profit from the books written on tenantry, and even the motives of the readers of reformist writing. The popular propaganda literature of the thirties is the special focus of Agee's attacks. The thirties had witnessed a proliferation of case worker reports, exposés, and worker narratives that attempted to graphically portray the true effects of the Depression. Because they were perceived as radical, these exposés often became the butt of criticism, particularly during the Hoover administration, when presidential wisdom held that merely ignoring the Depression would cure it. As William Stott points out, in the thirties a kind of "propaganda against propaganda enjoyed wide popularity."[4] But whereas conservative officials in the establishment and proponents of fundamental Lockean liberalism who questioned New Deal policies had been critical of documentary writers for falsifying reality by exaggerating the details of poverty, Agee criticizes these writers for their denial of, and insensitivity to, significant details.

In *Famous Men*, Agee repeatedly faults documentary writers for ignoring the diversity of tenant life and for making the tenant solely

an economic fact or datum. But Agee's anger is not directed only at
this narrow economic valuation. In fact, the major thrust of his attack
is against the very act of interpretation and the process of authorization inherent in it. He views interpretation as an authoritative, often
politically motivated attempt at finalized definition and reduction to
which most journalists, reformers, sociologists, and artists are prone.
His own efforts, he suggests, are against interpretation and definition.
While describing the household pets of tenants, for instance, Agee
reflects as follows:

> This naming of poultry is not common and indicates, if you like,
> the relative 'primitivism' of the Ricketts; though it also indicates
> less sociological and more attractive things about them; though
> these in turn are more difficult to define, or even to understand,
> and would be merely tiresome to those whose intelligence is set
> entirely on Improving the Sharecropper, and who feel there's no
> time to waste on petty detail. These same rapid marchers...will
> be equally uninterested in the fact that Mrs Woods's mother calls
> babies coons and baby chickens sings, or worse still will...some-
> how manage to capitalize it politically or against landowners as
> the unvanquishable poetry of the oppressed. (FM 215)

Agee scorns reformers who view the tenants only as objects in a pro-
gram of economic improvement because he feels they are merely
using the lives of tenants as a means for political ends. He criticizes
the dogmatism of these reformers and suggests instead that the end of
dogmatic ideology can mean the beginning of multiple perspectives.
Thus Agee is critical of writers who presume that labels like *primi-
tivism* are all-explanatory and more significant than the small and
diverse details of tenant life. Interpretation, for Agee, is a form of
dominance in that it accords a hierarchical privilege to the observer.
His own attempts, he suggests, are directed away from the subjugation of the subject that arises from the acts of interpretation and definition. In fact, he implies that by focusing on details generally ignored
by others as "tiresome" he is avoiding not only fixed definition but
also, ultimately, interpretation. The naming of poultry is an important
detail for him precisely because its significance is "difficult to define,
or even to understand."

   Accordingly, in *Famous Men*, Agee deliberately uses techniques
to direct his readers away from a single, dominant interpretation. He
seems to be even more self-conscious than Henry Adams and Jane
Addams about the fact that his voice is socially inscribed rather than

autonomous, partial rather than complete. Agee points out that his text is partial, rather than whole and complete, and that Walker Evans's photographs, which constitute Book I, are as important as his own writing in Book II. He also denies closure by presenting *Famous Men* as only the beginning, the first volume of a longer work titled *Three Tenant Families*. These deauthorizing devices, in addition to sections with titles such as "(On the Porch: 1," numerous paragraphs and chapters ending in colons, a chapter on aesthetics provocatively titled "Colon," chapters without titles, and footnotes that provide a countervoice to the text, suggest that the authorial voice is constantly open to dialogue.[5] It is also apparent that for Agee these techniques are not merely aesthetic. The transgressions of grammatical convention illustrate the extent to which traditional linguistic categories are philosophically dependent on concepts of unity and closure. Chapter titles embody completeness of meaning, an opening parentheses requires a closing one, and footnotes support the text. By violating these rules Agee suggests that his writing will privilege a dialogic openness and variability of meaning.

That is why Agee cannot privilege economic oppression alone as a matrix of interpretation. Other diverse voices—"psychological, semantic, traditional, perhaps glandular"—are to him equally valid and will always intervene (FM 208). Agee also questions the finality of his own voice by emphasizing that his analyses of the tenants can never be the final truth. His interpretation of George Gudger, he explains, "will only be a relative truth" because his own context, his role and bias as observer, will inevitably enter his description of the tenant farmer. Agee has both the social self-consciousness of a Jane Addams who worried about her own position and status in writing about the inner-city poor, and the philosophical self-consciousness of a Henry Adams about the relativity of all Truth statements. In fact, Agee goes on to challenge the reader: "Name me one truth within human range that is not relative and I will feel a shade more apologetic of that" (FM 239). Given this relativistic epistemology, Agee cannot claim a truth value for any of his propositions. *Famous Men* thus appears as a "book filled with anguished beginnings," one in which "we must give up looking for…a finished product in the old sense."[6] Indeed, Agee dramatizes the ongoing process of interpretation by rethinking his rhetorical strategies halfway through *Famous Men*. He proposes that he would now like to start using a language that partakes of different social contexts. "It would be an art and a way of seeing existence," he suggests, "based on…an intersection of astronomical physics, geology, biology, and (including psychology) anthropology, known and spoken of not in scientific but in human terms" (FM 245). Agee wishes to use a language that breaks the boundaries between discourses conventionally viewed as disparate. His desire to rethink science in "human terms" is also significant. Like Adams, who creatively interfused technology and Christianity, Agee is interested in taking the languages of different sciences out of their exclusive denotative paradigms into a cultural (or "human") narrativization where they can dialogically interact with other cultural languages.

Agee's belief in a culture constituted by difference rather than consensus and his distrust of monologic interpretation are evident in his detailed descriptions of the tenants. In the chapter "Clothing," for instance, Agee challenges and subverts monologic conceptions of the "typical," "normal," and "average" that are the mainstay of conventional documentary writing. There are "so many variants that one cannot name anything as 'typical'" (FM 262). The smallest details of tenant clothing are multiple signs in a world of ideological sign systems. Even the shoes of the tenants resist conformity to a standardized "average." Although economic hardship and physical discomfort force most tenants to cut their shoes, Agee explains how each shoe signifies the mark of its wearer, who cuts it differently. Some tenants cut their shoes to maximize comfort, and others cut them so artistically that the utility of the shoe is compromised. Similarly, the headgear of the tenants might signify both personality and relative social status. George Gudger's machinist's cap, in fact, suggests a reaction against the stereotypical image of the farmer with a straw hat; Ricketts's homemade hat, on the other hand, is indicative of his willingness to accept a social status beneath most tenants. Clearly, Agee wishes to explode the mythology of the "tenant" as a singular documentary entity and, by examining the details of tenant life through an intersection of economic, social, aesthetic, and psychological spheres, he stresses the multiplicity and polyglossia of every culture.

But although Agee is able to question and dialogize the totalizing labels applied to the tenants, he is constantly aware that his very status as a writer necessarily positions him above the tenants whose lives he is recording. No other writer of the personal-political narrative agonizes so much about the traditional social implications of being an aesthete. A comparison with Jane Addams is instructive here. Although Jane Addams was conscious of her problematic patrician status at Hull-House, she knew she could only *rethink* the oppositions between her class and that of the slum dwellers, not transcend them. But Agee exacerbates his dilemma by simultaneously acknowledging his role as artist and announcing his freedom to transcend the role. He tries to avoid the role of the intellectual and wishes instead to be perceived as one of the tenants. The problem for Agee is both ideological and aesthetic. He wants to nullify the social contexts that separate his voice from the tenants' voices; he also wants to place as much value on the ordinary language of the tenants as on what he perceives as "art." In order to achieve this oneness with the tenants, Agee emphasizes both his attempts to immerse himself in the lives of the tenants and to dissociate himself from "high" art. The former effort often takes the form of self-flagellation. Like Adams, who reiterated the cry of "failure" to demonstrate his educational success, Agee berates himself for using the tenants as materials for his work in order to finally suggest an extraordinary sensitivity through which he can claim a complete kinship with them. He repeatedly presents himself as an alien or spy, prying into the lives of the tenants. Yet in spite of (perhaps because of) this self-condemnation, Agee is able to purge himself of guilt and declare himself as one with the tenants.[7]

Similarly, he tries to distance himself from "art" by deliberately breaking generic conventions, by questioning accepted writing practices, and by attacking the proponents of sterile aestheticism. Agee questions the status of accepted literary conventions by using startling juxtapositions. *Famous Men* begins without introduction, preface, or even a title page with photographs by Walker Evans. These photographs constitute Book I of *Famous Men*, and the rest of the text constitutes Book II. By placing the photographs in this manner and implying that they are as significant as the three-hundred-odd pages of writing that follow, Agee questions the literary convention of privileging the written word. Agee also undertakes a subversive dismantling of cultural hierarchies. He prefaces Book II with excerpts from *King Lear* and Marx and explains that these two form the themes of the book. But, as if parodying the convention of using epigraphs from authoritative sources, Agee follows these immediately with extended excerpts from Louise Gudger's geography textbook, *Around the World With Children*. Shakespeare, Marx, and the third-grade geography textbook of a tenant child, Agee implies, can serve equally well as prefaces for his text. Or again, by printing the portions of newsprint that are scattered around the Gudger home as poetry, Agee suggests that even the scraps found in tenant homes can have aesthetic value. Such formal subversions undermine the authority of conventional learning and democratize art by inserting generic indeterminacy into traditional forms like the epigraph and the poem.

The attempts to present a dialogic authorial voice and to deprivilege the language of art are, however, secondary to a more important motivation for Agee. He assumes that these devices will liberate him from interpretation altogether and will generate a language that will be idea free.[8] Thus, despite his awareness of the diverse significances of each aspect of tenant life, Agee, through his belief in the possibility of a language and experience beyond a social context, bolsters the universalism endemic to liberal thought. He wants to present an *actuality* free from socio-ideological violation. Early in *Let Us Now Praise Famous Men*, Agee attempts to explain the nature of this nonmediated perception:

> For in the immediate world, everything is to be described, for him who can discern it, and *centrally and simply*, without either dissection into science, or digestion into art, but with the whole of consciousness, seeking to perceive it *as it stands:* so that the aspect of a street in sunlight can roar in the *heart of itself* as a symphony, perhaps as no symphony can: and all of consciousness is shifted from the imagined, the revisive, to the effort to perceive simply the *cruel radiance of what is.* (FM 11, italics mine)

Clearly, Agee does not discount perception or interpretation altogether because he sees everything as there to be "discerned." But he also suggests that there is an inherent actuality in things that precedes the ideological context of the observer and to which the observer can only respond transcendentally. It is significant again to note the rupture in the series between "science," "art," and "the whole of consciousness." Whereas the former are modes of discourse, the latter is a metaphysical abstraction. Agee's proclaimed search for a better type of interpretation (than the imagined or revisive) is only apparent. His assumption of an essence (the "what is") uncontaminated by the social-material world suggests instead a problematic attempt to do away with interpretation altogether. Agee's metaphysics indicate a belief in the possibility of words being ideologically neutral, mere transmitters of a nonmaterial essence. Such a condition, however, is hardly possible.[9] Even the conception of an idea-free language that can capture a primal essence is ideologically charged. It is, among other things, a response to materialist conceptions of language. Such a theory of discourse assumes that subjectivity and voice are autonomous constructs operating in isolation from society. As Richard King notes, Agee's aesthetics of unassisted consciousness belongs to a metaphysics of presence, a belief that "unmediated access can be gained to God, Truth, the Good, the Absolute, Reality, or whatever might serve as the 'god-term' in a religious or philosophical system."[10]

It is precisely the metaphysics of presence that gets to the heart of *Famous Men*. It bolsters Agee's search for a neutral language and determines his method of depicting the lives of the tenants. The main premise of Agee's philosophy is a transcendent belief in the uniqueness and holiness of each individual, which is of far greater significance than the social-material world a person inhabits. This is another reason why Agee abhors overtly socio-economic interpretations of the tenants. Such interpretations seem to him reductive totalizations that ignore the essential (holy) truth about the tenants that exists beyond socio-economic contextualization.It could be argued that by not restricting himself to economic analysis Agee forges an aesthetics whereby the tenants become more than economic integers and acquire their own unique voices. Agee certainly reiterates this intention. But the diminished significance of the socio-economic and the predominance accorded instead to the uniqueness, beauty, and holiness of each individual in *Famous Men* is largely a matter of replacing one privileged language with another. Although Agee assuredly subverts the narrow economic analyses of traditional documentaries, he does so only to accept most of the premises (and thus the social implications) of an old Anglo-American transcendental romanticism. By finding beauty and divinity in the commonplace, romanticists humbled themselves only in gesture. The romantic artist actually became the purveyor of Truth and the supreme decipherer. Whitman, in his moments of transcendence, becomes a prophet with hordes in his following. Emerson, in similar moments, literally metamorphoses into a see-er (a huge eyeball) as the currents of universal being circulate through him. In his quest to present the divine Truth about the tenants, Agee too becomes the romantic god-artist.[11] But transcending the social-material world, as we have seen with Thoreau, also means transcending social realities and conflicts, the different voices of Others altogether.

This is not to suggest that Agee ignores the complexities and differences in the social horizon. On the contrary, as we have seen, the book is rife with the multiple signifiers of tenant life. But although Agee provides details about many social aspects of the tenants—their work, education, and family structures—these are finally encapsulated by, and deemed inconsequential in comparison to, the moments of illumination when the divinity of each aspect of tenant life is revealed. These incandescent moments create unity and totality beyond the merely historical and temporal. For some critics it is this very lack of significance accorded to social factors that makes *Famous Men* attractive. Peter Ohlin, for instance, finds merit in the fact that Agee "refused to see the problem [sharecropping] in the facile terms of contemporary politics or sociology but tried to approach it, individualistically, and rebelliously, simply as a human being."[12] Ohlin recognizes Agee's subversion of the facile and oversimplified modes of many documentaries, but, like Agee, he assumes that to approach a subject in "human" terms is necessarily to disregard politics and sociology. What Ohlin here calls "human" is analogous to Agee's "human-divine," an essence that attempts to embody an asocial and apolitical abstraction.

Further, although Agee implies that by focusing on individual holiness he is able to depict the tenants nonideologically, the very workings of the text suggest otherwise. Human divinity itself is not presented only in an abstract context but very obviously in a Christian context. The Bible, like any other holy book, is a text in which different voices strive for ascendancy and which is dependent upon interpretive contexts. To make it function, as Agee often does, as an absolute and final answer, is to deny its textuality and to give it a privileged ahistorical and asocial normative status. The dialectic between the voices of the tenants and the biblical voice is present in the title of the book itself: the entire projected work called *Three Tenant Families* and the first completed volume, *Let Us Now Praise Famous Men*. And in the process of working out the dialectic, Agee privileges the biblical voice praising famous men over the voices of the three tenant families. Because Agee so frequently states his intent not to subordinate the voices of the tenants and criticizes reformist writing for doing so, it is necessary to see the process by which Agee himself absorbs the tenants' voices and the political implications of this approach.

The depiction of the uniqueness and holiness of every detail of tenant life suggests a democratic aesthetic wherein all the diverse aspects of the tenants are given importance. Samuel Hynes suggests that Agee's "Christian realist" mode accomplishes just that.[13] But in *Famous Men*, the discovery of holiness in everything is predicated on authorial control and moments of privatized transcendence. It is not surprising, therefore, that many descriptions of the tenants are preceded by moments of meditation or spiritual transcendence when the author is privy to the unity and divinity of the created world. J. A. Ward describes *Famous Men* as a "sociological analysis that turns into a mystical meditation."[14] It is finally the authoritative voice of mystical meditation that absorbs the sociological particular (the tenant). The synchronic, in other words, is secondary to, and predicated on, the diachronic, even though it is posited as its correction.

The chapter "I:" of "A Country Letter" exemplifies the dialectic between the voices of the tenants and the universalizing voice of the author. An important character in the chapter is Annie Mae Gudger's sister, Emma. It is with characterizations such as Emma's that Agee does, in fact, subvert the totalizing interpretations of reformist and journalistic writing that he so abhors. Emma does not appear as a typified product of the tenantry system but as a powerful figure involved in a complex of forces. She is part of the tenant poor, and her marriage to a shiftless carpenter in Cherokee City has not alleviated her poverty. Her dime store necklace, her paper suitcase, and the dilapidated truck in which she rides to Mississippi are all implicit indicators of the economic factors that compel her to return to her husband. She also lives within a social structure in which her status as a married woman is a supreme signifier ("She can't have fun with anyone else because she is married and nobody will have fun with her that way").

In addition to these economic and social contexts, there are also familial factors surrounding Emma. Emma's decision to marry early, Agee perceives, was partly the result of her father's (Bud Woods's) remarrying, which, in effect, displaced her. But despite the depiction of these overt forces surrounding Emma, Agee does not present her merely as a case study. Emma both partakes of and forcefully influences the social dynamics around her. It is in part because of her sexual attractiveness that her husband is insanely jealous of her. In fact, Emma's sexuality creates a complex psycho-sociological drama in the Gudger home. George Gudger is attracted to Emma and engages in a flirtation with her which his wife, Annie Mae, with due propriety, pretends not to notice. Agee himself confesses to being similarly captivated by Emma. It is as if Emma's voice momentarily controls the narrative, making Agee speak through her. The Emma story is an instance of the different voices the tenants are able to have precisely because they are presented in a social context. Agee can also enter the story as a participant (as he so often ardently wishes) because he does not discount his own social context, his difference from Emma. As a writer he has access to a social world far removed from the reaches of the tenants and cannot therefore claim a universal oneness with them. Emma is attracted to him and Walker Evans, Agee speculates, not because of their identity with the tenants but because of their differences from them. "Each of us is attractive to Emma," Agee reflects, "both in sexual immediacy and as symbols or embodiments of a life she wants and knows she will never have." They possess, for Emma, "the mystery or glamour almost of mythological creatures" (FM 61-62).

But while the Emma story presents an ideologically complex social picture not subject to control by the authorial voice, it is contained by a desocialized context in which the author appropriates a prophetic role. Agee begins the chapter by setting the context, in transcendental tradition, for divine inspiration. While everyone in the Gudger household is asleep, Agee enters the transcendent extra-temporal realm of universal truths. In this non-material, gnostic sphere, disconnected from earthly constraints (he particularly stresses his freedom from chronological time: "What day of month I do not know, which day of week I am not sure"), the prophetic author can feel such an "ultimate" "holiness of silence and peace" that he can confidently announce to the reader: "I can tell you anything within realm of God" (FM 51). This is a postulation of beginnings whereby the text is seen as removed from the sphere of production. Agee appears here as an effortless romantic creator rather than a producer of texts, a creator unbounded by time or space and empowered to roam the world at will. And the power of this voice controls and marginalizes the voices of all Others. To this voice, the Gudger home becomes a small instance of a universal pattern of seclusion and procreation. Like Whitman, wandering among sleepers in his night visions, Agee moves from particularized images of people in settlements, towns, and cities, "drawn inward within their little shells of rooms," to observations on the nature of human existence: "A man and a woman are drawn together upon a bed and there is a child and there are children: /.... This has been happening for a long while: its beginning was before stars," and, finally, to oracular pronouncements: "And these are the classic patterns, and this is the weaving, of human living: of whose fabric each individual is a part" (FM 54–56).

Given this consolidation of an abstract prophetic voice, the Gudger family, and to an extent even Emma, become mere instances of a cosmic pattern. In this transcendent sphere, where the author speaks as the prophet who sees a holiness and unity in the universe, the smallest details of the Gudgers' lives are arbitrarily deified and lose their social-material significance. The effect is the same as in any religion where finding holiness and beauty in the poor has as its hidden agenda a perpetuation of existing class structures. Antebellum writings about blacks repeatedly used this strategy. Similarly, in *Famous Men* the signs in the Gudger household become fixed signs that can signify only divinity and beauty, or "classic patterns," and that too through the author-prophet as their speaker. Thus, the Gudgers sleeping on iron beds and pallets on the floor signify in their rest an "indiscernible drawing-in of heaven"; Burt Gudger's whimpering becomes an "inarticulated soprano"; Annie Mae's whispered cajoling, "git awn back to sleep, they aint nothing agoin to pester ye," acquires a value that "anneals all fences of language and surpasses music"(FM 58). Comparing different aspects of the Gudgers to forms of music is also a mode of depoliticization and glorification. Music, to Agee, is an art form that, unlike writing, transcends all social contexts.

This continual translation of every aspect of the tenants into the language of beauty and divinity subordinates the tenants' voices as much as Franklin's translation of all ideologies into the language of business disempowered other voices. An even more pronounced form of authorial control, however, is Agee's overt appropriation of the tenants' voices. Agee often suggests that he *is* the supreme voice of the tenants. He not only claims to understand each person in the Gudger home intimately but also to know more about them than they themselves do. "I lie down inside each one," declares Agee, "as if exhausted in a bed, and I become not my own shape and weight and self, but that of each of them.... So that I know almost the dreams they will not remember, and the soul and body of each of these seven" (FM 58). The relation between the authorial voice and the voices of the tenants is one of power and control. Overall, this tendency toward universalized pronouncements gives the authorial voice powers that compel the multiplicity of tenant life to serve as an illustration of a "higher" truth (all is holy).

In emphasizing the divinity and beauty in the lives of the tenants, Agee was partly reacting to conventional documentaries, which often presented tenants as objects of pity. Erskine Caldwell, author of the famous documentary reportage on tenantry, *You Have Seen Their Faces,* and a special butt of Agee's scorn, suggested, for instance, that the economic pressures to which the tenants were subjected could hardly be conducive to the development of fine moral traits. According to Caldwell, the sharecropper thus lacked "most of the virtues that the human race...pats itself on the back for possessing." "A defeated, frustrated, resentful person in the latter years of his life," notes Caldwell, "is not likely to have a strong character" (FM 108). Caldwell's purpose in thus describing the sharecropper was obviously to create righteous indignation in the reader and to evoke sympathy for the plight of the sharecropper.[15] Agee, however, sees the portrayal of tenants as oppressed victims as belonging to the realm of ideology he wishes to see the end of. For him the tenants are not merely objects of sympathy but people who must be admired and respected in their own rights. But the depiction of the tenants falls short of Agee's stated intent. Although Agee views all the tenants as unique, their voices scarcely acquire a status that permits them to stand alongside and equal to the authorial voice.

In a sense, Agee's problem is similar to that of Thoreau's in *Walden.* While Thoreau criticized the conformity of his readers and urged them to find their own voices, he attempted to transcend the social-material world through an empowered, prophetic voice. Similarly, although Agee suggests that the tenants (unlike his readers, who are in turns vulgar, simplistic, and conventional) all have unique voices, the workings of the text repudiate this assertion.[16] It is surely a curious feature of *Let Us Now Praise Famous Men* that the author who claimed to have lived in intimate contact with the tenants never discovered that they had any beliefs, ideas, or opinions worth noting. What Agee actually discovered is best left to biographical speculation. I suggest that Agee's emphasis on a spiritual (nonmaterial) and cosmic context could in fact leave no room for the tenants' voices because an assertion of difference depends upon a recognition of a social-material context. The desocialized, cosmic context in *Famous Men* permits only two valid voices—the prophetic authorial voice and the biblical voice—which are compatible and are treated together as absolute.[17] The voices of the tenants are often entrapped between the authorial voice without which they cannot be embodied and the biblical voice that becomes a standard of judgment.

The subordinate status of the tenants' voices is particularly evident in chapter "II:" of "A Country Letter." The latter half of this chapter is presented literally as an intersection of the voices of different tenants, landowners, observers, and others. The implicit intent seems to be to expose and repudiate the typified, often hostile interpretations to which the tenants are subjected. There are observers, for instance, who merely categorize the tenants as wretched and filthy: "Fred Ricketts? Why that dirty son-of-a-bitch, he brags that he hasn't bought his family a bar of soap in five years"; "Why, Ivy Pritchert was one of the worst whores in this whole part of the country.... They're about the lowest trash you can find" (FM 79). There are landowners for whom the tenants are fortunate dependants: "Why times when I envy them. No risk, we take all the risk; all the clothes they need to cover them; food coming up right out of their land" (FM 80). For the conservative capitalists, the tenants are merely slothful and improvident: "None of these people has any sense, nor any initiative. If they did, they wouldn't be farming on shares" (FM 80).It is obvious that most of these interpretive voices reflect the ideology of self-reliant individualism which denies class difference and the fact of socio-economic exploitation. Against these interpretive voices, Agee juxtaposes the voices of the tenants themselves. These voices, however, are unable to participate in a dialogue with the voices of landowners and other observers because they are completely depoliticized. The tenants do not speak for themselves but chant in a chorus. Obviously such depictions of the "common folk" are paternalistic. The "idealiza-tion of the 'popular,'" says Michel deCerteau, "is made easier if it takes the form of a monologue. The people may not speak, but they can sing."[18] The idealization is made possible *because* the people are voiceless. Similarly, Agee's tenants chant together, unable to compre-hend the forces working on them. Without any realization of their roles in the economic structure, they can merely ask repeatedly, "In what way were we trapped? where, our mistake? what, where, how, when, what way, might all these things have been different, if only we had done otherwise?" (FM 78). Even when the tenants seem to speak in diverse voices by using the "I," the difference accorded to their voices is almost purely linguistic. Take, for example, the despairing voice of the tenant wife: "I wanted to make the house pretty...but now I just don't care any longer" (FM 79). This voice is ideologically no different from the collective helpless voices of the tenants. It fol-lows as an illustration of the general cry "How were we caught?"

In the context of political dialogue the tenants are clearly power-less, and their subordinate status is further apparent in the authorial appropriation of their voices. Here, for instance, is Agee's depiction of the language of two tenant children:

But *I* am young; and I am young, and strong...; and I am too young to worry; and so am I, for my mother is kind to me; and we run in the bright air like animals...the natural world is around us like a lake and a wide smile and we are growing...and one by one in the terrible emptiness and leisure we shall burn and tremble and shake with lust, and one by one we shall loosen ourselves from this place, and shall be married, and it will be dif-ferent from what we see, for we will be happy and love each other, and keep the house clean...and we will know how to do things right. (FM 80–81)

Although the grammatical markers indicate otherwise, it is obvious that it is not just the tenant children who are speaking here. Of course, in the Bakhtinian sense no words can completely belong to one speak-er because language always reflects and refracts other ideologies and other voices. But just because there is always dialogic potential in lan-guage does not mean that language cannot be used oppressively. The problem here is not one of verisimilitude but of authority. By simulta-neously presenting a simulacrum of the voices of tenant children and forcing them to adopt *his* language and ideology, Agee suggests that it is only through his articulations that the tenants can speak. The authorial voice (evident in phrases such as "we run in the bright air like animals" and "terrible emptiness and leisure") does not enter into dialogic relationships with the voices of tenant children, but demands instead that the latter accept its interpretational judgment.

The purpose of depoliticizing and disempowering the voices of the tenants becomes clear at the end of the chapter. The inarticulate ness, incomprehension, and powerlessness of the tenants' voices is legitimized by what we might call the "politics of divinity." The chapter ends with a vision of Jesus on the mountaintop blessing the poor, the meek, the merciful, and the persecuted. This special sanction to the poor and the meek does not function as Nietzschean *ressentiment* to privilege the tenants because they have already been rendered powerless in the text. The biblical text, "Blessed are the meek in spirit..." (Matthew 5: 1–12), becomes a point of closure, providing a definitive answer to "How were we caught?" It acts as a check on change and subversion of existing class structures. The use of the biblical text both reinforces the holiness-in-poverty interpretation that Agee authorizes when he speaks as a prophet and also suggests that holiness-in-poverty is not an interpretation but a universal truth. The Bible, like any other text, can be used in different (nonabsolute) ways, and Agee, by making Christ one of the unpaid agitators in his cast of characters early in the book, is well aware of this. But here the biblical text is demarcated as authoritative, and thus is separated from other voices. It functions, as Bakhtin calls it, as the "sanctified word," the "pious and inert quotation that is isolated and set off like an icon."[19] As such, it has a hierarchical status to which all other voices must submit.

The subordination of the voices of the tenants and the normative status given to the biblical text are recurrent features of *Let Us Now Praise Famous Men*. In the chapter " *Shady Grove, Alabama, July 1936*," the biblical text is again used to provide closure. Most of the chapter is devoted to a detailed description of a tenant cemetery. The graves marked with pine headboards, the numerous rows of narrow, small graves of tenant children, and the unmarked graves of the poor farmers are poignant signs of economic disinheritance within a social symbology. Here Agee places the tenants in a socio-economic context and recognizes the overwhelming oppression they are subject to. But he ends the chapter by inviting the tenants to join him as he invokes the Lord's Prayer as a final "cure" and "end" to the sorrows "whose beginnings are long begun" (439). The chapter ends with the text of the Lord's Prayer as the final interpretive authority. Similarly, the biblical text is deployed close to the end of the book, where Agee cites "Let Us Now Praise Famous Men" (Ecclesiasticus 44: 1–14) as an authoritative summation to the project of eulogizing the tenants (FM 445).[20]

If the tenants are scarcely permitted their own voices, it is partly because, despite his reverence for them, Agee considers them innocent and infantile. They are therefore incapable of ideological formulation. His interaction with George and Annie Mae Gudger, intimate as it might be, is one between "two plain people and one complex one" (FM 417). And although Agee castigates himself for "using" the tenants as materials for his work, they still remain for him people "innocent of such twistings as these which are taking place over their heads" (FM 13). Such associations are problematic and evoke uneasy resemblances with established conventions of depicting cultural Others—the routine characterization of African-Americans, for instance, as more moral, though less intellectual, than the whites.[21]

In light of this intellectual paucity attributed to the tenants, it is easy to see why the few attempts to introduce dialect in the text seem merely quaint. The language of dialect can acquire a validity only when it is conjoined with its own worldview, that is, when it is not conceived of in narrowly linguistic terms. The use of dialect in *Famous Men*, however, remains purely linguistic, because the tenants are conceived of as ideologically inarticulate. In fact, dialect often seems to function in the text merely to provide a contrast to normal linguistic usage. Take, for instance, Agee's conversation with the Ricketts children: "Then I said, taking care to say it to all three, Is your Daddy around? They said nawsuh he was still meetnen so was Mama but ParlLee was yer they would git her for me. I told them, No, thanks.... I just wanted to ask their Daddy would he tell me where Mr George Gudger lived. They said he didn' live fur, he lived jist a piece down" (FM 386). The dialect here has little social significance because it is framed by an analysis that denies the tenant children adequate socialization and treats them merely as a species to be revered. Watching the children as they come running to him, "panting with the grinning look of dogs," Agee can only exclaim, "Jesus, what could I ever do for you that would be enough." Given this suggested ideological voicelessness of the tenant children, the dialect can only function linguistically. Further, although the dialogue is presented as reported speech, there is no attempt made to attribute different parts to the various tenant children. Instead, the dialect is presented as a collective voice which functions merely as an illustration of linguistic idiosyncracies to be exhibited, much like they are in the tradition of local color.

The depiction of the tenants as divine yet ideologically voiceless is in fact not a contradiction. Analyzing Agee's treatment of the tenants, particularly his disinclination to censure them, Alan Holder suggests that Agee, "reacting against a general feeling of condescension toward the tenants, tried to canonize them.... In the process, his subjects were placed in a racial and moral vacuum. He placed them in a political one as well."[22] Whether Agee should have been more critical of the tenants is an issue of moral arbitration. What is important in Holder's observations is the connection he draws between the act of canonization and depoliticization. Agee could canonize the tenants only when he placed them in a socio-political vacuum. In this vacuum, arbitrary and universalized canonization was possible because the tenants could only be abstract biological (rather than social) individuals and thus be ideologically voiceless. Agee's disinclination to allow the tenants their own voices in *Famous Men* is also a necessary consequence of adopting the politics of transcendence. Because Agee, like his predecessor, Thoreau, adopts a prophetic authorial voice beyond society, history, and ideology, there can hardly be other valid voices to dialogize the text.

To suggest that *Famous Men* is totally governed by a singular, dominant authorial voice, however, is to ignore some of the internal stratification of the work. Many of Agee's aesthetic theories are in fact attempts to introduce multiple voices in the text. Agee often brings to the forefront an acknowledgment of the text as constructed artifact and emphasizes the process of writing itself. By ending the book with a promise to the reader that more will follow, Agee questions the closure of his own narrative and the totality of his articulations. But alongside these radical, dispersive impulses are stronger, cohesive ones. The assumption that there is an absolute reality prior to ideological violation and the valorized status often given to the biblical text are attempts to consolidate logocentric constants despite an awareness of ideological dispersion. In fact, the use of religion in the book itself testifies to both monologic and dialogic modes. The transcription of the writing in the Gudger family Bible (which smells of human excrement) and the redefinition of the altar and tabernacle as parts of the Gudger home, for instance, recreate religious signification through the use of nontraditional signifiers. They are attempts to open up and dialogize the language of religion. However, the treatment of the biblical text and the language of religion as normative (the daily rituals of the tenants are beautiful to Agee *because* they are as sacred as the mass) points to a monologic totalization.

Famous Men illustrates the particular dilemma of dispossessed radicals in the Roosevelt era when faced with taking a stance toward political programs. Although these radicals were sharply critical of free-market interpretations of poverty, their suspicion of all political theories and policies extended to the very programs of the New Deal that they could have supported. Thus, in the attempt to get beyond ideology, Agee risks appearing like a contented liberal. The problem in *Famous Men* is not that Agee does not follow a particular party line. In fact, in the narratives of Mailer and Kingston we will see how the resistance to defined and organized politics can be extremely effective. Agee's problem is the denial of ideology and the need for the stability and coherence of a spiritual or metaphysical sphere of Truth. The realm of spirituality becomes the constant for Agee as was the realm of culture for Henry James. The space outside ideology is conceived of as the place of transcendence and revelation. And because this space is seen as originary, outside society and history, Agee's subversions of the narrow and consensual definitions of the tenants fall short of their radical intent.

8

Toward a Politics of Difference: Linguistic Otherness in *The Armies of the Night*

Let the old men ask sourly, 'Out of Apathy—into what?' The Age of Complacency is ending. Let the old women complain wisely about 'the end of ideology.' We are beginning to move again.

J. S. Mills[1]

There could not have been a more propitious intellectual climate for questioning the liberal-capitalist consensus than the one in which *The Armies of the Night* was written. Whereas Agee wrote within a limbo created by the denial of ideology, Mailer wrote at a time when the intellectual Left was realizing and articulating a radical challenge to the liberal-capitalist ideology. Just as thinkers of the New Left were formulating a shift from reformist to utopian politics, radical changes were taking place both at home and abroad. In the Third World the decade had been marked by rapid decolonization; in the United States the "colonized" blacks were agitating for their rights; and in Paris, May 1968 loomed ahead. In *The Armies of the Night* Mailer took the occasion of the 1967 march on the Pentagon (which had symbolically affirmed the right to dissent) to deliver a severe and wide-ranging indictment of the cultural uniformity and ideological repressiveness of postindustrialist capitalist society.

Mailer's questioning of bureaucracy, organizational structures, and dogmatic political groups and his vision of a politics of radical difference in *The Armies of the Night* are supported by the philosophy of the New Left. The strength of the New Left was in the breadth of its analyses and its Foucauldian sensitivity to the means as well as ends of revolutionary activity. All spheres of life were politicized and subject to scrutiny, and the structures of all movements and groups were examined. Marcuse saw the power of the New Left in what he called the "Great Refusal," the ability to "recognize the mark of social repression even in the most sublime manifestations of traditional culture, even in the most spectacular manifestations of technical progress."[2] The fact that the New Left did not endorse any fixed programs was, in fact, its particular strength.[3]

In *Advertisements for Myself* and "The White Negro" Mailer had anticipated some of New Left thought. But Mailer cannot be thought of as belonging to the New Left if we see the New Left in terms of traditional, even reformist, politics. If one thinks in those terms (where allegiance to all "leaders" has to be sworn), we might take Mailer's criticisms of Paul Goodman in *The Armies of the Night*, for example, as indicative of his dissociation from the New Left. But this kind of subversive, satiric, deflation, even of people with politics one might be sympathetic of, is a strategic move that questions the power of political hierarchies. It is a recognition of the fact that the style of the politics is as important as the "message." In seeing *The Armies of the Night* through the politics of the New Left, I am not, therefore, putting a party definition on Mailer but rather suggesting that New Left politics provide an enriching context for the text. In *The Armies of the Night* we see how Mailer translates his distrust of organization and hierarchy, and his suspicion of all forms of consensus, into a text that both acclaims difference and is, in its own voicings, subversively egalitarian.

Many of Mailer's writings had been motivated by a polemical impulse similar to that of previous writers of the personal-political narrative. Mailer's announcement in *Advertisements for Myself* to "settle for nothing less than making a revolution in the consciousness of our time" could well have been voiced by Thoreau or Agee .[4] Like Mailer, Thoreau and Agee were determined to challenge the culture of liberal capitalism and to radically reshape the ideologies of their readers. Thoreau questioned his readers' acceptance of the values of market society and urged them to assert their difference from it. Agee attacked the absolutism inherent in the restrictive definitions applied to tenants and entreated instead an attention to the specificity and significance of each individual. In a different manner, James criticized the standardization of American capitalist democracy and posited instead an ideal of cultural refinement. But despite their critiques of cultural consensus, many of these writers maintained a commitment to an ahistorical and asocial humanism. Rhetorically, the dialogic questioning of consensus was simultaneous with a univocal and authoritative authorial voice. Thoreau celebrated a spiritual reality and spoke as prophet, Agee invoked a mystical divinity, and James conserved a concept of high culture and an inviolate American identity.

Mailer is, by no means, completely apart from the culture of liberalism, but he is sufficiently distanced from it to question some of its basic assumptions. Most importantly, Mailer questions the concept of the unified subject at the core of liberal ideology by speaking through a voice that resists being singular or whole. Mailer's polemic in *The Armies of the Night* is predicated on an authorial voice that is continually diverse and multiple and that stresses the numerous (borrowed) literary and ideological voices within it. It is a voice, at once singular and plural, that erases its own demarcations and lays little claim to the wholeness or finality characteristic of a culture of consensus. Mailer dramatizes the intensely social and interactive nature of all utterances. He continually celebrates the linguistic and ideological mediacy of his own voice and also demonstrates the ideological absolutism, the totalitarianism that is generated when any language is conceived of as original and self-sufficient.

In *Let Us Now Praise Famous Men*, Agee is also aware of the relativity and temporality of his articulations. But although he is conscious of writing within a politically charged context, and indeed within the contexts of documentary writing and literature as institutions, he attempts, problematically, to create a language that is free of all ideology. He assumes that his voice can be free of its inevitable interactions with other social voices. The result is the creation of an authoritative (though not ideologically neutral) voice. Mailer, on the other hand, like Adams, welcomes the entry of different ideologies into his language. There are, however, differences between Mailer's and Adams's articulations. Adams searches for ruptures and multiplicities within all systems of knowledge, but does so as a student or historian, that is, as a professional intellectual. Adams seems to need the role of professional intellectual as a pedestal from which to view his age. With Mailer, however, professionalism is of dubious value. If he philosophizes, he wants to do so in a Nietzschean manner by breaking the rules of the game, by playing philosophy, by proceeding like Nietzsche's genuine philosopher, "unphilosophically," "unwisely," "imprudently," and "play[ing] the wicked game."[5] Thus the continual flaunting of his prejudices and petulances is central to Mailer.[6] Mailer is aware that he cannot dissociate himself from the social contexts through which he speaks. That is why belief in a fixed ideology or ideological neutrality is all the more difficult for Mailer and why a politics of difference is necessary. It is important, therefore, to examine the nature of Mailer's polemic against fixed ideologies—both of the Old Left and the warmongers—and then to see the extent to which the workings of the text generate a politics of difference.

We must remember that the arena of the "political," as suggested in *The Armies of the Night*, is not restricted to a specific administrative policy or party ideology. For Mailer, there is no aspect of society that can be separated from the political. Like many thinkers of the American Left in the sixties, Mailer engaged in a radical politicization of social, psychological, and cultural spheres. As Jean Radford suggests, the "end of ideology" occasioned by Stalinism abroad and the consolidation of unions in America shifted the focus of American radicals in the sixties from considerations of Left or Right to criticism of the centralized state and its power to impose political conformity.[7] No less significant was the discovery by the New Left of the Marx of the *Economic and Philosophical Manuscripts*, the thinker interested as much in culture and alienation as in economic laws. Criticisms of cultural totalitarianism therefore gained increasing attention over theses of economic exploitation. Mailer, too, is more concerned with socio-cultural centralization than with particular party politics.

Furthermore, like many thinkers of the New Left, Mailer deliberately risks the charge of being labeled indiscriminate. For Mailer the threat of ideological standardization demands an effective opposition which can only be generated by a recognition that all spheres of life are politically permeated and therefore need to be protected from totalitarianism. As Mailer puts it in *Advertisements for Myself*, "politics as politics interests me less today than politics as a part of everything else in life" (AN 271). Above all, the "everything else" for Mailer includes literature. The power of ideological consensus and the proliferation of media that reinforce it demand that the writer undertake the task of political reawakening. The need to address a wide readership is therefore a paramount concern in *The Armies of the Night*. Reflecting on the role of the writer while on the bus with the prisoners of the march, Mailer writes the following:

> As the power of communication grew larger, so the responsibility to educate a nation lapped at the feet.... And one had become a writer to find a warm place where one was safe—responsibility was for the pompous, and the public servants; writers were born to discover wine. It was an old argument and he was worn with it— he had written a good essay once about the failure of any major American novelist to write a major novel which would reach out...to a major part of that American audience brainwashed by Hollywood, T.V., and *Time*. (AN 178–79)

Key elements of the authorial voice in *The Armies of the Night* are revealed here. Although Mailer envisions himself as the educator of his readers, he is aware that his voice is in competition with the more potent voices of mass media. He is also conscious of, and mocks, the assumptions of authorial privilege involved in adopting the voice of a national educator ("responsibility was for the pompous"), but he is simultaneously cognizant that the use of a purely "aesthetic" voice is less a deauthoritative tactic than a politically expedient one which ensures the writer a modicum of political safety. But, more importantly, the separation of the literary and political horizons is a mute acceptance of the structures through which power is exercised. Power is consolidated by keeping separate different areas of knowledge and by denying the politically permeated nature of all activities. Mailer's response to the ideological conformity perpetuated by mass media (the instruments of business power) is therefore not to retreat into an apolitical aestheticism or mysticism, as did Agee, but to attempt to rupture the ideological constants of his readers by adopting an aggressively political voice as he had in *The Presidential Papers* and *Cannibals and Christians*. Through this voice Mailer launches an attack on the existing political hegemony and advocates a politics of difference.

A frequent butt of Mailer's criticism is the ideology of unconditional patriotism, the belief of most Americans that "America-is-always-right." It is an ideology so deeply entrenched in the national character that it has acquired a normative status, and even quasi-radical critics of the liberal consensus have been unable to dissociate themselves from it. Mailer's perception of this ideological consensus in America is, of course, hardly a novelty. As we know, Tocqueville had commented on the ideology of patriotism that disallowed any censure of national institutions. Patriotism as a culturally debilitating phenomenon was also the subject of Sinclair Lewis's *Babbitt*. Much later, John Updike in *The Coup* used the American relief agent, Gibbs (who arrives with potato chips and milk powder as American aid to a drought-stricken region in Africa), to caricature the idea that America can set everything right.

Mailer's contribution to this ongoing cultural critique is his attempt to deconstruct the language of patriotism by exposing it as an expedient social conditioning that serves the political ends of the power structure. Simplistic patriotism of the America-is-always-right type, Mailer points out, is perpetuated by strategic political iconography and reinforcement by the mass media: "The brain is washed deep, there are reflexes: white shirts, Star-Spangled Banner, saluting the flag. At home is corporation land's whip—the television set" (AN

281). Patriotism, in other words, is able to operate as a transcendental signified, an unquestioned value, only because it is continually and insidiously transmitted as such. Mailer is also aware that the language of patriotism needs to be presented as absolute because of political necessity. Bakhtin's observations on the correlation between language and politics are important here. He points out that "a unitary language gives expression to forces working toward concrete verbal and ideological centralization, which develop in vital connection with the process of sociopolitical and cultural centralization."[8] Political centralization, Bakhtin suggests, demands a unitary language that will consolidate it. Mailer arrives at a similar conclusion about the function of the language of patriotism. He sees that the language of patriotism is not a politically innocent affirmation of faith but a means of centralizing power within the country by deeming the protestors aberrant, for example, and, abroad, by translating the ideology of American exceptionalism into a right to subdue Vietnam. The way to deconstruct this language is therefore to expose its vested ideologies and the immediate political ends it serves.

Frequently, Mailer illustrates how the America-is-always-right ideology translates itself into politically specific terms. The Pentagon, for example, is an "authoritative embodiment" of the principle that "America was right, America was might, America was the true religious war of Christ against the Communists" (AN 311). Here, by syntactically equating the patriotic absolute ("America was right") with affirmations of American power ("America was might") and cold war rhetoric (the religious war), Mailer implies that the language of patriotism is politically expedient. Political support for the military-industrial complex and wars, Mailer suggests, is consolidated by recourse to the rhetoric of patriotism. At other times, Mailer offers travesties of the patriotic principle at work within the context of the march. The law enforcement personnel often become living representations of this principle. Observing the Marshal who intervenes in an authoritarian fashion in his altercation with a Nazi marcher, for instance, Mailer comments: "The Marshal's emotions had obviously been marinating for a week in the very special bile waters American Patriotism reserves for its need.... He was in agonies of frustration because the honor of his profession kept him from battering every prisoner's head to a Communist pulp" (AN 164). Mailer's description of the Marshal's patriotic fury is obviously hyperbolic. But, more importantly, it deconstructs and deprivileges the language of patriotism by subjecting it to a comic contextualization. Patriotism, here, is deprived of its abstract Truth status by being associated with concrete bodily functions (the creation of bile) and by the suggestion that it is a vulgar means of inciting appropriate political hatred. Furthermore, by relating the idea of smashing prisoners' heads into communist pulps to patriotic faith, Mailer makes the grotesquely violent act function as a consequence of the patriotic principle and its ancillary paranoia, "The Reds are coming." Mailer engages here in what Marcuse calls "linguistic therapy," the attempt to reshape the political vocabulary of the establishment by stripping it of its "false neutrality" and moralizing it in terms of the Refusal.[9] The comic demythologizing and politicizing of the key words of patriotism serve to expose its ideological investments and reveal it as a language of power consolidation.

The language of patriotism is able to function as absolute, Mailer suggests, because most Americans are politically apathetic and lack the ability to question it. Guinivere in *Barbary Shore*, content to know nothing about politics, and the turnkey at the Post Office in *The Armies of the Night*, who typifies to Mailer "that infernal American innocence which could not question one's leaders," are representatives of an unthinking majority easily seduced by simplistic patriotism (AN 191). As with writers who claim an aesthetic disinterestedness, this seemingly apolitical majority merely strengthens the existing power structure. The march against the Pentagon, on the other hand, is a politicized protest against the various means of maintaining the current political center—the Pentagon, the law enforcement agencies, and the politicians in power. However, many of the protesters also seem to Mailer to perpetuate their own forms of authority and structure. They believe in causes and particular forms of politicization which they hold to be sacrosanct. For Mailer, such forms of protest cannot be truly revolutionary because they do not leave room for political difference. In fact, in *The Armies of the Night*, Mailer rejects organized politics altogether. He had fantasized about being an underground leader or guerrilla, Mailer writes, because he had "scorned the organizational aspects of revolution, the speeches, mimeograph machines, the hard dull forging of new parties and programs, the dull maneuvering to keep power, the intolerable obedience required before the over-all intellectual necessities of each objective period" (AN 94).

It is Mailer's contempt of accessories like speeches and mimeograph machines which seems to suggest that his aversion to organized politics is the petulant reaction of a facile hipster. Indeed, to some critics, Mailer's dismissal of organized revolution is merely a justification of political inactivism. Referring to Mailer's criticisms of "alphabet soup organizations," Robert Meredith, for instance, finds

Mailer's repudiation of parties and organizations a "pseudo-hip form of dropout opportunism." "Revolutions," says Meredith, "are made, in part, by organizations and orders of men in extended struggles, and they are prepared for, in part, by organizing and organizers and organizations."[10] Meredith's suggestion that Mailer rejects organized parties simply because they use organization is a true but limited interpretation of Mailer's politics. Mailer criticizes these parties not merely because they are organized (although that is part of it) but because the organizational aspects are instruments for maintaining an authoritative unity. This need to be vigilant of organizational structures has been keenly felt by many political philosophers. Foucault warned about the appearance of the state apparatus even in seemingly serial organizations such as people's courts, Sartre about the antidemocratic implications of organization in revolution, and Marcuse about administration as a form of domination.[11] The New Left was particularly sensitive to the structure and style of its politics because it did not want to replicate the hierarchies of the establishment. Mailer is similarly suspicious of organized parties because they wear the vestments of power. The forging of new "programs" (which can become programmatic), the need to maintain "power," and the "obedience" before a cause are all aspects that attest to a faith in a politics of identity. The creation of new slogans like *programs, power,* and *obedience* become the framework for the monologic affirmation of a "true" party or cause; they also imply a belief in final solutions that will solve or unify the anarchy of political dialogue.[12] The creation of absolute structures, Mailer suggests, can only generate absolute forms of thought.

It is Mailer's distrust of singular and authoritarian political voices that prompts his criticism of many of the participants and parties involved in the march. Like Thoreau, who created character-ideologues whose social-material ideologies he could mock, Mailer creates typified characters whose political monologism he can deride. (Of course, the differences between Thoreau's and Mailer's authorial positions are numerous. The author who issues attacks on the "mass of men" is a Homeric figure, whereas the author who scoffs at organized parties is a media-hungry, slovenly, unshaven drunk.) The protestor who to Mailer seems most to embody organized revolution, and hence political absolutism, is Walter Teague. Unlike most protestors, Teague makes his temporary imprisonment serve his ideological ends. After resting in the crowded prison cell, Teague uses the evening to lecture the prisoners on the organizational shortcomings of the march. He continues his oratory the next morning to criticize

Dellinger for suppressing the real militants and ends his incarceration by drafting a letter itemizing the flaws of the National Mobilization. Overtly, Teague's polemic thus champions dissent and seems to be directed against the established leadership of the march. However, Teague's voice itself seems to Mailer to operate within a framework of mass identity and authoritarianism. Mailer shows the falsity of the revolutionary pretensions of this voice by exposing and typifying its absolutism. He is averse to Teague's rhetoric because of its rhetorical fixity. Teague's indictment of the march, says Mailer, "was too easy—it had all the firm impact of all the sound-as-brickwork-logic of the next step—he had heard Communists and Trotskyists expatiating on social problems...with just this same militant, precise, executive command in analyzing the situation, the same compelling sense of structure" (AN 202).

Of course, part of Mailer's response to Teague's proselytizing stems from his distrust of rationality as an adequate guide to societal problems.[13] For Mailer, the systematic liquidation of millions of Jews by orderly process was a horrendous culmination of the fetish of rationality. But Mailer is also critical of the language of reason because it assumes that its articulations are based on a perfected system of comprehension. Formal logic claims universal validity for its methods and therefore cannot admit dispersion. Teague's rhetoric seems to Mailer to partake of this kind of universality. It moves through well-defined steps of logic sanctioned by the Old Left. In presuming the applicability of the same dogmas to diverse social problems, it also assumes a normative and absolute status. In his analysis of Teague's polemic, Mailer points to the necessary conjunction of language and ideology. The verbal features of a language are in themselves ideological, and a language that rests upon fixed verbal structures cannot be ideologically differentiative.[14] As Mailer later surmises, he feels "the pinch of the hanging judge" in Teague's critique of the march, primarily because of Teague's "certainty" (AN 216). Teague's polemic provides immediate and decisive analyses, and leaves little room for doubt or contingency.[15]

Mailer further subverts what he perceives as Teague's political absolutism by subjecting him to mock analysis and definition. He ridicules Teague's act of falling asleep immediately on reaching the prison cell, for instance, by defining him as a "professional" who works, sleeps, and thinks revolution twenty-four hours a day (AN 181). Professionalism, with its associations of objectivity, competence, surety, and the ethos of an ever stronger corporation land, is a designation of power and control. That is why Mailer playfully privileges

amateurism over professionalism. Having typified Teague as a professional, Mailer, as if parodying Teague's absolutism, uses this designation as all-explanatory. Teague's overt lack of resentment at Mailer's
opposition to his letter criticizing the National Mobilization can be
conclusively explained by this term. As Mailer concludes, "Teague
gave no sign of rancor. Teague was a professional" (AN 223). Similarly, Mailer mocks Teague's "professional" lecturing of the prisoners by
designating him the "First Preceptor" conducting the "Occoquan Free
School for Transient Nascent Revolutionaries" (AN 215). By putting
the finalized and organized aspects of Teague's rhetoric to parodic
use, Mailer deprivileges the consensual rhetoric of party politics.

Throughout *The Armies of the Night* Mailer continues to attack
what he perceives as attempts to create ideological homogeneity. He
mocks the utopian politics of "liberal technologues" who aim to put
an end to all human conflict; he ridicules the "scholarly Socialist" edi-
tors of *Dissent* prone to publishing standardized "polemical gravies."
His own preference is for a politics of radical heterogeneity, one without ideological constants. Analyzing what he calls the "political aesthetic" of the New Left, Mailer writes the following:

> Just as the truth of his material was revealed to a good writer by
> the cutting edge of his style (he could thus hope his style was in
> each case the most appropriate tool for the material of his expe-
> rience) so a revolutionary began to uncover the nature of his
> true situation by trying to ride the beast of his revolution.... The
> future of the revolution existed in the nerves and cells of the
> people who created it and lived with it, rather than in the sancti-
> ty of the original idea.... What seemed significant here, was the
> idea of a revolution which preceded ideology; the New Left had
> obviously adopted the idea for this March. (AN 104)

Mailer is most attracted to the New Left because it seems to operate
without ideological constants and rejects the ideal of consensus. It
questions the authoritative nature of established political languages
by refusing to define any ideological ends. Like many radicals of the
sixties, Mailer has little faith in a politics dictated by dogma. As Morris Dickstein points out, the New Left turned from the belief in definitive causes to a commitment to "spontaneity and the personal here-
and-now" (AN 105). In a sense Mailer, like Agee, wishes to give voice
to the voiceless. Whereas Agee wished to give voice to the tenants
themselves rather than to sociologists or reformers of tenant life,
Mailer wishes to give voice to the experiential, "the nerves and cells

of the people," rather than to abstract theories. But Mailer does not essentialize the experiential as Agee essentializes the tenants. The politics of personal testament can easily change from a subversion of logical absolutes to the creation of a new set of absolutes: spontaneity and instinct. But Mailer is aware of the ideological implications of glorifying a privileged psychosensual politics and is careful, therefore, to circumscribe the interpretational validity of the experiential. The radical who participates in revolutionary activity without following a proclaimed ideology does not by this token have access to an ultimate political solution. He can only "begin to discover" his true situation by "trying" to immerse himself in revolution. The language of experiential politics is a viable alternative to the language of dogma, but it is by no means a final and absolute solution.

What is even more important in the above analysis of New Left politics is Mailer's explicit connection of the political with the aesthetic. It implies a recognition that the verbal features of language are not politically innocent. (It was by demonstrating the vested political interests inherent in the language of organized revolution that Mailer was able to expose its absolutism.) Indeed, Mailer suggests that interpretation ("the truth of his material") follows and is predicated on the verbal constructs of a language or what he calls "style." Furthermore, Mailer's equation of the aesthetic not merely with the political in the general sense but with ideologically decentered revolutionary activity suggests his commitment to a dispersive aesthetics. Like the New Left revolutionary who proceeds without a sacrosanct ideology, and who is continually engaged in discovering rather than finally defining the political, Mailer wishes to speak in a language that celebrates incompletion. It is through such a language that Mailer begins to articulate a politics of difference.

The impulse toward verbal and ideological dispersion is clearly evident in the authorial voice in *The Armies of the Night*. Although Mailer envisions himself as a national educator, he does not, like the practical educator Franklin or the spiritual educator Thoreau, rely on a unified and autonomous voice. Mailer's sense of subjectivity in *The Armies of the Night* is social, and he acknowledges the traces of different literary, social, philosophical, and political voices in his own ideological formulations. The ideological dispersion of the authorial voice is immediately obvious in the multiple guises in which it appears. Like James in *The American Scene*, who used different author-characters as social interpreters, Mailer also presents himself as a succession of different characters who participate in and analyze the politics of the march. But James's author-characters are all observers who serve to consolidate ideals of cultural refinement and a fixed American identity. Mailer's characterizations, on the other hand, are acknowledgements of the diverse social horizons within which his voice operates. Characterizations like the "beast," the "snob," or the "showman" suggest Mailer's antagonistic awareness of the media and celebrity world in which he participates. Some, like the "novelist," the "historian," and the "comic-hero," invoke the literature and criticism establishments. Still others, such as the "General," the "Left Conservative," and the "existentialist," operate within the sphere of political commentary.

These overt characterizations, however, are only the surface features of the hybridized nature of the authorial voice. The authorial voice in *The Armies of the Night* is all dialogic: it constantly refracts other voices, replaces one language with another, and subjects all these languages to disruptive commentary and questioning.[16] Richard Poirier, who sees Mailer's language as predicated on the instability of his voice, finds an "interplay of voices" in any sentence of Mailer's.[17] Mailer is, for Poirier, a most accomplished "ventriloquist of styles."[18] Poirier's observations on Mailer's language are apt descriptions of the multivoicing at the center of the text. Mailer is able to free himself from a unitary language precisely *because* he ventriloquizes. This ventriloquism of language as an acknowledgement of linguistic otherness is an important dispersive feature of novelistic prose. By speaking through different languages, without giving itself up to any of these languages, the authorial voice in *The Armies of the Night* foregrounds its intertextuality.

The ideological indeterminacy of the authorial voice is evident in much of what may be called the "inner speech" in *The Armies of the Night*, which takes the form of a dialogic interaction of voices. Likening his march past the Washington Monument to the excitement of his combat experiences, for instance, Mailer writes the following:

> A zany part of him had been expecting...he would lead an army (The lives of Leon Trotsky and Ernest Hemingway had done nothing to dispel this expectation).... Probably there were very few good wars (good wars being free of excessive exhaustion, raddled bowels...and computerized methods) but if you were in as good shape for war as for football, there was very little which was better for the senses. They would be executing Ernest Hemingway in effigy...for having insisted on this recognition, they would even be executing him in Utope City on the moon, but Mailer now sent him a novelist's blessing (which is to say, well-intended but stingy) because Hemingway after all had put the

key on the table. *If it made you feel good, it was good.* That and
Saint Thomas Aquinas' "Trust the authority of your senses"
were enough to enable a man to become a good working amateur philosopher, an indispensable vocation for the ambitious
novelist since otherwise he is naught but an embittered entertainer, a storyteller, a John O'Hara! (Born January 31, same birth-
day as Mailer). (AN 106–7)

I quote this passage at length because it illustrates the deep-seated linguistic stratification, the diversity of voices, within the authorial voice
in *The Armies of the Night*. Mailer's language here is predicated on a
series of voices, all of which are intermingled and which resist final-
ization. Mailer adopts the voices of an army leader, an amateur
philosopher, an ambitious novelist, and an embittered entertainer.
And these voices are not merely different voices adopted by the
author in turn, voices that are independent of each other. Instead,
they are positioned in dialogic relationships where they comment on
and interact with each other. The voice of the army leader, for
instance, is mocked by metamorphosis of that voice into that of an
amateur philosopher, a transformation which suggests that theoretical
justifications of war are phony. Similarly, the voice of the ambitious
novelist is deprived of its honorific status by the suggestion that it is
merely an expedient guise for the voice of the embittered entertainer.
Further, the authorial voice is also split between the voice of the meditative writer and the parenthetical voice of the interpretive critic. This
device of using parenthetical critical commentary is also a recurrent
dialogizing feature of *The Armies of the Night*. It points both to an
awareness of writing as a continual process of interpretation and to a
recognition of the semantic open-endedness of any articulation. The
voice of the interpretive critic, for example, serves to modify and
question the voice of the meditative writer. The validity of the
apotheosis of Hemingway's theories on the senses is questioned by
the interpretive voice's suggestion that the meditative writer is more
concerned with professional status (and is therefore "stingy" in offering praise) than with searching for viable theories. In like manner, the
writer's scorn of storytellers like John O'Hara is ridiculed by the critic's implication that the writer has more in common with John O'Hara
than he thinks.

But although these multiple characterizations and parenthetical
voices indicate Mailer's freedom from a unitary language and culture
of consensus, a more potent means of affirming ideological difference
is the celebration of linguistic mediacy. It is significant that a medita-

tion which begins by presenting the author as a leader progresses by acknowledging other voices: Trotsky, Hemingway, and Aquinas. The inclusion of antecedent voices within the philosophical theorizations of the authorial voice, here and elsewhere in the text, suggests Mailer's awareness of the socially and historically permeated nature of language. Instead of denying the echoes of numerous voices within his own, Mailer welcomes them and continually speaks through other voices. This mixture of voices reflects Mailer's rejection of the unified, autonomous subject of capitalism in favor of a subjectivity that is formed by otherness. The inclusion of these voices is also not a validation of prior authority. Mailer does not hold these antecedent voices to be originary or sacrosanct. By simultaneously quoting from Hemingway and Aquinas and subjecting the quotes to comic contextualizations, Mailer acknowledges their functional significance, but he also deprives them of a privileged status. Hemingway's slogan about the morality of feeling "good," for instance, is made to caricature itself by being verbally associated with good wars (free of raddled bowels) and good physical shape (for playing war or football). Further, the sensual theories of both Hemingway and Aquinas are mockingly slighted by the suggestion that they are fit instruments for amateur philosophizing. Thus, although Mailer acknowledges the validity of prior voices, he does not nostalgically conceive of them as originary or absolute. Unlike the monologic languages of patriotism and organized revolution discussed earlier, Mailer suggests that his language has no ideological constants. It is a language where the process of supplanting one ideological voice with another is continuous.

If Mailer rejects the authoritative privileges of the polemical voice by acclaiming ideological proliferation and change, he also ruptures the boundaries of his language by questioning the closure of his articulations. Mailer's theorizations about war in the above passage, particularly his comments about the gross physical discomforts during war, are explicitly related to the chronicling of his war experiences in *The Naked and the Dead*. The comic polemic against the builders of "Utope City" is a continuation of his diatribe against "liberal technologues" initiated in an earlier chapter, "The Liberal Party." The positioning of the authorial voice within a system of references to previous and present articulations is a dramatization of New Left politics in action. No formulation is complete or separate in itself, and every utterance is related to numerous other utterances. The deliberate inclusion of a chapter titled "Why Are We in Vietnam?" in *The Armies of the Night*, for example, deliberately questions the closure of Mailer's book bearing that title.

Mailer's commitment to ideological difference is also evident in the double-voiced structure of *The Armies of the Night*. The decision to write two narratives of the march against the Pentagon suggests Mailer's awareness of the impermanence of all inscriptions.[19] All language, to Mailer, is subject to revision and reinterpretation. Indeed, a major function of Book II is to generate counterinterpretations of the march that contest the articulations of Book I. While waiting to be released from Occoquan prison in the first narrative, for instance, Tuli Kupferberg's refusal to stay away from the Pentagon at the risk of courting further imprisonment seems to Mailer to imply ideological fixity. Kupferberg's "moral ladder," as Mailer calls it, is then only an escape from guilt and nausea. "One ejected oneself from guilt by climbing the ladder" (AN 219). In the second narrative, however, climbing the moral ladder is translated into an act of courage. Within the context of the protestors who, despite being beaten by the police, continue their late vigil outside the Pentagon, it becomes a necessary and commendable assertion of political will. "The rite of passage was invoked, the moral ladder was climbed, they were forever different in the morning than they had been before the night" (AN 311–12). Similarly, Mailer subjects media accounts of the march to different interpretations through strategic recontextualization. Take, for example, Jimmy Breslin's story about the physical and verbal abuse perpetrated on the soldiers by unruly protestors. In Book I, the story, following Mailer's own observations about the insensitivity of protestors who insist on being dragged by tired, hernia-suffering soldiers, and the raucousness of the nonpacifist protestors, seems tacitly to confirm Mailer's speculations. In Book II, however, by deliberately juxtaposing the Breslin story with what he perceives to be a biased account of police brutality from the *National Guardian*, Mailer implicitly equates the two and suggests that the Breslin story is similarly exaggerated.

The device of multiple characterization, the acknowledgement of one's language always being "borrowed," and the introduction of opposed analyses serve to dialogize the authorial voice in *The Armies of the Night*. These techniques dramatize Mailer's freedom from a unified voice and suggest that his commitment to ideological difference is present as much in the structure of his articulations as in his endorsement of the diverse groups that conglomerated for the peace march. Mailer is also aware that the hegemony of organized politics is consolidated by the use of a privileged and sacrosanct political language. Mailer's alternative to a politics of absolute causes is to posit a language (and consequently an ideology) that rests on a series of shifting binaries. Mailer's political analyses in *The Armies of the Night* are frequently grounded in these binaries, which to Mailer represent a "schizophrenia" within both American culture and himself. Some of these binaries are "concept" versus "obscenity," "rationality" versus "instinct," "technology" versus "mystery," and "professional" versus "amateur." Through these dualisms, Mailer attempts to generate political dialogue and to question ideological fixity. As Richard Poirier points out, Mailer's politics and language oscillate between these dichotomies without giving themselves up to either. Mailer, for example, introduces "concepts" and corrects them by "sudden slangy intrusions."[20] The same is true of many of Mailer's political observations. He sees that the hippies who have conglomerated to march for an unknown (mysterious) end, and whom he therefore admires, are, in their drug taking, also products of a "technology" that he detests in principle. He cannot, therefore, completely separate *mystery* and *technology* and privilege merely the first term.

More importantly, his use of binaries also questions the idea of a privileged political language. Mailer seems as concerned to reinterpret and recontextualize his terms as he is to deploy them as analytical modes. Take, for instance, the use of *obscenity* in "A Transfer of Power." Obscenity is first associated with lasciviousness (the common man is "obscene as an old goat"). Then obscenity becomes part of a subversive "humor" that deflates "overblown values." Next, it operates as a necessary adjunct to "concept." ("All the gifts of the American language came out in the happy play of obscenity upon concept.") It shifts later to become a literary device which enables Mailer in *Why Are We in Vietnam?* to "kick goodbye" to the "literary corset of good taste." Finally, obscenity is used to explain the moral debilitation (obscenity "resides in the quick conversion of excitement to nausea") of Lyndon B. Johnson (AN 61–62). Mailer often undertakes similar efforts to redefine his key terms. *Technology*, for example, is associated not merely with mechanization but with corporations, political organizations, capitalism, the Wasp mentality, ideological certainty, and language devoid of moral content.

If Mailer continually redefines his terminology, it is because he is aware that linguistic rules are permeated with politics. He revels, therefore, in presenting arguments based as much on puns as on logic. He intimates his aversion to reporters, for instance, by referring to them as "Luce-ites" and then "Loo-sights" (AN 43). He describes, repeatedly, the efforts of censors to suppress his obscene language and proceeds to repeat the obscenities. These plays with language, like Jerry Rubin's pronouncement, "The Yippies are Marxists.... We follow in the revolutionary tradition of Groucho, Chico, Harpo, and

Karl," are not denials of serious politics.[21] Just as the New Left priori-
tized seemingly "marginal" movements, Mailer's purpose is to foreground what has been perceived as trivial and deviant and thus to
question the ethics and politics of the literary center.

Mailer's radical critique of liberal capitalism comes during a
period of civil unrest when the politics of every organization and
movement are under question, and when, in literature, modernist aestheticism is suspect. But although Mailer participates, in *The Armies of
the Night*, in oppositional politics, he cannot completely dissociate
himself from ideas of consensus in the culture, and we see the author
agonizing over the very differences he has celebrated. Mailer's view of
cultural dualisms, for example, suggests traces of a nostalgia for some
sort of cultural consensus. Although Mailer does privilege difference
by shifting between a series of binaries, he still views cultural
schizophrenia as a disease that needs curing. But schizophrenia can be
designated as a disease only by creating standards that demarcate
acceptable and unacceptable behavior. Indeed, as Deleuze and Guattari have shown, the need for cultural hegemony and authoritative
wholeness demands that disruptive schizophrenic thought remain
outside the demarcated limits of acceptability. The schizophrenic completely ruptures wholeness because he does not attempt to reconcile
disjunctions. Instead, he puts them to "affirmative use. He is and
remains in disjunction."[22] Although Mailer recognizes and deploys
disjunction, he does not always put it to affirmative use. He often
views disjunction as a lack of wholeness. His frequent statements on
the necessity of the two halves of America to come together attest to
some need for a liberal, humanistic core of values. The center of America, Mailer decides, is insane, because Americans have been living in a
state of schizophrenia by being both devout Christians (believing in
"Mystery") and residents of corporation land (believing in "Technology"). "The country had been living with a controlled, even fiercely
controlled schizophrenia which had been deepening with the years.
Perhaps the point had been passed. Any man or woman who was
devoutly Christian and worked for the American Corporation, had
been caught in an unseen vise whose pressure could split their minds
from their souls" (AN 211). It is significant that Mailer analyzes the
abnormality of schizophrenia by resorting to the traditional dualism
between the mind and the soul. The soul, in this case, is a universal
that promises wholeness; schizophrenia is the disease that threatens to
rupture it. Indeed, Mailer fears the possible anarchy that will be
wreaked once schizophrenic thought passes the point of control.

This nostalgia for wholeness is also apparent, to a degree, in

Mailer's deification of the American past. Despite his belief in ideological difference, the past is, to some extent, a constant in its virtues, ideological stability, and heroism. The testimonials to a purer American past in *The Armies of the Night* are frequent. For Mailer, "American civilization" has "moved from the existential sanction of the frontier to the abstract ubiquitous sanction of the dollar bill" (AN 179); it has deviated from its foundations, which were "its love and trust in Christ" (AN 239). Indeed, the need for cultural unity even leads to excessively wishful historical reconstruction. The Hay-Adams hotel in Washington, D.C., for instance, reminds Mailer of the times of Henry Adams, "when men and events were solid, comprehensible, often obedient to a code of values, and resolutely non-electronic" (AN 69). Anyone familiar with the multiplicities of Adams's *Education* would be compelled to question Mailer's analysis.

The significance of Mailer's observations, however, is not in their possible exaggeration but in his valorization of the past as a repository of values. The past becomes a standard of evaluation, and it is this authoritative status that Mailer utilizes to analyze the march. Although Mailer acclaims the subversiveness of the march, his admiration for it often takes the form of comparing the march to venerated events in the past. The Civil War, in particular, is used as an event full of meaning (a signified) to which the march can be profitably related. Mailer likens the confrontation between the marchers and soldiers to Matthew Brady's Civil War pictures. He commemorates the last of the protestors who keep a late vigil outside the Pentagon by associating them with Civil War soldiers. In fifty years, Mailer thinks, the day of the march "may loom in our history large as the ghosts of the Union dead" (AN 105). Such comparisons are suggestive of more than cultural and historical amnesia. In *The Armies of the Night* they function as devices that allow Mailer to link the march with what he perceives as respectable American history.[23] They provide Mailer with a narrative of ideological constants within an ideology of difference.

It is perhaps this retention of some ideological constants in *The Armies of the Night* that has caused some critics to view the book as an attempt at unification. Stanley Gutman, for instance, suggests that Mailer "begins with divisions which, through dialectical confrontation, are eventually united into a coherent whole."[24] Although Gutman is right in perceiving the moves toward unification in *The Armies of the Night*, his view that Mailer endorses cultural unity ignores much of the linguistic stratification in the text. Mailer ends the book with a prophetic description of America heavy with child, but leaves indeterminate and open the results of this birth. And just as he assumes this prophetic voice, he also undercuts it by suggesting that his prognostication about the future of America is very consciously a metaphor "delivered" to the reader. The mediacy of the authorial voice, the celebration of incompletion, and the continual questioning of all unitary languages and ideologies in *The Armies of the Night* signal Mailer's freedom from a consensus and allow him to articulate a politics of difference. Such a politics is energized by its commitment to change, its belief in serial political structures, its endorsement of the coexistence of diverse, even opposed cultural values, and its denial of social consensus.[25] In *The Armies of the Night* both the play of voices and the overtly stated agenda reach their most differentiative form within liberal discourse.

Polemics and Dialogics in *The Woman Warrior:* A Radical Challenge

How does the marginal writer of the personal-political narrative approach the issues of bourgeois homogeneity, liberal individualism, community, and difference? How does the fact of writing from outside the dominant culture affect the polemical stance of the authorial voice? How do the Bakhtinian concepts of voice and dialogism, as we have pursued them so far, translate themselves in these texts? Obviously, to follow the fullest implications of these questions would require a book-length study. I have chosen Maxine Hong Kingston's *The Woman Warrior* for analysis because it is not only a personal-political narrative by a marginal writer, written through a perspective of marginality, but also a radical narrative which questions the unified and autonomous subject of liberal capitalism and demonstrates the effectiveness of a politics of difference. It is also a useful text with which to rethink some of our terms of analysis because it specifically foregrounds the concerns of voice, authority, and dialogic intertextuality and emphasizes issues of race and class.

Let us first examine some of the issues of marginality and race as they relate to issues of subjectivity, consensus, and authority. As we have seen in Jane Addams's *Twenty Years at Hull-House,* the fact that the text is authored by a woman does not place it outside the dominant culture. *Twenty Years* still has some investment in the liberal consensus. Addams's questioning of this consensus occurs at moments in the text when she contextualizes and relativizes her voice as privileged patrician, as disempowered woman. Similarly, not all texts by racial Others subvert or challenge the dominant culture. These texts can be radical challenges only if they do not replicate the modes of unity and universality that constitute authoritative power structures.[1]

In recent years theories of femininity and race have increasingly been concerned with these issues of definition and subversion. What has been perceived as "white" feminism, for example, has been criticized for treating white, bourgeois conceptions of womanhood as universal, while slighting the concerns of women of color. Alice Walker's use of the term *womanist* to designate the concerns of black women is well known. Women of color have seen the facts of race and colonialism as more important in their lives than the singular patriarchal oppression emphasized by white feminists. This vocabulary of common oppression, Bell Hooks argues, might well be an appropriation of a radical vocabulary by liberal women.[2] However, although it is politically important to stress the difference of race, it is equally important to be wary of the totalizing implications of strict racial and ethnic categories. If marginalized groups are to be politically effective, they have to subvert the concepts of unity, coherence, and universality and force a recognition of the values of multiplicity and diversity upon the dominant culture. Feminists of color are recognizing that to accept categories of white versus black or Western versus Asian as absolutes is to fall victim to the very hierarchical thinking by which marginalized groups have been oppressed by being designated as "Other." Floya Anthias and Nira Yuval-Davis argue, for instance, that "political struggles...which are formulated on an ethnic or sexual essence...[are] reactionary."[3] It is important, therefore, to recognize difference as a crucial strength and not to theorize about marginalized groups in terms of unity or definition.[4] *The Woman Warrior* is a radical challenge to the liberal consensus because Kingston is able to speak from her marginalized position without resorting to a singular definition of it.

Kingston critiques the dominant culture, its marginalization and impoverishing definitions of Others, but does so from a position of radical instability which questions the very notions of identity and universality. Of course, Kingston's position as a Chinese-American is one of separation and exclusion from the consensual culture of competitive, atomistic, liberal individualism. The very Franklinian industry and frugality of Chinese immigrants was, in fact, viewed in America as aberrant and degenerate because these immigrants supported extended families. Kingston's position in relation to the dominant culture is therefore very different from Jane Addams's complex position. But although Kingston, unlike Jane Addams, speaks from within a group that is being marginalized, instead of from the outside, she does not conceive of this group in essentialized terms. *The Woman Warrior* is a personal and polemical text but one fundamentally concerned with questioning singular definitions of racial, national, and sexual identity.

Kingston's text is a collection of "memoirs" of Kingston's experiences of growing up in an immigrant family in Stockton, California.

Kingston reveals the squalor and poverty of Chinatowns, the endemic racism, the traumas of acculturation in a hostile environment, and her own attempt to subvert gender hierarchies by imaginative identification with the woman warrior. But although *The Woman Warrior* is a polemic against the subjugation of women and the racial hostility experienced by Chinese-Americans, the polemic does not emanate from a clearly defined authorial voice. Voicing is a complex issue in the text. The very act of speaking involves breaking through the gender and race barriers that suppress voicing from the margins. But the voice Kingston speaks through is not isolated and autonomous. It refracts, echoes, and is creatively conjoined with the numerous voices with which it interacts. This undefined basis of narration dramatizes Kingston's determination not to create singular definitions of ethnic identity in order to combat the impoverishing stereotypes to which Chinese-Americans are subject. She does not wish to postulate the foundations of a new hierarchy.

It is clear at the very outset that the act of articulation itself will be a major concern in the book. Kingston begins her memoirs with a secrecy oath imposed on her by her indomitable mother, "You must not tell anyone," and a moral drawn from the story of the adulterous aunt who has been banished from family memory: "Don't humiliate us. You wouldn't like to be forgotten as if you had never been born."[5] Kingston is aware of the temerity involved in her very act of writing. To articulate herself she must break through the numerous barriers that condemn her to voicelessness. The unnamed narrator thus begins her recollections with the act of listening rather than speaking. Sworn to silence, she hears the tale of the unnamed aunt who gives "silent birth" to "save her inseminator's name" (WW 13). Like Jane Addams's descriptions of her guilt and inadequacy during her childhood, this initial story establishes the denial of expression women are condemned to in patriarchy and the cultural stranglehold the narrator must fight in order to express herself. The narrator here is a present-day prototype of the "madwomen" of the nineteenth century, whispering their secrets from patriarchal attics.[6] "Go away and work," her mother tells her. "Whispering, whispering, making no sense. Madness...I shut my mouth, but I felt something alive tearing at my throat" (WW 233).[7] She feels the agony of silence, the "pain in [her] throat" that comes from holding back the two hundred things she has to tell her mother (WW 229).

But the anxiety of articulation is also peculiarly a racial one. Kingston is sensitive to the brutality and degradation experienced by Chinese immigrants. *China Men* records the heroism of Chinese rail-

road workers and sugarcane planters who survive hostility and violence. Living in a culture that had for long grouped Orientals with
imbeciles and denied Chinese immigrants legal and naturalization
rights, the present-day immigrants in *The Woman Warrior* still live in
fear.[8] Immigrants thus "guard their real names with silence" and even
after years of living in America avoid signing innocuous permission
slips for their children at school (WW 6, 194). The narrator realizes
that "silence had to do with being a Chinese girl" (WW 193). In the
American school she is overcome by dumbness, her voice reduced to
a whisper. In the Chinese school she finds her voice, but it is strained
one: "You could hear splinters in my voice, bones rubbing jagged
against one another" (WW 196).

These vivid accounts of being tortured by silence are metaphors
for the particular limitations the marginal writer must overcome in
order to be heard. African-Americans had to demonstrate their very
humanity by being able to write when public strictures expressly for-
bade schooling for them.[9] Even so gifted a writer as Ralph Ellison felt
compelled to "prove" his artistry by emulating the modernists. And
the unnamed, invisible narrator of *Invisible Man* could only discover
his identity underground, in a Manhattan city sewer. Kingston's
voicelessness is a symbolic expression of the culture's refusal to give
her voice legitimacy. But the alternative to this disempowerment,
Kingston knows, is not to create a "true" Chinese woman's voice or to
define a singular Chinese identity to celebrate, but to question the
very political structures that make positions of power and powerlessness possible. Just as Jane Addams problematized theories of oppression and Mailer celebrated the heterogeneous nature of the march on
the Pentagon and the refusal of the New Left to define political ends,
Kingston speaks for the marginalized by questioning the very idea of
definition. Kingston deconstructs monologic oppositions between
American and Chinese, male and female, and most importantly
between self and Other by articulating herself through a language in
which opposed and diverse voices constantly coexist. By doing so,
Kingston questions the values of the autonomous self necessary to liberal thought and simultaneously presents the dialogic community as
the realm of radicalism, hope, and possibility.

The tale of Fa Mu Lan, the legendary swordswoman who took
her father's place in battle, fought gloriously, returned victorious, and
lived obediently thereafter with her parents, is a fascinating and complex narrative of multiple voicing and gender reconstruction. Like
most of the stories in the book, this one is not an "original." But
Kingston revels in retelling tales, deriving her inspiration from the

community of tellers before her rather than from defining her own autonomous voice. The tales of swordswomen become part of the imagination of children as they listen to the adults "talk-story." Brave Orchid, the narrator's mother, recreates for her, in turn, the most adventuresome of the swordswomen tales. "Night after night my mother would talk-story until we fell asleep. I couldn't tell where the stories left off and the dreams began, her voice, the voice of the heroines in my sleep" (WW 24). The narrator remembers her own participation in the continuation of folklore: "As a child I had followed my mother about the house, the two of us singing about Fa Mu Lan.... I had forgotten this chant that was once mine, given me by my mother, who may not have known its power to remind" (WW 24). The origins of the tale are communal and familial, and the narrator's continuation of it attests to the relatedness of her voice to other voices. But this community does not force univocal visions upon its members. It is obvious that the intents of Brave Orchid's and the narrator's tales vary greatly; but the fascinating aspect of the tale is the narrator's ability to tell her own tale both in opposition to, and in harmony with, Brave Orchid's tale.

The folkloric intent of the tale is the strengthening of the institution of the family. Girls are reminded that growing up as wives or slaves is a mark of mediocrity, of failure. They have the potential to be "heroines, swordswomen." But the task of the swordswoman is similar to that of a wife: maintaining the family honor. The swordswoman "got even with anybody who hurt her family" (23).[10] Brave Orchid's version emphasizes filial devotion and obedience to the patriarchal order. Fa Mu Lan is "the girl who took her father's place in battle...and returned alive from the war to settle in the village" (WW 24). The authorial voice will both dialogically challenge certain familial values and retain others. The conflictual role of the narrator within the institution of the family is evident from the beginning. The girl (with whom the narrator identifies) decides to begin her tutelage under the old man and woman of the mountains after hearing their arguments. The old man challenges her: "You can go pull sweet potatoes, or you can stay with us and learn how to fight barbarians and bandits." The old woman continues: "You can avenge your village.... You can be remembered by the Han people for your dutifulness" (WW 27). A complex structure of oppositions is built up here. The girl leaves her family to seek her future alone but finds solace in a substitute household; the new family invites her to transgress her traditional role as a female and become a fighter, but the purpose of this transgression is to fight barbarians (read: outsiders); and she must always maintain strict filiality.

But soon within the tale, gender oppositions and family structures become less clear. The old man and woman become, for instance,
an embodiment of perennial, natural forces, always changing but
always in harmony. They are the dancers of the earth everywhere, two
angels, perhaps an infinite number of angels. "They were light; they
were molten, changing gold—Chinese lion dancers, African lion
dancers in midstep.... Before my eyes, gold bells shredded into gold
tassels that fanned into two royal capes that softened into lions' fur"
(WW 32). It is important to recognize that even radical texts do have
moments of affirming some transcendent visions as a polemical means
of undermining cultural hierarchies. Kingston here attempts to move
beyond gender difference to a higher "unity" beyond gender. But this
vision is only an initial move in the attempt to question traditional definitions of gender and deny gender hierarchies.[11] The couple often
appear like young lovers. He appears as a "handsome young man"
and she as a "beautiful young woman" who in spring "dressed like a
bride" (WW 33–34). But to the girl the manner of the couple suggests
that "the old woman was to the old man a sister or friend rather than a
wife," because they do not reduplicate patriarchy. Having problematized traditional gender roles, Kingston presents the complex figure of
the swordswoman ready for battle. As she leaves her village, she is at
once the knight in shining armor who rides on her talismanic white
horse and the departing bride who receives gifts like wedding presents
(WW 42). She wears men's clothes and ties her hair back in manly fashion and is complimented on her beauty: "How beautiful she looks"
(WW 43). Her husband appears before her during battle not as titular
head of the family but as the lost part of the androgyne, "the childhood
friend found at last" (WW 46). With her pregnancy, the swordswoman's gendering is finally most complicated. She looks like a powerful
man, carries the inscription of her family's revenge on her back and
her baby in the front.

Through her retelling of the tale, Kingston, in addition to questioning gender roles, also recreates the role of avenger for her purposes. She needs to be the female avenger and the avenger of the family.
Thus, the woman warrior out in battle avenges not only the wrongs to
her village but also the hierarchical genderizing to which she has been
subject. In a scene of ironic misspeak, the swordswoman alights at the
house of a rich baron and announces herself as a "female avenger."
The baron, misunderstanding the appellation, tries to appeal to her
"man to man." "Oh come now. Everyone takes the girls when he
can.... 'Girls are maggots in the rice.' 'It is more profitable to raise
geese than daughters.' He quoted to me the sayings I hated" (WW 51).

The legend of the swordswoman becomes the personal story of the Chinese-American girl enraged at the misogynist proverbs she constantly hears in the immigrant community. But Kingston does not separate her voice from that of the community. She also wishes to avenge the hardships of her family, their loss of their laundry in the process of urban renewal, and the pervasive racism to which the Chinese are subjected. "The swordswoman and I are not so dissimilar," the narrator realizes. "What we have in common are the words at our backs.... And I have so many words—'chink' words and 'gook' words too" (WW 63).

Kingston deals with the necessity of maintaining and creating multiple ideological positions, of always letting the numerous voices echo in her own articulations. For Kingston this refraction of other voices is an affirmation of community and diversity just as it was for Mailer. Thus it is appropriate that the final story of the book emphasizes differences and communicative interaction. "Here is a story my mother told me...recently, when I told her I also talk story. The beginning is hers, the ending, mine" (WW 240). As opposed to the beginning of the book, where the mother silences her, here the narrator emphasizes how their voices are inextricably and dialogically linked, even if they are different.[12] This relationship of mutuality becomes even more interesting in view of the fact that what the narrator presents as a single story is, compositionally, two stories. The first, in all probability the mother's story, is about the indomitable grandmother whose word is inevitably proven right, and therefore obeyed by the community. She fearlessly commands the household to accompany her to the theater, and true to her prediction, the bandits attack the theater that night, leaving the house safe. Brave Orchid and the grandmother, we guess, are spiritual and physical kin. Kingston's story, based on the songs of Ts'ai Yen, is about the importance of achieving mutually creative understanding of the Other. Ts'ai Yen, the embodiment of marginality, perseveres, even in an alien environment, to understand and be understood by her captors. "Her words seemed to be Chinese, but the barbarians understand their sadness and anger" (WW 243). But Ts'ai Yen also seems remarkably similar to the mother that has so vigorously been fleshed out in the book—captive in a strange land, who fights when needed and whose children do not speak her language. "She spoke it to them when their father was out of the tent, but they imitated her with senseless singsong words and laughed" (WW 242). These strong resemblances suggest that the two stories are integrally related to each other. Brave Orchid is both an indomitable matriarch, protector of the family, and a captive in a strange land, straining to be heard.

The authorial voice as it emerges in *The Woman Warrior* is thus highly provisional, always full of echoes of other voices, and never autonomous. Kingston does not merely wish to appropriate power and write an authoritative "marginal" text. She wishes to celebrate marginality as a position of writing and not to postulate a new source of authority or a new hierarchy. Virginia Woolf, certainly the progenitor of modern women's writing, consciously tried to avoid the traditional stable and authoritative "I." In *A Room of One's Own*, which Kingston echoes, Virginia Woolf said, "'I' is only a convenient term for somebody who has no real being...call me Mary Beton, Mary Seton, Mary Carmichael or by any name you please" (103).[13] Denying universality, absolute values, and a monologic, autonomous self are crucial to writings of all marginal groups that wish to radically assert their difference, not only from the politics, but also the power structure, of the dominant group.

Just as it is important for Kingston to treat gender as a site of difference, it is vital for her to treat race too as a play of differences. Indeed, to view *The Woman Warrior* as a book about an essential, abstract, female self beyond culture and society is to miss the point entirely.[14] The immigrant experience is an integral part of the book. Kingston is sensitive to the dehumanizing and monologic definitions to which Chinese-Americans are subject and is determined not to perpetuate the same by merely inverting the hierarchies. At the base of such definitions is the destructive binary logic which hierarchically divides male and female, self and other, white and nonwhite. Edward Said has compellingly demonstrated how such hierarchies have operated in depictions of the "Oriental" as the passive and denatured Other.[15] In *The Woman Warrior* Kingston will question and undo the oppositions that make such sterile racial definitions possible.

The narrator of *The Woman Warrior* is uniquely positioned to dialogically question racial oppositions. She is the daughter of Chinese immigrants for whom America is temporary exile, and China home, but who nevertheless will stay in America. Her only reality is America, but it is the America of the margins (Kingston makes no bones about Stockton being a racial and economic ghetto). She goes to Chinese school and to American school. Her own undefinable position is a metaphor for the way in which ethnicity will operate: "I learned to make my mind large, as the universe is large, so that there is room for paradoxes.... The dragon lives in the sky, ocean, marshes, and mountains; and the mountains are also its cranium.... It breathes fire and water; and sometimes the dragon is one, sometimes many" (WW 35).

Reed Dasenbrock describes *The Woman Warrior* as a "multicultural" text, one that is not only explicitly about a multicultural society but one which is also implicitly multicultural in "inscribing readers from other cultures inside [its] own textual dynamics."[16] Kingston's dialogic questioning of racial and cultural oppositions is multicultural in the latter sense—implicitly so, and highly fraught with political significance. On an obvious level, Kingston obviously creates clear cultural oppositions, indeed, as if she were speaking in the voice of the monocultural reader. American life is logical, concrete, free, and guarantees individual happiness; Chinese life is illogical, superstition ridden, constricted by social roles, and weighted down by community pressures. The American school teaches that an eclipse is "just a shadow the earth makes when it comes between the moon and the sun"; the Chinese mother prepares the children to "slam pots and lids together to scare the frog from swallowing the moon" during the next eclipse (WW 197). American culture promises the young girl opportunity for excellence if she gets straight A's. She can go to college. But she also has the freedom to be a lumberjack in Oregon. In China the girl fears she will be sold as a slave; or within the immigrant community she will be married off to a "Fresh Off the Boat Chinese." Indeed, the structure of hierarchical oppositions is so cleverly set up that the narrator's growth might be equated with being fully "American."[17]

But Kingston sets up these hierarchies only to subvert and make undecidable these monologic oppositions. "To make my waking life American-normal, I turn on the lights before anything untoward makes an appearance. I push the deformed into my dreams, which are in Chinese, the language of impossible dreams" (WW 102). But just as the conventional American reader might begin to feel at ease with the comfortable hierarchy (American-normal, Chinese-deformed), Kingston challenges it. "When the thermometer in our laundry reached one hundred and eleven degrees on summer afternoons, either my mother or my father would say that it was time to tell another ghost story so that we could get some good chills up our backs" (WW 102). American-normal reality gets so nightmarish that Chinese ghost stories are needed to chase it away into imaginary chills. Not only is the cultural hierarchy subverted, but the traditional associations of logicality and dreams are suspended. Similarly, Kingston questions other oppositions. If revolutionary China is a nightmare of ruthless disciplinary violence, Stockton, California, has its own gratuitous slum violence. "The corpses I've seen had been rolled and dumped, sad little dirty bodies covered with a police khaki blanket" (WW 61). The No Name aunt, who is punished for transgressing her social role as wife and daughter-in-law, has her American counterpart in another aunt. Moon Orchid comes to America at the behest of her sister Brave Orchid to claim the Americanized husband who has abandoned her. Her fate: insanity.

In fact,the very subtitle of the book, "Memoirs of a Girlhood Among Ghosts," is designed to question cultural oppositions. Reed Dasenbrock sees the use of the term *ghost* in the book as a "Shlovskian defamiliarization not so much of the word as of our self-concept" because as non-Chinese readers we are forced to question our perceptions of ourselves.[18] *Ghosts* is perhaps the most dialogically used term in the book because it describes the experience of living within both Chinese and American cultures. Kingston has said that ghosts are "'shadowy figures from the past' or unanswered questions about unexplained actions of Chinese, whites, and Chinese in America."[19] *Ghost* is an appellation used for any concept that defies clear interpretation. The narrator lives in a double ghost world—that of the China of legends, rumor, history, and ancestors she does not know, and that of an American world full of its own ritual ghosts. Thus we have Brave Orchid, at once conjurer and shaman, the exorciser of ghosts; the No Name aunt to whose wandering ghost the narrator is drawn; and the numerous American ghosts—Taxi Ghosts, Bus Ghosts, Police Ghosts, Fire Ghosts, and Garbage Ghosts. The continued use of the term across cultures denies not the idea of difference but that of hierarchical separation and thus definition.

Kingston's questioning of oppositions and her resistance to definition are intensely political strategies. For the Asian woman who is often pathologized by singular definition (most commonly as the "passive," unemancipated woman), such a dialogic stance is often a strategy of survival.[20] It was necessary for Franklin to distinguish between good and bad citizens because he wished to create a cohesive citizenry. Thoreau retained the concept of an autonomous, spiritual self in order to maintain some separation of culture from the market. James relied on hierarchical oppositions between culture-beauty-aristocracy on the one hand and barbarity-chaos-democracy on the other in an attempt to save some concept of a cohesive American identity. Kingston, on the other hand, problematizes and subverts racial definitions in order to reveal the dangers of maintaining them. Ironically, many of the early reviews of the book reflected the very essentialized definitions Kingston was fighting. The appraisals reflected, to use Edward Said's term, *Orientalism*. A *Publisher's Weekly* critic praised the book for its "myths rich and varied as Chinese brocade" and prose that "achiev[ed] the delicacy and precision of porcelain."[21] Another critic claimed to be confused by the depiction of some Chinese women as aggressive and others as docile, suggesting that Chinese women have a singular identity.[22] Suzanne Juhasz, writing for a scholarly journal, saw Kingston's retention of a "traditional literary style" a result of her need, as a daughter of immigrants, to prove her English language skills.[23] As these reviews suggest, Kingston's position in the literary world is more clearly implicated in her marginality, more political than are the positions of the writers we have discussed so far.

Kingston operates out of this position to dialogize cultural definitions. She presents Chinese culture as a multiplicity of heterogeneous voices that she does not attempt to unify or contain. Thus she uses traditional myths to write a narrative that is deliberately antimythic. Myths, as many of the modernists saw, could play the conservative function of creating and preserving cultural unity. In his essay on Joyce, T. S. Eliot explained the mythic method as "a way of controlling, of ordering, of giving a shape and significance to the immense panorama of futility and anarchy that is contemporary history...a step toward making the modern world possible for art, toward...order and form."[24] It is possible for the mythic method to create order, shape, and form because myths conventionally serve a stabilizing function in society.[25] Kingston, well aware of the traditional function of myths, uses them in order to subvert this function.

Kingston begins with the story of No Name Woman to suggest that all myths and legends are contingent upon some cultural necessity. Brave Orchid relates this family myth as a warning to her daughter, but the narrator realizes its fictitious aspect. There is the logical improbability of her mother having witnessed the attack when she and the aunt were not living in the same household. But this problem in ambiguity does not trouble Kingston because such an uncertainty allows her the freedom to continue the process of recreating the myth. With this initial move Kingston questions the privileged access to truth that myths claim and sets the stage for further destabilization of the function of myths. The choice of the story is also significant: "She observes the custom of ancestor worship in such a way as to destroy its fundamental principle, that of maintaining patriarchal descent intact."[26] Similarly, Kingston narrates the legend of Fa Mu Lan through her own identification with it and makes its patriarchal moral about filial piety incidental. The purpose of the tale in Kingston's text is to create uncertainty. Fa Mu Lan can represent the female avenger, but she can also represent a continuation of patriarchy as Brave Orchid, to an extent, does. Ts'ai Yen's tale about her captivity by barbarians and her return home becomes a tale of intercultural understanding rather than, as it is traditionally received, an ethnocentric tale about Chinese cultural superiority.[27] More importantly, in *The Woman Warrior* myths do not solve moral and cultural conflicts but create them. Chinese myths abound with misogynistic rituals—smearing bad daughters-in-law with honey and tying them on ant nests, keeping ash ready near a birthing bed in order to suffocate a potential female child, and so on. Kingston deliberately presents historical facts and exaggerated legends as if both are equally true and thus questions the truth status of both myth and history. She keeps up the uncertainty by never settling on the validity of these myths. Like the cryptic appellation "Ho Chi Kuei," which means anything from "centipede" and "grain sieve" to "good frying," all that the narrator can glean from her mother about the social validity of myths is that Chinese people "like to say the opposite" (WW 237–38).

The Woman Warrior thus subverts all forms that have the potential of creating consensus and poses a radical challenge to the very concepts of universalism and cultural unity. Myths here create contradictions and confusions. Kingston writes polemically as a Chinese-American woman confronting and battling with the patriarchal, white American culture, but she does so from a position that is radically unstable. She writes as a woman but destabilizes the concept of gender; she speaks as a Chinese-American but questions racial definitions. Authorship therefore becomes a complicated question because Kingston refuses to give us a traditional position from which she articulates. This does not mean that the text is apolitical or socially meaningless. Gender and race are important to Kingston, but not as transcendent and true categories. Kingston does not dismiss or destroy these categories but radically transvalues them by making them dialogically interactive. Because she subverts these categories only in relation to the monologic definitions imposed by the dominant culture and does not attempt to lay the foundations of another system, the concept of the polemical authorial voice here becomes a complex one. The association of the authorial voice with power and authority that we have been working with thus far becomes highly problematic. Although the very act of writing implies some authority, power and authority are not present in the same manner for writers who consciously write out of their marginality as for those who have some investment in the consensual, dominant culture.[28] Authority with the marginal writer is likely to be something seized rather than simply available. That is why voicing is such a crucial concern for Kingston. Henry Adams might present himself as a manikin, a mere geometrical figure incapable of volition, but he still speaks as a representative victim of his age and an interpreter of the oncoming twentieth century. A comparison with Jane Addams is also instructive. Although Jane Addams articulates her doubts, hesitancies, and feelings of worthlessness, she still uses the latter part of her narrative to speak as the objective social scientist viewing her subjects from a somewhat empowered position. For Kingston, however, neither the representativeness of a Henry Adams nor the stance of a Jane Addams is possible or desirable.

In embracing a voice and self implicated in a community of voices and in rejecting a stable, autonomous voice, *The Woman Warrior* offers a powerful challenge to the culture of liberal capitalism and the bourgeois concept of the individual subject. Reading such marginal texts in their relations to the liberal-capitalist consensus thus offers alternative possibilities for the study of political expression. However, crucial reconceptualizations will be necessary before such analyses can be undertaken. As a first step, it will be necessary to dissociate the authorial voice from sanctioned authority. Second, deauthoritative devices and dialogic self-questionings will have to be reinterpreted in the context of particular cultural and social suppressions. Third, the very nature of polemical writing will have to be redefined within the parameters of social constraints operating to delimit literary and polemical expression by cultural Others.

Postscript

Our analysis of different writers' use of personal-political narratives to dialogically question the ideology of liberal capitalism, even as they were bound to aspects of liberal thought, raises theoretical questions about concepts like 'dominant power structures' and 'subversive politics' which need to be addressed. Was it at all possible for these writers to radically challenge the culture to which they belonged? Do subversions of dominant ideologies ultimately participate in the very structures through which these ideologies are maintained? Any analysis of power or ideology today must come to terms with these questions.

Two thinkers who have fundamentally challenged simple oppositions like the 'dominant' and the 'oppressed' as a means of thinking about social structures are Gramsci and Foucault. Gramsci's concept of 'hegemony' is a way of thinking about power in terms of consensus. Hegemony, as opposed to domination, suggests that the power of existing political systems is constituted not by force but by consensus, that everyone has investment in the current hegemony.[1] Foucault similarly redefines power as something which is not imposed on the individual from the outside but which traverses the social body. Power, according to Foucault, is not merely negative and repressive but "induces pleasure, forms knowledge, produces discourse." Foucault provocatively asks, "If power were never anything but repressive...do you really think one would be brought to obey it?"[2] Both Gramsci's and Foucault's reformulations have brought significant complexity and sophistication to analyses of power structures. However, we must also be wary of the fact that concepts like the 'circulation of power' can be too easily used to contain all radicalism and to deny the importance of all moments of subversion.

Throughout this study I have examined the attempts of writers to question the consensus of liberal capitalism, both rhetorically and in terms of manifest content, and have analyzed the various ways in which writers have introduced ideological difference into their narratives. The strength of these questionings and subversions has been in the relative refusal of writers to define an oppositional political agenda in the recognizable structures of the dominant ideology. These texts have been most subversive when writers have recognized the contextuality of their own articulations and have given play to shifting authorial voices. Obviously, the radicalism of these strategies is relative. James's changing voices, for example, represent a challenge of difference only when seen against the depiction of American democracy as standardized; Kingston's deconstructions of race and gender definitions are similarly subversive only in relation to the restrictive definitions she sees prevalent in the culture. But the fact that a politics of subversion is always relative and depends upon its positioning against a dominant ideology does not mean that the two can merely be collapsed, that a subversive politics is merely an aspiration towards the center. As Edward Said points out, "If power oppresses and controls and manipulates, then everything that resists it is not morally equal to power.... Resistance cannot equally be an adversarial alternative to power and a dependent function of it, except in some metaphysical, ultimately trivial sense."[3] Foucault is actually not neutral about power, as he is sometimes taken to be. Foucault's notion of power as "something which circulates" is a brilliant demonstration of how power works in ways most of us are unaware of—covertly and insidiously. He does not give up the notion of oppression and is interested in seeing how "mechanisms of power have been...invested, colonized...by ever more general mechanisms and by forms of global domination."[4]

Bakhtin's notion of the dialogic is based on a similar awareness of the realities of power and social struggle. Although by the time Bakhtin had written "Discourse in the Novel" he had moved from thinking in terms of a monologic and dialogic opposition to thinking of language as inherently dialogic, he continued to see dialogism as a subversive force. Dialogism could only be understood in relation to a dominant or unified ideology or to the "rock bottom truths" that it questioned and relativized.[5] Indeed, Bakhtin's criticisms of official and authoritative discourse continue throughout his career, as do his valorizations of terms such as *carnival, heteroglossia,* and *polyphony,* all of which sound a familiar theme of subversion. Again, it is important to point out that these terms are relational rather than absolute.

In my discussions of all the writers, I have argued that the strength of the oppositional stance lies in its dialogic questionings rather than in its definitional agenda. I have, therefore, valorized the dialogic moments in these texts: Franklin's attacks on figures of authority; Thoreau's carnivalizations of the business culture; James's stance as the bewildered and questioning observer of American democracy; Henry Adams's search for break and ruptures within scientific and social theories and his opening up of the languages of science and religion to each other; Jane Addams's splitting of her own voice and her attempts to complicate the boundaries between high and low culture; Agee's rewriting strategies and his dialogic questionings of the definitions of tenants; Mailer's multiple voices and his subversion of the language of patriotism; and Kingston's radically undefined voice which questions unified concepts of race and gender. I have suggested that the radicalism of these texts was inhibited from freer expression by the writers' inability to dissociate themselves from individualism and universalism. These latter beliefs were manifested in problematic stances: expressions of transcendence and the creation of prophetic authorial voices by Thoreau and Agee, for instance, and romanticizations of a stable American history by Mailer.

However, the very presence of dispersive moves in the works of quasi-liberal writers suggests that possibilities for a politics of difference exist even within the dominant culture. Limitations of space keep me from fully addressing the question of the efficacy of such a politics. I will only suggest that because concepts like the unified subject and transhistorical values have too often been linked with power, dominance, and control, we need to maintain an active suspicion of these concepts.[6] Patriarchal and imperialist thinking, for example, depend upon the notion of "shared" values to propagate a singular idea of "civilization" and to demarcate as aberrant and Other all those who resist these values. It is no surprise that the resistance to the unified subject and universal values has come, in recent years, from the most disempowered of groups—women of color. We need, therefore, a politics of difference that thrives on diversity and that makes problematic the definitional boundary between self and Other, one's own voice and the voices of Others, that makes oppression possible. The rhetorical expression of such a politics, even in a muted manner, in works by liberal American writers suggests an uneasiness with the idea of an oppressive and essential Americanness which can only be seen as hopeful.

Notes

Preface

1. Bakhtin's critical enterprise has involved breaking the dichotomy between language and ideology by refusing to see any separation between them. V. N. Volosinov (/Bakhtin) states, "The domain of ideology coincides with the domain of signs.... Whenever a sign is present, ideology is present too. *Everything ideological possesses semiotic value.*" V. N. Volosinov, *Marxism and the Philosophy of Language*, trans. Ladislav Matejka and I. R. Titunik (Cambridge, Mass.: Harvard University Press, 1973), p. 10. Raymond Williams has also seen Volosinov's theories of language as the best alternative to the "partial theories of expression and objective system." Raymond Williams, *Marxism and Literature* (New York: Oxford University Press, 1977), p. 35.

2. Jameson's concept of ideology of form is a way of seeing texts as socially and culturally significant artifacts *because* of the way they are constructed. Jameson sees "formal processes as sedimented content in their own right, as carrying ideological messages of their own, distinct from the ostensible or manifest content of the works." Fredric Jameson, *The Political Unconscious: Narrative as a Socially Symbolic Act* (Ithaca, N.Y.: Cornell University Press, 1981), p. 99.

Chapter One

1. See Richard Poirier, *A World Elsewhere* (New York: Oxford University Press, 1966).

2. The essays in *Ideology and Classic American Literature* reflect the new, more politicized American literary criticism. See Sacvan Bercovitch and Myra Jehlen, eds., *Ideology and Classic American Literature* (New York: Cambridge University Press, 1986).

3. John Gray, *Liberalism* (Minneapolis: University of Minnesota Press, 1986), p. 23.

4. John P. Diggins, *The Lost Soul of American Politics: Virtue, Self-Interest, and the Foundations of Liberalism* (New York: Basic Books, 1984), p. 14.

5. Intellectual historians have variously seen Hobbes and Spinoza as either liberals or liberal precursors. John Gray, for example, sees them only as precursors because both believe that ignorance and slavery are man's natural condition. See Gray, *Liberalism*, p. 11.

6. Alexis de Tocqueville, *Democracy in America*, ed. Phillips Bradley, vol. 1 (New York: Knopf, 1980), p. 243.

7. Ibid., p. 263.

8. Louis Hartz, *The Liberal Tradition in America: An Interpretation of American Political Thought Since the Revolution* (New York: Harcourt Brace, 1955), p. 9.

9. Ibid., p. 11.

10. Tocqueville, *Democracy in America*, vol. 2, p. 99. Robert Shulman also sees Tocqueville's analysis as a criticism of capitalism's privatizing and alienating power. "For Tocqueville 'democracy' is a shorthand word for the individualism, competitiveness, and restless mobility of an open, egalitarian, nontraditional market society." Shulman, *Social Criticism and Nineteenth Century American Fiction* (Columbia: University of Missouri Press, 1987), p. 29

11. Hartz, *The Liberal Tradition in America*, p. 56.

12. Daniel J. Boorstin, *The Genius of American Politics* (Chicago: University of Chicago Press, 1953), p. 6.

13. See Herbert Marcuse, *An Essay on Liberation* (Boston: Beacon Press, 1969), pp. 10–11; Jameson, *The Political Unconscious*, pp. 293–96; Nancy Chodorow "Family Structure and Feminine Personality" in *Woman, Culture and Society*, ed. Michelle Z. Rosaldo and Louise Lamphere (Stanford, Calif.: Stanford University Press, 1974), p. 44; and Carol Gilligan, *In a Different Voice* (Cambridge: Harvard University Press, 1982), p. 17.

14. M. M. Bakhtin, *The Dialogic Imagination: Four Essays*, trans. Caryl Emerson and Michael Holquist (Austin: University of Texas Press, 1981), p. 300.

15. The problems of positing a value-free criticism are painfully obvious to women and racial minorities, who cannot buy into notions of universality. Most feminist critics use the denial of objectivity as a starting point for their analyses. Judith Fetterly, for example, begins her account of the resisting reader with the slogan "Literature is political" and goes on to emphasize the need for a "different subjectivity." See Judith Fetterly, *The Resisting Reader: A Feminist Approach to American Fiction* (Bloomington: Indiana University Press, 1978), p. xi. Similarly, Edward Said has shown how the concept of neutrality has in fact worked with impunity to create ostensibly "true" images of the Oriental as lazy, sly, and lecherous. Edward Said, *Orientalism* (New York: Pantheon Books, 1975).

16. Jameson, *The Political Unconscious*, p. 20.

17. Terry Eagleton, *Criticism and Ideology: A Study in Marxist Literary Theory* (London: Verso Press, 1978), p. 70.

18. Williams, *Marxism and Literature*, p. 97.

19. For Jameson, form is sociological in nature, like content in the realm of superstructure. See Fredric Jameson, *Marxism and Form: Twentieth Century Dialectical Theories of Literature* (Princeton, N.J.: Princeton University Press, 1971), pp. 329–31. Jameson's own ideological analyses throughout *The Political Unconscious* are analyses of form.

20. Jameson, *The Political Unconscious*, p. 99.

21. Jacques Derrida, *Positions*, trans. Alan Bass (Chicago: University of Chicago Press, 1981), pp. 15–16.

22. Jacques Derrida, *Of Grammatology*, trans. Gayatri Chakravorty Spivak (Baltimore, Md.: Johns Hopkins University Press, 1974), p. 3.

23. Jameson, *The Political Unconscious*, p. 10.

24. Like Todorov, I see Bakhtin as the major author of the works which have appeared under his name and under the names of Medvedev and Volosinov. See Tzvetan Todorov, *Mikhail Bakhtin: The Dialogic Principle* (Minneapolis: University of Minnesota Press, 1984), p. 11. The authorship issue is still a matter of debate. Morson and Emerson have recently concluded that Bakhtin did not write the books under the names of Volosinov and Medvedev. However, they argue that Bakhtin heavily influenced, and was influenced by, these Marxist works and that the sociological emphasis of his later works might have been a response to the challenge of his friends. "Faced with the challenge of a sophisticated sociological poetics, based to a considerable extent on Bakhtin's own ideas, Bakhtin appears to have responded with theories of language and literature that were sociological without being Marxist." Gary Saul Morson and Caryl Emerson, Eds., *Rethinking Bakhtin: Extensions and Challenges* (Evanston, Ill.: Northwestern University Press, 1989), pp. 48–49. In any event it seems clear that Bakhtin was heavily influenced by Marxism.

25. Graham Pechey, "Bakhtin, Marxism and Post-Structuralism," in *Literature, Politics and Theory: Papers from the Essex Conference, 1976–84*, ed. Francis Barker, Peter Hulme, et al. (New York: Methuen, 1986), p. 106. More critics are noting this similarity between Bakhtin and Derrida. See Allon White, "Bakhtin, Sociolinguistics and Deconstruction" in *The Theory of Reading*, Ed. Frank Gloversmith (New York: Barnes & Noble, 1984), p. 139.

26. Bakhtin, *The Dialogic Imagination*, p. 259. Although Bakhtin accepts many elements of Marxist thought, such as the social nature of the psyche, he is critical of crude Marxist attempts to posit an immediate and unchanging

economic structure. Such Marxists, says Bakhtin, often "move too quickly from the separate ideological phenomenon to conditions of the socioeconomic environment." See P. N. Medvedev/M. M. Bakhtin, *The Formal Method in Literary Scholarship: A Critical Introduction to Sociological Poetics* (Baltimore, Md.: Johns Hopkins University Press, 1978), p. 15.

27. David Carroll, "The Alterity of Discourse: Form, History, and the Question of the Political in M. M. Bakhtin," *Diacritics* 13 (Summer 1983): 68.

28. Volosinov, *Marxism and the Philosophy of Language*, p. 10.

29. Roland Barthes, *The Pleasure of the Text* (New York: Hill & Wang, 1973), p. 30. Barthes sees ideology as something that can and should be overthrown. "It is quite inconsistent," says Barthes, "to speak of a 'dominant ideology,' because there is no dominated ideology: where the 'dominated' are concerned, there is nothing, no ideology, unless it is precisely...the ideology they are forced...to borrow from the class that dominates them.... It is the subversion of all ideology which is in question" (p. 32). There are two assumptions in this concept of ideology: (a) that culture works as repression and (b) that there can be a structureless cultural model.

30. Caryl Emerson, "The Outer Word and Inner Speech: Bakhtin, Vygotsky and the Internalization of Language," *Critical Inquiry* 10 (1983): 247.

31. Susan Stewart, "Shouts on the Street: Bakhtin's Anti-Linguistics," in *Bakhtin: Essays and Dialogues on His Work*, ed. Gary Saul Morson (Chicago: University of Chicago Press, 1986), pp. 53, 52.

32. Emerson, "The Outer Word and Inner Speech," p. 248.

33. Besides being apolitical, theories focusing on the reader assume that a text has one or more readers or addressees, whether or not they are overtly mentioned. But although these theorists offer interesting observations on hypothetical readers, most of them assume that readers can be separated into finite and discrete categories. Thus Gibson posits readers and mock readers and Rabinowitz differentiates between actual audience, authorial audience, and so forth. See Walker Gibson, "Authors, Speakers, Readers and Mock Readers" in *College English* 11 (1949–50): 265–69; and Peter Rabinowitz, "Truth in Fiction: A Reexamination of Audiences," *Critical Inquiry* 4 (1977): 121–41. The question of addressees in a text is a complex one. Although Gerald Prince in *Narratology* goes farther than many narratologists in seeing that some texts have a number of different addressees (Prince calls them "narratees"), his approach poses two main problems. First, he sees some texts as having a single addressee. Second, even in the case of multiple addressees, he assumes that all the addressees can be identified and isolated. Although Prince's observations on hierarchizing narratees and pitting them against each other are useful, it is necessary to modify his approach. Bakhtin has

shown how each utterance, even each word, has one or more addressees or listeners. Every utterance in a text is a response to other utterances—social, political, moral, or literary. A text cannot therefore have a reader or two main readers. See Gerald Prince, *Narratology: The Form and Functioning of Narrative* (New York: Mouton Press, 1982).

34. See M. M. Bakhtin, *Problems of Dostoevsky's Poetics*, ed. Caryl Emerson (Minneapolis: University of Minnesota Press, 1984) p. 5.

35. Bakhtin, *The Dialogic Imagination*, p. 46.

36. While analyzing a passage from Dostoevski's *Crime and Punishment*, for example, Bakhtin comments, "All words in it are double-voiced, and in each of them a conflict of voices takes place." See Bakhtin, *Problems of Dostoevsky's Poetics*, p. 74.

37. It is interesting to compare Barthes' notion of voice to Bakhtin's. For Barthes words do not have to raise the question of authority. The modern text is one in which "voices are so treated that any reference is impossible: the discourse, or...the language, speaks: nothing more.... In the classic text the majority of utterances are assigned an origin." See Roland Barthes, *S/Z*, trans. Richard Miller (New York: Hill & Wang, 1974), p. 41. Barthes obviously sees the identification of voice as repressive. For Bakhtin, however, it is impossible to do away with the voice. In fact, what Barthes calls "codes" in *S/Z* is closer to Bakhtin's notion of voice.

38. Bakhtin, *Problems of Dostoevsky's Poetics*, p. 196.

39. Bakhtin, *The Dialogic Imagination*, p. 349.

40. Bakhtin's notion of the dialogic has rightly been interpreted as a celebration of difference. Kristeva was the first to see dialogism as a theoretical breakthrough—an introduction of intertextuality. See Julia Kristeva, *Desire in Language: A Semiotic Approach to Literature and Art*, trans. Thomas Gora, Alice Jardine, and Leon S. Roudiez (New York: Columbia University Press, 1980), p. 66. Paul DeMan similarly sees dialogism as "a principle of radical otherness" (in Morson and Emerson, *Rethinking Bakhtin*, p. 109). Bakhtin sees dialogism, the potential of words to always carry echoes of other words, as an essential part of language. In this sense, language is always dialogic and always a medium of liberation. There are obviously problems with this formulation which Bakhtin does not address. We need to recognize that just because language always has a dialogic potential does not mean that language cannot be used monologically or for authoritarian purposes. In fact, as we will see in our analysis of liberal personal-political narratives, there is often an impulse to suppress voices of others when these voices seriously threaten cultural unity.

41. Cecil F. Tate, *The Search for a Method in American Studies* (Minneapolis: University of Minnesota Press, 1973), p. 130. Tate commends American lit-

erary scholars for not giving up the "original goal to study American culture systematically as a whole and yet do justice to its individual facets," but he addresses himself largely to their assumptions of holism (pp. 6–7). The works he examines are Roy Harvey Pearce's *The Continuity of American Poetry*, Henry Nash Smith's *Virgin Land* , J. W. Ward's *Andrew Jackson, Symbol for an Age*, and R. W. B. Lewis's *The American Adam*. Interestingly, Tate himself views race and gender studies as "aimless proliferation" that fragment what should rightly be a "total vision of man" (p. 132).

42. Russell J. Reising, *The Unusable Past: Theory and Study of American Literature* (New York: Methuen, 1986), p. 17. Russell J. Reising provides an incisive analysis of the tradition of essentialist theses about American literature and also the paternalism of much criticism on minority writing. To prove that Richard Wright can be read as a romancer, says Reising, "reveals little beyond the fact that marginal figures can always be made to conform to the literary standards of what are seen as homogenous cultural traditions" (p. 9).

43. Cathy N. Davidson, *Revolution and the Word: The Rise of the Novel in America* (New York: Oxford University Press, 1986), p. 256.

44. John Carlos Rowe has, for some time, questioned the proclivity of Americanists towards unified studies. He points out that even critical efforts to recuperate marginal texts have "many of the presuppositions about artistic coherence, literary expression, poetic style." John Carlos Rowe, *Through the Custom House: Nineteenth Century American Fiction and Modern Theory* (Baltimore, Md.: Johns Hopkins University Press, 1982), p. 6.

45. In practice all these critics concentrate almost exclusively on the radical innovativeness of the works of the sixties, an innovativeness resulting from rapid social change. This causal reasoning, which leads to a limitation of scope, might stem from a tendency common to literary critics of perceiving the period of their concern as the time of social upheaval. As Barbara Foley observes, there is a "myopia" and "chauvinism" behind the claim put forth by these critics that "contemporary American reality is more horrific than that of other ages or places" ("Fact, Fiction, and 'Reality'" *Contemporary Literature* 20 [1979]:p. 394).

46. John Holowell finds that "New Journalism" works combine fictional techniques with the detailed observations of journalism. See John Holowell, *Fact and Fiction: The New Journalism and the Nonfiction Novel* (Chapel Hill: University of North Carolina Press, 1977), p. 10. To John Hellman these "fables of fact" combine journalism and fabulation; see John Hellman, *Fables of Fact: The New Journalism as the New Fiction* (Urbana: University of Illinois Press, 1981), p. xi. For Ronald Weber these "literary nonfiction" works use fictional techniques "while remaining fully factual"; see Ronald Weber, *The Literature of Fact: Literary Nonfiction in American Writing* (Athens: Ohio University Press, 1980), p. 2. For Mas'ud Zavarzadeh these "fictual" works are "bi-referential," poised between fact and fiction; see Mas'ud Zavarzadeh, *The*

Mythopoeic Reality: The Postwar American Nonfiction Novel (Urbana: University of Illinois Press, 1976), pp. 56–57.

47. Zavarzadeh sees the nonfiction novel as having a "zero degree" of interpretation. The nonfiction novelists, according to Zavarzadeh, offer no judgments on their material. I am skeptical of accepting Zavarzadeh's "zero-degree" thesis because I do not think such neutrality is possible and also because the very titles, like *In Cold Blood* and *The Armies of the Night*, attest to the presence of some form of interpretation.

48. René Wellek separates the factual from the literary by associating the latter with a world of imagination, one in which things "are not literally true." See René Wellek and Austin Warren, *Theory of Literature* (New York: Harcourt Brace, 1962), p. 25. Robert Scholes distinguishes between what he calls the empirical and the fictional, a distinction maintained by Northrop Frye in his terms *assertive* and *literary*. See Robert Scholes and Robert Kellog, *The Nature of Narrative* (New York: Oxford University Press, 1966), reprint 1981, pp. 13–15, and Northrop Frye, *Anatomy of Criticism: Four Essays* (Princeton, N.J.: Princeton University Press, 1957), p. 74. Barbara Foley suggests that the definition for mimesis be contractual but still makes interpretation dependent upon the recognition of factuality and fictionality. Foley is aware of the theoretical issues raised by concepts like 'factuality' and 'fictionality' but wishes to retain them partly because she wishes to resist what she sees as the poststructuralist fetishization of textuality by bringing in some notion of the referent. See Barbara Foley, *Telling the Truth: The Theory and Practice of Documentary Fiction* (Ithaca, N.Y.: Cornell University Press, 1986), pp. 40, 18.

49. Hayden White has shown how the writing of histories begins with a deep poetic structure. Historians choosing to give explanation by emplotment, for instance, identify the kind of story to be told—romance, tragedy, comedy, or satire. Hayden White, *Metahistory: The Historical Imagination in Nineteenth-Century Europe* (Baltimore, Md.: Johns Hopkins University Press, 1973), p. 7. White's illumination of a poetic act in historiography suggests that the notions of 'factuality' as applied to history need re-vision. The classification of works according to whether they are "true" is also put into question by speech-act theory. John L. Austin shows how even statements (which were traditionally viewed as being either true or false), have an illocutionary force and are subject to infelicities. "The traditional 'statement,'" he concludes, "is an abstraction, an ideal, and so is its traditional truth or falsity." John L. Austin, *How To Do Things With Words* (Cambridge: Harvard University Press, 1962), p. 147.

50. See Robert F. Sayre, *The Examined Self: Benjamin Franklin, Henry Adams, Henry James* (Princeton, N.J.: Princeton University Press, 1964), pp. ix, 4. A good approach to autobiography is offered by James Olney, who uses the term *autobiography* as a point of departure to study different versions of self-validation in a series of texts, including Eliot's *Four Quartets* and Jung's *Mem-*

ories, Dreams, Reflections. James Olney, *Metaphors of Self: The Meaning of Autobiography* (Princeton, N.J.: Princeton University Press, 1972).

51. Albert E. Stone, *Autobiographical Occasions and Original Acts: Versions of American Identity From Henry Adams to Nate Shaw* (Philadelphia: University of Pennsylvania Press, 1982), pp. 19–20.

52. Two interesting recent studies on American autobiography are
those by Paul John Eakin and Arnold Krupat. Eakin explores the thematiza-
tion of the self being constituted by language in works such as Mary
McCarthy's *Memoirs of a Catholic Girlhood* and Maxine Hong Kingston's *The
Woman Warrior.* Krupat applies poststructuralist notions of 'self' and 'subject'
to American Indian autobiography, where he points out that the opposition
between individual and society does not exist. Paul John Eakin, *Fictions in
Autobiography: Studies in the Art of Self-Invention* (Princeton, N.J.: Princeton
University Press, 1985); Arnold Krupat, *For Those Who Come After: A Study of
Native American Autobiography* (Berkeley: University of California Press, 1985).

53. I am thinking here of fictional works such as Steinbeck's *The Grapes
of Wrath*, Ellison's *Invisible Man*, Doctorow's *The Book of Daniel*, and so forth.
Personal narratives that are not overtly political would include Gertrude
Stein's *The Autobiography of Alice B. Toklas*, Hemingway's *A Moveable Feast*,
and so forth.

Chapter Two

1. See Charles W. White, *Benjamin Franklin: A Study in Self-Mythology*
(New York: Garland, 1987), pp. 123–24, for a discussion of this letter and the
significance of the pseudonym. White sees this letter as the beginning of
Franklin's conscious development of a nationalistic identity.

2. Diggins, *The Lost Soul of American Politics*, p. 20.

3. Benjamin Franklin, The *Writings of Benjamin Franklin*, ed. Albert
Henry Smyth (New York: Macmillan, 1905–1907), vol. 9, pp. 161–63.

4. William B. Wilcox, "Franklin's Last Years in England: The Making of
a Rebel" in *Critical Essays on Benjamin Franklin*, ed. Melvin H. Buxbaum
(Boston, Mass.: G. K. Hall, 1987), p. 104.

5. See Vernon Louis Parrington, *The Colonial Mind* (Norman: University
of Oklahoma Press, 1987), p. vi; orig. pub., 1927.

6. In a letter to John Adams, for example, Jefferson wrote, "The essence
of virtue is doing good to others, while what is good may be one thing in one
society, and its contrary in another." Thomas Jefferson to John Adams, Octo-
ber 14, 1816, in *The Adams-Jefferson Letters: The Complete Correspondence
Between Thomas Jefferson and Abigail and John Adams*, ed. Lester J. Cappon

(Chapel Hill: University of North Carolina Press, 1959), p. 492. Like Franklin, Jefferson associated virtue with utility, but he also realized that utility was extremely variable. He thus concluded that "men, living in different countries, under different circumstances, different habits, may have different utilities." Jefferson to Thomas Law, June 13, 1814, in *The Portable Thomas Jefferson*, ed. Merrill D. Peterson (New York: Viking, 1975), p. 543.

7. Quoted in Hartz, *The Liberal Tradition in America*, p. 81.

8. For an interpretation of the *Autobiography* as belonging to the genre of the conduct book, see Bruce Ingham Granger, *Benjamin Franklin: An American Man of Letters* (Ithaca, N.Y.: Cornell University Press, 1964), p. 211. Bernard Cohen sees the *Autobiography* as a moral tale about self-improvement and altruism; see Bernard Cohen, *Benjamin Franklin: His Contribution to the American Tradition* (New York: Bobbs Merrill, 1953), p. 68. Charles Sanford sees it as a secularized Pilgrim's Progress; see Charles L. Sanford, "An American Pilgrim's Progress," in *Benjamin Franklin and the American Character*, ed. Charles Sanford (Lexington, Mass.: D. C. Heath, 1955), p. 71. Franklin's view of the instructional value of his *Autobiography* is evident in the manner in which he presents his moral errata as mistakes from which young people can learn. Franklin added these errata to the manuscript after the bulk of Part I had been completed. See P. M. Zall, "A Portrait of the Autobiographer as an Old Artificer," in *The Oldest Revolutionary: Essays on Benjamin Franklin*, ed. J. A. Leo Lemay (Philadelphia: University of Pennsylvania Press, 1976), p. 57.

9. Benjamin Franklin, *The Autobiography of Benjamin Franklin*, ed. Leonard W. Labaree (New Haven: Yale University Press, 1964), p. 164. All subsequent references will be made parenthetically in the text (BF).

10. Max Weber, *The Protestant Ethic and the Spirit of Capitalism*, trans. Talcott Parsons (New York: Scribner's, 1958), p. 51.

11. Noah Webster included a condensed version of the *Autobiography* in his *Biography For the Use of Schools* (1830). Thomas Mellon attributed his decision to quit the farm and enter banking to his reading of the *Autobiography* and had one thousand copies of the book printed to be handed out to young men needing advice. Harvey O'Connor, *Mellon's Millions* (New York: 1933), pp. 4–5; cited in Labaree, "Introduction," in the *Autobiography*, p. 10.

12. White, *Benjamin Franklin*, (New York: Garland Press, 1987), p. 4.

13. Few critics have taken seriously Franklin's explanation at the end of Part I of the *Autobiography* that the 1775 section was a private correspondence to his son and that the rest, following the dictates of his friends, was written for the public at large. J.A. Leo Lemay points out that because Franklin's son would hardly have needed the advice, the "Dear Son" address is a literary ploy in the tradition of the conduct book that makes "the assumptions of age and experience on the part of the writer and youth and inexperience on the part of the audience, more logical." J. A. Leo Lemay, "Benjamin Franklin," in

Major Writers of Early American Literature, ed. Everett Emerson (Madison: University of Wisconsin Press, 1972), p. 238.

14. Edwin G. Burrows and Michael Wallace point out that the image of the Empire as a family was so consistently used that it came "close to being the very *lingua franca* of the Revolution." Edwin G. Burrows and Michael Wallace, "The American Revolution: The Ideology and Psychology of National Liberation," *Perspectives in American History* 6 (1972): 168.

15. Franklin, *Writings,* vol. 7, p. 26.

16. John Adams, *Works,* ed. Charles Francis Adams (Boston: Little, Brown & Co., 1856), vol 1, pp. 662–63.

17. Gary B. Nash suggests that the theme of social control permeates colonial thinking because of this perceived threat. See Gary B. Nash, *Class and Society in Early America* (Englewood Cliffs, N. J.: Prentice Hall, 1970), pp. 5–7.

18. Diggins, *The Lost Soul of American Politics,* p. 37.

19. Many critics have attempted to place Franklin's project of arriving at moral perfection within a Puritan tradition but have found important ideological differences. David L. Parker views the project as a Puritan conversion experience but points out that no Puritan would have tolerated Franklin's accommodation of virtue to self-interest. See David L. Parker, "From Sound Believer to Practical Preparationist: Some Puritan Harmonics in Franklin's *Autobiography,*" in *The Oldest Revolutionary: Essays on Benjamin Franklin,* ed. J. A. Leo Lemay (Philadelphia: University of Pennsylvania Press, 1976), p. 75. Robert Sayre's thesis that the project demonstrates yet another of Franklin's masks, that of the "*naif* philosophical quaker" is more interesting. See Sayre, *The Examined Self,* pp. 26–28. However, I do not agree with Sayre's suggestion that Franklin adopts a number of provisional identities in the *Autobiography.* To think of the narrator as having a number of identities all equally valid is to conceive of the *Autobiography* as a polyphonic text with multiple voices not subject to control by a dominant voice. But the *Autobiography* derives its force from an impulse to control other voices within the ideology of liberal capitalism.

20. Richard E. Amacher argues that Franklin's projects for public improvement attest to a belief in social concern over the values of personal gain. See Richard E. Amacher, *Benjamin Franklin* (New York: Twayne, 1962), p. 23.

21. Tocqueville, *Democracy in America,* vol 2, p. 121. For an opposing view of Franklin's notion of "doing good," see Beidler, who argues that although Franklin mixes the notion of doing good with an "institutionalized social religion of enlightened self-interest" he writes as a Christian rhetor justifying his god-given talents. Philip D. Beidler, "The 'Author' of Franklin's *Autobiography,*" *Early American Literature* 16 (1981–82): 260–61.

22. Robert Shulman, *Social Criticism and Nineteenth Century American Fictions* (Columbia: University of Missouri Press, 1987), p. 108.

Chapter Three

1. Leonard N. Neufeldt has done a useful survey of the types of success manuals available in America during Thoreau's lifetime. Sixteen such guide-books were published between the time Thoreau entered Harvard and the time he completed the final revisions of *Walden*. The majority of these guides to success went through multiple printings and editions. Leonard N. Neufeldt, *The Economist: Henry Thoreau and Enterprise* (New York: Oxford University Press, 1989), pp. 134–35.

2. Between 1820 and 1860 the proportion of Americans living in cities rose by 800 percent. See Michael T. Gilmore, *American Romanticism and the Marketplace* (Chicago: University of Chicago Press, 1985), p. 2.

3. Bray Hammond, *Banks and Politics in America from the Revolution to the Civil War* (Princeton, N.J.: Princeton University Press, 1957), p. 327.

4. Bray Hammond, "Jackson, Biddle and the Bank of the United States," *Journal of Economic History* 7 (1947): 2, 9. Cited in Hartz, *The Liberal Tradition in America*, p. 138.

5. Ralph Waldo Emerson, "Self-Reliance," in *Selections from Ralph Waldo Emerson: An Organic Anthology*, ed. Stephen W. Whicher (Boston: Houghton Mifflin, 1957), p. 149.

6. Raymond Williams, *Culture and Society: 1780–1950* (New York: Harper & Row, 1958), p. 34.

7. David Leverenz argues that the American Renaissance writers' alienation from the marketplace is an alienation from "prevailing norms of manly behavior" which equate manhood with competition and aggression. See David Leverenz, *Manhood and the American Renaissance* (Ithaca, N.Y.: Cornell University Press, 1989), pp. 3–5. Leverenz's argument is a compelling one although Thoreau does not fall neatly into the male-denial paradigm. As I will argue later, Thoreau creates a gender dichotomy in "Higher Laws" and views femininity as something to be suppressed.

8. Henry David Thoreau, *A Week on the Concord and Merrimack Rivers*, ed. Carl F. Hovde et al. (Princeton, N.J.: Princeton University Press, 1980), p. 96.

9. Henry David Thoreau, *The Writings of Henry David Thoreau*, vol. 13, ed. Bradford Torrey and Francis Allen (Boston: Houghton Mifflin, 1906; reprint AMS Press, 1968), p. 79.

10. David S. Reynolds, *Beneath the American Renaissance: The Subversive Imagination in the Age of Emerson and Melville* (New York: Knopf, 1988), p. 98.

11. David S. Reynolds in *Beneath the American Renaissance* has interestingly shown that Thoreau (along with other writers of the American Renaissance) was very much a product of his age and that his writings were in the tradition of popular reform (pp. 98–100).

12. Henry David Thoreau, *Walden*, ed. Lyndon Shanley (Princeton, N.J.: Princeton University Press, 1971), p. 71. All subsequent references will be made parenthetically in the text (W).

13. Bakhtin, *Problems of Dostoevsky's Poetics*, pp. 122–23.

14. I have made this argument about Thoreau's language in my essay "Carnival Rhetoric and Extra-Vagance in Thoreau's *Walden*," *American Literature* 58 (March 1986): 33–45. For another analysis of Thoreau's parodies of the language of business culture, see Leonard N. Neufeldt's "*Walden* as Parody," in his *The Economist*, pp. 156–90.

15. Charles R. Anderson also notes the reader-directed language of *Walden*. Thoreau "keeps up a running attack against those who are asleep, finally limiting his audience to the few who are really awake and aware of life's possibilities." See Charles R. Anderson, *The Magic Circle of Walden* (New York: Holt, Rinehart, 1968), p. 158.

16. Joseph J. Moldenhauer, *The Rhetoric of Walden*, Ph.D. dissertation, Columbia University, 1964, p. 136. Moldenhauer makes a distinction between Thoreau's refutations of attitudes directly expressed by characters who interrogate him and Thoreau's refutations of his readers' vocabulary through paradox. I do not find that distinction useful because whether a character directly questions the author or whether these questionings take the form of commonly held ideologies that Thoreau refutes, we can clearly see two voices in opposition with each other. It makes little difference whether these ideologies are in discernible (external) or hidden (internal) quotation marks. See Moldenhauer, "The Extra-Vagant Maneuver: Paradox in *Walden*," *Graduate Journal* 6 (1964): 132–46.

17. Staughton Lynd, for example, finds a very close similarity between Thoreau's critiques and Marx's analysis of alienation in *Economic and Philosophical Manuscripts*. *Intellectual Origins of American Radicalism* (New York: Vintage, 1968), pp. 93–96.

18. Though such overt characterizations appear most frequently in "Economy," it is probably because it is the longest chapter in *Walden*. A look at the proportion of characterizations to the length of chapters gives some indication of the continual use of this method. (The first number in the following parentheses indicates the length of the chapter; the second, the number of characterizations in the chapter.) "Economy" (78, 20); "Where I lived..." (18, 4); "Reading" (12, 4); "Sounds" (18, 2); "Solitude" (11, 3); "Visitors" (15, 5); "Bean-Field" (12, 4); "The Village" (6, 2); "The Ponds" (28, 4); "Baker Farm" (9, 2); "Higher Laws" (13, 2); "Brute Neighbors" (15, 1); "House Warming" (18, 5); "Former Inhabitants..." (15, 1); "Winter Animals" (11, 1); "The Pond in Winter" (17, 3); "Spring" (21, 0); "Conclusion" (13, 7).

19. Lawrence E. Buell, *Literary Transcendentalism: Style and Vision in the American Renaissance* (Ithaca, N.Y.: Cornell University Press, 1973), pp. 76–85.

20. Moldenhauer, "The Extra-Vagant Maneuver," p. 137.

21. Benjamin Franklin, "The Way to Wealth," in *Benjamin Franklin: The Autobiography and Other Writings*, ed. Jesse Lemisch (New York: Signet, 1961), p. 190.

22. Jacques Derrida, *The Archaelogy of the Frivolous: Reading Condillac*, trans. John P. Leavey, Jr. (Pittsburg, Penn.: Duquesne University Press, 1980), p. 128.

23. Stanley Cavell, *The Senses of Walden* (New York: Viking, 1972), p. 61.

24. Friedrich Nietzsche, *Beyond Good and Evil*, trans. Walter Kaufmann (New York: Random House, 1966), p. 2.

25. Richard Bridgman argues that "the feminine was virtually a non-existent gender for him [Thoreau], except when he was complaining about its trivialities." Richard Bridgman, *The Dark Thoreau* (Lincoln: University of Nebraska Press, 1982), p. 5.

26. Although different stylistic criteria can be used to define aphorisms, there is a general consensus about their function. Aristotle in *Rhetoric* describes a maxim as a "statement...not about a particular fact...but of a general kind...about questions of practical conduct, courses of conduct to be chosen or avoided." Aristotle, *Rhetoric and Poetics*, trans. W. Rhys Roberts (New York: Modern Library, 1954), p. 135.

27. Ralph Waldo Emerson, *The Complete Works of Ralph Waldo Emerson*, ed. Edward W. Emerson, vol. 2 (Boston: Houghton Mifflin, 1968), p. 108.

28. Bakhtin, *Problems of Dostoevsky's Poetics*, p. 25.

29. See Buell, *Literary Transcendentalism*, pp. 30–36.

Chapter Four

1. Quoted in Sidney Lens, *Radicalism in America* (New York: Thomas Y. Crowell, 1966), 219.

2. Mikhail Bakhtin has used the social density of the novel as a means of formulating a theory of language.

3. Maxwell Geismar in his *Henry James and the Jacobites* (Boston: Houghton Mifflin, 1963) was the earliest of James critics to criticize the limited social scope of James's novels.

4. Lens, *Radicalism in America*, p 218.

5. The native populace was threatened by these new immigrants and often persecuted them. In New Orleans, for example, the assassination of a

police chief who had incurred the enmity of the Mafia led to the lynching of eleven innocent Sicilians. See Morison, *The Oxford History of the American People*, (New York: Oxford University Press, 1965), pp. 794, 813.

6. Henry James, *English Hours* (Cambridge, Mass.: Riverside Press, 1905), pp. 73–74.

7. The conservative implications of James's concept of culture have been noted by many critics. Marius Bewley finds James inclined toward "a conservative, a *conserving*, political establishment." Irwing Howe says of *The American Scene* that "for all its brave recognitions of change [it] is a conservative book. In motivation, if not always perspective, it is often elegaic, a journey backward in time, where all is fixed and irrevocable" See Marius Bewley, *Masks and Mirrors: Essays in Criticism* (New York: Atheneum, 1970), p. 120, and Irwing Howe, *Decline of the New* (New York: Harcourt Brace, 1970), p. 114. For an analysis of the political implications of James's imagery, see Robert L. Gale, *The Caught Image: Figurative Language in the Fiction of Henry James* (Chapel Hill: University of North Carolina Press, 1964).

8. Henry James, *The American Scene*, ed. Leon Edel (Bloomington: Indiana University Press, 1968), p. 159. Subsequent references will be made parenthetically in the text (AS).

9. Robert H. Wiebe, *The Search for Order, 1877–1920* (Westport, Conn.: Greenwood Press, 1967), p. 77.

10. The need to separate James's "ideas" from his art and to view James's works only on aesthetic terms has, of course, a long history in James criticism. T.S. Eliot had pronounced James to have had "a mind so fine that no idea could violate it." *Selected Prose of T. S. Eliot* ed. Frank Kermode (London: Faber, 1975), p. 151. Joseph Warren Beach, the first influential critic of James's works, said, "Neither politics nor literature, neither religion, morality, nor social questions make the subjects of his discourse.... His people seem to have no theories." See Joseph Warren Beach, *The Method of Henry James* (Philadelphia: Albert Saifer, 1954), p. 99.

11. Peter Buitenhuis, *The Grasping Imagination: The American Writings of Henry James* (Toronto: University of Toronto Press, 1970), p. 188.

12. William Thomas Burtner, *Ideal and Actual Society: Theme and Technique in Henry James's The American Scene*. Ph.D. dissertation, Miami University, Ohio, 1973, p. 58.

13. Alwyn Berland suggests that James consecrated culture to replace for his age the religious sanctions no longer available. See Alwyn Berland, *Culture and Conduct in the Novels of Henry James* (New York: Cambridge University Press, 1981), p. 19.

14. Although James does not use the word *capitalism* in his analysis, his comments on the working of what he calls "democratic institutions" involve

an examination of capitalistic social features. He notes, for instance, the link between individualism and aggressive money-making, the social control exercised by big business, and so forth.

15. Georg Lukács, *History and Class Consciousness*, trans. Rodney Livingstone (Cambridge: MIT Press, 1971), pp. 86–87. Commodification is a constant concern in James's novels as well. In *The American Scene* commodities seem to have their own world and operate like people, and in James's fiction people define themselves through commodities. As Jean Christophe Agnew puts it, "The world of *The Golden Bowl* is a reified world. James represents the relation between characters as a relation between things, luxurious and rarefied things to be sure, but things nonetheless." See Jean Christophe Agnew, "The Consuming Vision of Henry James," in *The Culture of Consumption: Critical Essays in American History, 1880–1980,* ed. Richard Wightman and T. J. Jackson Lears (New York: Pantheon Books, 1983), p. 97. Peggy McCormack sees an increasing sophistication in James's treatment of reification. In James's later works characters not only discover a reified world but recognize their participation in it. Peggy McCormack, "The Semiotics of Economic Language in James's Fiction," *American Literature* 58 (1986): 547.

16. Richard S. Lyons, for instance, deals collectively with these voices and finds that the third-person characterizations, "together with the use of the past tense, give that implicit division between author and character—James present and James past—on which the sense of incipient drama so much depends." See Richard S. Lyons, "In Supreme Command: The Crisis of Imagination in Henry James's *The American Scene*," *New England Quarterly* 55 (1982): 518. Lyons, in other words, assumes that the use of the third-person characterizations is necessarily indicative of double voicing.

17. David Seed suggests that these voices undercut the self absorption of the authorial voice. See David Seed, "Penetrating America: The Method of Henry James's *The American Scene*," *Amerikastudien* 26 (1981): 346. But Seed does not demonstrate how the observations of the mooning observer differ from that of the ancient contemplative observer. Instead of seeing how these voices work in the text, he assumes that they create dispersion. William F. Hall points out that the passive voice of the "ancient contemplative person," which is adequate for observing rural New Hampshire, is unable to cope with urban America and is therefore replaced by the "restless analyst." See William F. Hall, "The Continuing Relevance of Henry James's *The American Scene*," *Criticism* 13 (1971): 153.

18. In *The American Scene* James uses the term *alien* to refer to the newly arrived immigrant.

19. Ross Posnock makes an impassioned case for seeing James's observations on aliens and Jews as instances of self-projections and expressions of intersubjectivity. According to Posnock, James values "non-identity, difference, and heterogeneity." Ross Posnock, "Henry James, Veblen and Adorno:

The Crisis of the Modern Self," *Journal of American Culture* 21 (1987): 35. Posnock is right in identifying some of the qualities James espouses; however, James's political stance is much more ambiguous than Posnock suggests. The cultural interest of the text, in fact, lies partly in the conflict between the values James espouses aesthetically (heterogeneity, etc) and his political timidity before ethnic and racial difference.

20. Stuart Johnson suggests that because of the aliens James's "relation to his subject is...radically destabilized. His subject is noncentered." See Stuart Johnson, "American Marginalia: James's *The American Scene*," *Texas Studies in Language and Literature* 24 (1982): 87.

21. Alan Trachtenberg finds that James's response to the immigrants at Ellis Island "reveals a set of snobbish biases" but stresses that "the form James gives his experiences, not his particular ideas, is the chief value of his book...not *what* he thinks but *how*." Trachtenberg in *"The American Scene:* Versions of the City" in *Massachusetts Review* 8 (1967), p. 294.

22. Buitenhuis, *The Grasping Imagination*, pp. 189–90.

23. See, for example, Burtner, *Ideal and Actual Society*.

24. James's relationship to feminism is too large and complex an issue to be taken up here. For an overview of the feminist criticism on James, see John Carlos Rowe's "Feminist Issues" in his *The Theoretical Dimensions of Henry James* (Madison: University of Wisconsin Press, 1984). Rowe suggests that James's complex portrayals of women are possible because of his identification with their marginal and powerless situations (p. 90).

25. David L. Furth, for instance, views James's response to the tomb as a departure from preconceived aesthetic standards to an aesthetic grounded on present American experience. For William F. Hall it exemplifies James's developed tolerance for the "public nature of American society." See David L. Furth, *The Visionary Betrayed: Aesthetic Discontinuity in Henry James's The American Scene* (Cambridge: Harvard University Press, 1979), p. 37, and William F. Hall, "The Continuing Relevance of Henry James's *The American Scene*," p. 156.

Chapter Five

1. Henry Adams, *The Education of Henry Adams*, intro. D. W. Brogan (Boston: Houghton Mifflin, 1961), p. 21. All subsequent references will be made parenthetically in the text (E).

2. John P. Diggins, "Who Bore the Failure of Light: Henry Adams and the Crisis of Authority," *New England Quarterly* 58 (1985): 172.

3. Many critics have noted that Adams's reiterations about failure rein-

force a moral superiority. See, for instance, Denis Donoghue, "The American Style of Failure," *Sewanee Review* 82, No., 3 (1974): 415 and B. L. Reid, "The View From the Side," *Sewanee Review* 88 (1980): 228.

4. In an excellent examination of the *Education*, John Carlos Rowe shows how the paradoxical structure of the book undermines Adams's dialectical thought and his desire for historical coherence. See John Carlos Rowe, *Henry Adams and Henry James: The Emergence of a Modern Consciousness* (Ithaca, N.Y.: Cornell University Press, 1976), pp. 97–112.

5. Ernest Samuels, "Notes," in Henry Adams, *The Education of Henry Adams*, ed. Ernest Samuels (Boston: Houghton Mifflin, 1973), p. 574.

6. Adams frequently resorts to an a posteriori generalization of his own experiences. Perhaps the most obvious instance of forced generalization is Adams's account of his boyhood visit to President Taylor. After ascribing his lack of awe at visiting the president to the fact that his family was always familiar with presidents, he writes, "Every one thought alike whether they had ancestors or not. No sort of glory hedged Presidents as such" (E 46–47).

7. David L. Minter, *The Interpreted Design as a Structured Principle in American Prose* (New Haven, Conn.: Yale University Press, 1969), p. 132.

8. Rowe, *Henry Adams and Henry James*, pp. 110–12. Many other critics also see Adams's realization of multiplicity as a tragic one, an insight forced rather than willed. Melvin Lyon points out that Adams "presents each new area of experience as if he had entered it naively, expecting to find unity and coherence, only to find fall in some form." Melvin Lyon, *Symbol and Idea in Henry James* (Lincoln: University of Nebraska Press, 1970), p. 115.

9. The structure of the book also denies notions of order and unity. There is an overt building up of contrasts in the titles of chapters. "Treason," for example, is followed by "Diplomacy," "Indian Summer" by "The Dynamo and the Virgin," and "The Height of Knowledge" by "The Abyss of Ignorance." The narrative also moves through digressions as different subjects vie for ascendancy. Some critics have seen the structure as a reflection of the cultural confusion portrayed in the book. See Richard Ruland, "Tocqueville's *De La Democratie in Amerique* and *The Education of Henry Adams*," *Comparative Literature Studies* 2 (1965): 200. Vern Wagner sees the internal inconclusion and circumlocution as part of a strategy of humor. See Vern Wagner, *The Suspension of Henry Adams: A Study of Manner and Matter* (Detroit, Mich.: Wayne State University Press, 1969), pp. 109–12.

10. William Graham Sumner, *What Social Classes Owe to Each Other* (New York: Harper & Row, 1920), pp. 16–17.

11. For Asa Gray's reactions to Darwinian evolution, see Richard Hofstadter, *Social Darwinism in American Thought* (Boston: Beacon Press, 1955), p. 18.

12. Ibid., p. 30.

13. James M. Mellard, "The Problem of Knowledge and *The Education of Henry Adams*," *South Central Review* 3 (1986): 62. Mellard sees Adams as a theorist of history who sought to ally himself with the new Einstenian principles and who realized the "fictiveness" of our conceptions of reality (p. 62).

14. William V. Spanos argues that the linear, Aristotelian plot has been part of an "essentialist" Western humanist tradition that assumes a problem-solution perspective to existence. The phenomenological/existential tradition in literature questions this straightforward, causal perspective. See William V. Spanos, *Repetitions: The Postmodern Occasion in Literature and Culture* (Baton Rouge: Louisiana State University Press, 1987), pp. 14–20.

15. For an account of Adams's antislavery efforts and his sympathy toward workers' movements in England, see William Dusinberre, *Henry Adams: The Myth of Failure* (Charlottesville: University Press of Virginia, 1980), pp. 36–37. Dusinberre, however, sees the *Education* as one of Adams's weakest works—philosophically weak, scientifically inexpert, and repetitive (pp. 210–13).

16. Sacvan Bercovitch, *The American Jeremiad* (Madison: University of Wisconsin Press, 1978), pp. 194–95.

17. Jean Francois Lyotard, *The Post Modern Condition: A Report on Knowledge*, trans. Geoff Bennington and Brian Massumi (Minneapolis: University of Minnesota Press, 1984), p. 25.

18. Ibid., p. 25

19. Adams's prayer to the dynamo has largely been seen as an ironic gesture which emphasizes his alienation from science. Ferman Bishop, for example, writes that here "obviously Adams is being ironical: he is expressing the fact that he understands the dynamo as a phenomenon and feels its importance at the same time." Ferman Bishop, *Henry Adams* (New York: Twayne, 1979), p. 116.

20. Henry Adams, *Mont Saint Michel and Chartres* (Boston: Houghton Mifflin, 1913), p. 261.

21. Paul Elmer More, *A New England Group and Others* (Boston: Houghton Mifflin, 1921), p. 123.

22. Bakhtin, *The Dialogic Imagination*, p. 367.

23. Rowe, *Henry Adams and Henry James*, p. 64.

24. A good analysis of the reacting reader demanded by the *Education* is offered by Earl N. Harbert. I agree with Harbert's view that the *Education* works to provoke the reader by offering questions rather than answers, but I am skeptical of his suggestion that the *Education* is didactic and that Adams provides casebook examples of his experiences to the reader. See Earl N. Harbert, "*The Education of Henry Adams*: The Confessional Mode as Heuristic Experiment," *Journal of Narrative Technique* 4 (1974): 3–18.

Chapter Six

1. Daniel Levine offers a good analysis of this mythologizing of poverty in "Environmentalism: The Culture of Poverty" in his *Jane Addams and the Liberal Tradition* (Westport, Conn.: Greenwood Press, 1971), pp. 126–43.

2. Andrew Carnegie, "The Advantages of Poverty," *Nineteenth Century* 29 (March 1891): 365–85.

3. Julia Kristeva, "La femmme, ce n'est jamais ça," *Tel Quel* 59 (1974), p. 24. Quoted in Toril Moi, *Sexual/Textual Politics: Feminist Literary Theory* (New York: Routledge), p. 164.

4. Allen F. Davis sees Addams at the time of her visit to Europe in 1883 as "the product of her background and education. She was the Victorian young lady, the epitome of American feminine innocence that Henry James was so fond of depicting." Allen F. Davis, *American Heroine* (New York: Oxford University Press, 1973), p. 35. Given the severe depression and mental anxieties Addams had gone through by this point, she can hardly be thought of as innocent. It is more relevant and interesting to view ladyhood as a repressive, if necessary, social facade which masked the anxieties attendant upon her position as an educated, thinking, yet socially powerless person.

5. Sandra M. Gilbert and Susan Gubar, *The Madwoman in the Attic: The Woman Writer and the Nineteenth-Century Literary Imagination* (New Haven: Yale University Press, 1979), p. 61.

6. Mary Jo Deegan, *Jane Addams and the Men of the Chicago School, 1892–1918* (New Brunswick: Transaction Books, 1988), p. 7. Deegan points out the continuity between Addams's earlier views on society, built on feminine values, and her wartime pacifism.

7. Jane Addams, *Twenty Years at Hull-House* (New York: Macmillan, 1910), p. viii. All subsequent references to the work will be made parenthetically (TY).

8. I will discuss the political implications of the relationship between feminism and visions of community later in the chapter. The closeness of Bakhtin's concept of dialogism to feminine concepts of subjectivity was initiated by Kristeva and is being increasingly recognized by feminist theorists like Patricia Yaeger and Dale Bauer. Feminists have long argued that because girls' development does not take place through the Freudian process of radical separation, women are inherently comfortable with social concepts of self. Jean Wyatt argues, for example, that "women are more comfortable vaulting over ego boundaries to fuse with what is outside than are men because what Freud calls the 'oceanic feeling' is built into their primary definition of self." See Jean Wyatt, "Avoiding Self-Definition: In Defense of Women's Right to Merge (Julia Kristeva and Mrs Dalloway)," *Women's Studies* 13 (1986): 119.

9. Although Addams was unsure about calling herself a socialist, many of her ideas were socialist in nature. She was also influenced by her lifelong friend and socialist, Charlotte Perkins Gilman, whose writings, such as *Women and Economics* she read enthusiastically. Addams's hesitancy in proclaiming herself an outright socialist probably had more to do with her genteel concern for conventions than with her ideas or social programs. As W. D. Howells noted, socialism "smel[t] to the average American of petroleum, suggest[ed] the red flag, and all manner of sexual novelties, and an abusive tone about God and religion." Quoted in Joseph Dorfman, *The Economic Mind in American Civilization*, vol. 3 (New York: Viking, 1946–59), p. 152.

10. James Dougherty, "Jane Addams: Culture and Imagination," *The Yale Review* 71 (1982): 374.

11. The overt rhetoric of goodwill on the part of social ameliorists has been nowhere more compellingly shown as in studies of colonial discourse, which have demonstrated the demonology and manichean aesthetics at work in the attitudes of colonizers and missionaries. The works of Edward Said, Franz Fanon, and Abdul Jan Mohammed are particularly concerned with these issues.

12. Cited in Deegan, *Jane Addams and the Men of the Chicago School*, p. 261.

13. Helene Cixous, "Castration or Decapitation?" *Signs* 7 (1981):52. Originally published as "Le Sexe ou la tete?" *Les Cahiers du GRIF* 13(1976): 5–15.

14. The question of what defines women's experiences has been the subject of much theoretical debate. Many feminists have found evidence to suggest that male and female psychologies are inherently different. Carol Gilligan's *In a Different Voice* (Cambridge: Harvard University Press, 1982) suggests, for instance, that women are more concerned about interpersonal contacts and community than men. However, these models run into problems the moment we question the gender categories by introducing racial difference.

15. Arlette Laguiller in an interview by Jacqueline Aubenas in *Les Cahiers du GRIF*, March 1975. Reprinted in Elaine Marks and Isabelle de Courtivron, *New French Feminisms* (New York: Schocken, 1980), p. 121.

16. This marginalization is obviously apparent in fiction as well, though in a somewhat indirect manner. Alice Walker's *Meridian* becomes politically conscious at the cost of complete separation from her body as she becomes rigid and goes into catatonic stupors; Celie finds herself unable to talk to anyone other than an abstract God. Toni Morrison ends *The Bluest Eye* with Pecola talking alone with her image in the mirror.

17. Peggy Stinson, "Jane Addams," in *American Women Writers: A Critical Reference Guide from Colonial Times to the Present*, ed. Lina Mainiero (New York: Frederick Ungar, 1979), p. 21.

18. Simone de Beauvoir, "Introduction" to *The Second Sex* (New York: Vintage, 1974). Cited in Marks and de Courtivron eds., *New French Feminisms*, p. 44.

19. See Julia Kristeva, "La femme ce n'est jamais ça" *Tel Quel* 59 (1974), p. 21; and Monique Wittig, "One is Not Born a Woman" in *Feminist Issues* I, No. 2 (1981), pp. 50–51.

20. Addams believed that if women participated more in public spheres society itself would be transformed. She sought franchise for women on those grounds. In one of her most successful essays on the need for women's franchise, Addams satirically questions the value of male universal franchise. "Can we, the responsible voters, take the risk of wasting our taxes by extending the vote to those who have always been so ready to lose their heads over mere military display?... Would not these responsible women voters gravely shake their heads and say that as long as men exalt business profits above human life, it would be sheer folly to give them the franchise." Jane Addams, "If Men Were Seeking the Franchise," in *Jane Addams: A Centennial Reader*, ed. Emily Cooper Johnson (New York: Macmillan, 1960), pp. 108–10.

21. The idea that femininity as marginality has aspects in common with other forms of marginalization is an important one for many feminists. Kristeva has long been a proponent of theorizing women's struggles in the same manner as struggles of other groups or classes. "Call it 'woman' or 'oppressed classes of society', it is the same struggle, and never one without the other." "La femme, ce n'est jamais ça," *Tel Quel* 59 (1974), p. 24. Quoted in Moi, *Sexual/Textual Politics*, p. 164.

Chapter Seven

1. Daniel Bell, *The End of Ideology: On the Exhaustion of Political Ideas in the Fifties* (New York: Free Press, 1960), pp. 369–70. Daniel Bell's classic formulation of the end of ideology as action, the end of chiliastic hopes for the generation between the 1930s and the 1950s, explains the mood of intellectuals without radical causes. This feeling is a beginning point for Agee, the reason for not providing economic or sociological interpretations. However, Agee moves from here to the more questionable idea that interpretation and ideological thought can be avoided altogether.

2. See Hartz, *The Liberal Tradition in America*, pp. 260–65. When asked about what his social philosophy was, Roosevelt said that he was a Democrat and a Christian (p. 263).

3. James Agee and Walker Evans, *Let Us Now Praise Famous Men* (Boston: Houghton Mifflin, 1961), p. xv. All subsequent references will be made parenthetically in the text (FM).

4. William Stott, *Documentary Expression and Thirties America* (New York: Oxford University Press, 1973), pp. 21–22.

5. There are numerous examples of footnotes which question the text. In "(On the Porch: 2," for instance, Agee writes, "It is not in the nature of journalism even to approach any less relative degree of truth. Again journalism is not to be blamed[2] for this." Footnote 2 reads: "Why not" (FM 234).

6. Eugene Chesnick, "The Plot Against Fiction: *Let Us Now Praise Famous Men*," *Southern Literary Journal* 4, No. 2 (1971): 54.

7. Perhaps the clearest example of this self-flagellation followed by a complete immersion with the tenants is Agee's description of his return to George Gudger's house after leaving earlier in the evening. While walking back to the house, Agee is overcome with guilt as he thinks of his intrusion: "I now felt shy of them yet somehow as if I knew why I possessed or was soon to possess them…. I have no right, here, I have no real right, much as I want it, and could never earn it, and should I write of it, must defend myself against my kind" (FM 410). But by the time he is with the Gudgers, Agee can say, "There is a particular sort of intimacy between the three of us which is not of our creating and has nothing to do with our talk, yet which is increased in our tones of voices…in their knowledge how truly friendly I feel toward them, and how seriously I am concerned to have caused them bother" (FM 417).

8. Victor Kramer lauds Agee's interpretational neutrality and his achievement of pure documentary expression. Agee's effort "is placed on demonstrating the dignity of persons he knew. Just as with the photographs of Evans, the purpose is to chronicle a way of life, not to suggest how to change it." See Victor Kramer, *James Agee* (New York: Twayne, 1975), p. 84.

9. Bakhtin explains, for example, that "there are no 'neutral' words and forms—words and forms that belong to 'no one'…. All words have the 'taste' of a profession, a genre, a tendency, a party, a particular work, a particular person…. Each word tastes of the context and contexts in which it has lived its ideologically charged life." See Bakhtin, *The Dialogic Imagination*, p. 293.

10. Richard King, *A Southern Renaissance: The Cultural Awakening of the American South, 1930–1955* (New York: Oxford University Press, 1980), p. 315. Although King provides an excellent reading of *Let Us Now Praise Famous Men* in light of Agee's aesthetics and his depoliticization of the tenants, his analysis reaches overly reductive psycho-autobiographical conclusions. He suggests, for instance, that Agee's quest in the book is really for a restitution of the time prior to his father's death (pp. 228–31).

11. Alfred T. Barson finds Agee influenced by the subjectivist British romanticism and the experiential American romanticism, both of which privilege the writer as priest and prophet. See Alfred T. Barson, *A Way of Seeing: A Critical Study of James Agee* (Amherst: University of Massachusetts Press, 1972), pp. 27–28.

12. Peter Ohlin, *Agee* (New York: Ivan Obolensky, 1966), p. 5.

13. Samuel Hynes presents a very sympathetic reading of Agee's treatment of the tenants but does not deal with the transcendent impulses in the text. He calls Agee a "Christian realist" who "strove to realize in his writing the divinity in each individual, by treating each person as he was; no one in this book is mythologized." See Samuel Hynes, "James Agee: *Let Us Now Praise Famous Men*," in *Landmarks of American Writing*, ed. Hennig Cohen (New York: Basic Books, 1969), pp. 332–33.

14. J. A. Ward, *American Silences: The Realism of James Agee, Walker Evans and Edward Hopper* (Baton Rouge: Louisiana State University Press, 1985), p. 17.

15. Many documentary writers in the thirties presented the poor as objects of pity. Michael Gold, for instance, began *Jews Without Money* (New York: Avon Books, 1965) with a caricatured account of the congestion and turmoil in East Side Street. "People pushed and wrangled in the streets. There were armies of howling pushcart peddlars. Women screamed, dogs barked and copulated. Babies cried" (p. 5).

16. Amy Godine offers a procedural explanation of Agee's problem. She suggests that Agee's curious assertions about worshipping an "actuality" create a moral dilemma. "Why write about Gudger at all and not his landlord," asks Godine, "all things being equal before the sheer stunning fact of actuality?" See Amy Godine, "Notes Toward a Reappraisal of Depression Literature," *Prospects* 5 (1980): 235. Thus Agee's method itself negates the possibility of the tenants being other than illustrations of aesthetic principles.

17. Even biographical studies acknowledge the unifying function of religion in the text. See Mark A. Doty, *Tell Me Who I Am: James Agee's Search for Selfhood* (Baton Rouge: Louisiana State University Press, 1981), pp. 52–54.

18. Michel deCerteau, *Heterologies: Discourse on the Other*, trans. Brian Massumi (Minneapolis: University of Minnesota Press, 1986), p. 122.

19. Bakhtin, *The Dialogic Imagination*, p. 69.

20. It should not be assumed that any biblical reference implies an authoritative and normative move. Both of Agee's novels—*A Morning Watch* and *A Death in the Family*—are preoccupied with religion, but the status given to scripture varies with each use. Here I am concerned with scripture which provides closure and becomes authoritative.

21. George M. Frederickson refers to this strategy as romantic racialism. See his *Black Image in the White Mind: The Debate on Afro-American Character and Destiny, 1817–1941* (New York: Harper & Row, 1971).

22. Alan Holder, "Encounter in Alabama: Agee and the Tenant Farmer," *Virginia Quarterly* 42 (1966): 199. Agee's idealization of the tenants has been noted by both his critics and admirers. Lionel Trilling saw a "failure

of moral realism" in Agee's "inability to see these people as anything but good." See Lionel Trilling, "An American Classic," *The Mid-Century* 16 (September 1960): 7. Kenneth Seib suggests that Agee saw the tenants as folk heroes. See his *James Agee: Promise and Fulfillment* (Pittsburgh: University of Pittsburgh Press, 1968), p. 54.

Chapter Eight

1. J. S. Mills, "The New Left." Quoted in Peter Clecak's *Radical Paradoxes: Dilemmas of the American Left: 1945–1970* (New York: Harper & Row, 1973), p.33.

2. Herbert Marcuse, *An Essay on Liberation* (Boston: Beacon Press, 1969), p. ix.

3. The political effectiveness of the New Left has been debated and critiqued by many people and is ultimately linked to the whole question of a poststructuralist politics. One of the most effective cases for the political effectiveness of the New Left has been made by Michael Ryan. Ryan argues that the New Left's strength is precisely its diversity and diffuse nature. Ryan argues that the binarism posited between a unified, authoritative (effective) and anarchic (ineffective) politics is simplistic. "There are alternatives to this simplistic binary. It is possible to combine a sense of commonality amid diversity, firmness of resistance, and aggressivity of attack with a plurality of different struggles." Michael Ryan, *Marxism and Deconstruction: A Critical Articulation* (Baltimore, Md.: Johns Hopkins University Press, 1982), p. 216.

4. Norman Mailer, *The Armies of the Night* (New York: New American Library, 1968), p. 17. All subsequent references will be made parenthetically in the text (AN). The similarity between Thoreau's and Mailer's polemical attempts to awaken their readers has been noted by many critics. See Morton L. Ross, "Thoreau and Mailer: The Mission of the Rooster," *Western Humanities Review* 25 (1971): 47–56. See also Warner Berthoff, "Witness and Testament: Two Contemporary Classics," in *Aspects of Narrative*, ed. J. Hillis Miller (New York: Columbia University Press, 1971), pp. 189–92.

5. Nietzsche, *Beyond Good and Evil*, p. 125. For the crucial importance of play as politics in Nietzsche, see Imafedia E. Okhamafe, "Heidegger's *Nietzsche* and Nietzsche's Play: The Question of Wo(man), Christianity, Nihilism, and Humanism," *Soundings* 71 (1988): 536, 548–49.

6. Mailer's continual parading of his ego is a deliberate strategy directed against the images of the objective and distanced scholar/thinker and the reclusive artist.

7. Jean Radford, *Norman Mailer: A Critical Study* (New York: Harper & Row, 1975), p. 54. Radford sees this move toward cultural criticism as an

unfortunate deviation from "truly political criticism." Radford faults *Advertisements for Myself* for being only cultural (and therefore apolitical) criticism and commends *The Armies of the Night* for being more political. Although I agree with Radford's assessment that the later work deals more with specific party politics, I do not think it signals a break from what Radford calls "cultural criticism." I also find Radford's separation between "political" and "cultural" criticism arbitrary and conservative. See Radford, pp. 54–55, 68–74. Peter Clecak in *Radical Paradoxes* faults the New Left for its wide scope, its attempts to subject everything to the criterion of egalitarianism (p. 252).

8. Bakhtin, *The Dialogic Imagination*, p. 271.

9. Marcuse, *An Essay on Liberation*, pp. 8–9.

10. Robert Meredith, "The 45–Second Piss: A Left Critique of Norman Mailer and *The Armies of the Night*," *Modern Fiction Studies* 17 (1971): 444–45. Although Meredith rightly criticizes Mailer for his elitist scorn of mediocrities in "alphabet soup" organizations and for his visions of male supremacy, his overall assessment of Mailer's reaction against organized politics is narrow. Meredith also chides Mailer for seeing revolution only in the "continuum of repression" and points out that its "authentic dimension" is that of "liberation." I suggest that Mailer's politics in *The Armies of the Night* is not tied to the master narrative of either repression or liberation. Mailer's rejection of ideological constants is also a rejection of master narratives. See Meredith, pp. 444–47.

11. See Michel Foucault, *Power/Knowledge: Selected Interviews and Other Writings*, trans. Colin Gordon et al. (New York: Pantheon Books, 1980), p. 2; Jameson, *Marxism and Form*, p. 269; and Herbert Marcuse, *One Dimensional Man: Studies in the Ideology of Advanced Industrial Society* (Boston: Beacon Press, 1964), p. 32.

12. Mailer's criticism of organized politics is similar to Michael Ryan's analysis of the politics of the "Left's Right" to which Robert Meredith seems to belong. The Left's Right posits an absolute binary opposition between absolutism and anarchy and repudiates the New Left for choosing the latter. Ryan suggests that the Left's Right wishes to see these excesses curbed by a return to the values of "the family, patriarchy, authority, party discipline." See Ryan, *Marxism and Deconstruction*, p. 215.

13. Marcuse has a similar distrust of rationality and the seemingly objective conclusions generated by it. He feels that (traditional) Marxist theory has been unable to entertain utopian speculation "for fear of losing its scientific character" (*An Essay on Liberation*, p. 3).

14. Repudiation of formal logic is inevitable in all dialogic texts. Julia Kristeva notes that "Menippean discourse develops in times of opposition against Aristotelianism, and writers of polyphonic novels seem to disapprove of the very structures of official thought founded on formal logic." See Julia

Kristeva, *Desire in Language: A Semiotic Approach to Literature and Art*, trans. Thomas Gora, Alice Jardine, and Leon S. Roudiez (New York: Columbia University Press, 1980), p. 85.

15. Walter Teague is an example of the particular nature of Mailer's criticism. Mailer dislikes only an aspect of Teague's politics—his programmatic sense of organization. Teague's arrest for carrying a concealed weapon, Mailer is convinced, is a frame-up.

16. For an analysis of Mailer's changing viewpoints in *Armies*, see Jennifer Bailey, *Norman Mailer: Quick-Change Artist* (New York: Barnes & Noble, 1979), pp. 88–93.

17. Richard Poirier, *Norman Mailer* (New York: Viking, 1972), pp. 48, 54.

18. Ibid., p. 81.

19. I choose not to deal with the two books of *The Armies of the Night* in terms of *novel* and *history* because I do not see the two as fixed entities. Many critics, however, use these terms as evaluative criteria for the text. Warren French, for example, is convinced that unless the book can be categorized as either fiction/nonfiction or novel/history, it cannot be appropriately critiqued. *The Armies of the Night*, he finally decides, must be read as history rather than as a novel. See Warren French, *Norman Mailer* (New York: Twayne, 1978), pp. 109–13. Peter Bufithis, on the other hand, finds the book novelistic and historical because it simultaneously "describes the *effects* of the march" on Mailer and it "scrupulously describes the *facts* of the march." Peter Bufithis, *Norman Mailer* (New York: Frederick Ungar Co., 1978), p. 86. Mailer has provided the ground for such criticism by subtitling his book "History as Novel, The Novel as History." But Mailer himself does not conceive of *novel* and *history* as completely separate entities. In fact, many of his theorizations on the two seem designed to challenge the critical assumptions behind these separations. Mailer deliberately creates these separations and undermines them. Although he suggests that Book I is more novelistic and Book II more historical, he mocks those who believe in these divisions. "Practical usage," says Mailer, "finds flavor in such comfortable opposites" (AN 284). In fact, Mailer's theorizations about history and the novel in the middle of Book II seem designed to deconstruct these oppositions. Here, Mailer announces his intention to relinquish the conceit of writing history and to enter the realm of "intuitive speculation." But the rest of Book II (the last thirty-six pages) seems decidedly historical if measured by the standards of "comfortable opposites." The fact that it is proliferated with transcriptions of newspaper accounts (six in all) suggests that Mailer does not believe in strict generic categorization.

20. Richard Poirier, "The Ups and Downs of Mailer" in *Norman Mailer: A Collection of Critical Essays*, ed. Leo Braudy (Princeton, N.J.: Prentice-Hall, 1972), p. 171.

21. Cited in Clecak, *Radical Paradoxes*, p. 259.

22. Gilles Deleuze and Felix Guattari. *Anti-Oedipus: Capitalism and Schizophrenia*, trans. Robert Hurley et al. (Minneapolis: University of Minnesota Press, 1983), p. 76.

23. Joseph Wenke links these invocations of the Civil War with Mailer's essential Americanness, "the deep well of patriotism from which his bitter criticism of America has always sprung." Joseph Wenke, *Mailer's America* (Hanover, N.H.: University Press of New England, 1987), p. 150. Wenke sees all of Mailer's work as a reflection of his Americanness. "Mailer's subject is preeminently America: throughout his work he is involved in trying to discover our identity as a nation by relating the promise and the debasement of the millennial idea of America" (p. 3). Wenke, in other words, sees Mailer as an American Jeremiah. Such an interpretation is certainly workable for *The Armies of the Night*, but the very use of the Jeremiah paradigm raises important ideological questions. Sacvan Bercovitch had identified the jeremiad as the major mode of American literature, one in which, as Wenke puts it, the subject is the conflict between the vision of America as the place of God's chosen people and the actuality of America (p. 2). The problem with such a paradigm, if taken as "real" rather than functional, is that it tends to create the myth of a singular national literature and contains the idea of dissent and radicalism within a nationalistic "tradition." We need only to look at much of black writing to see the absense of a jeremiad tradition.

24. Stanley Gutman, *Mankind in Barbary: The Individual and Society in the Novels of Norman Mailer* (Hanover, N.H.: University Press of New England, 1975), p. 190.

25. It should be clear that I am dealing with the commitment to cultural difference only in *The Armies of the Night*. Mailer has often publicly proclaimed his homophobia and resistance to feminism. Kate Millett deals extensively with this aspect of Mailer in *Sexual Politics*. The body of Mailer's works is so large and variable that few generalizations can be made. However, *The Armies of the Night* is a unique conjuncture of the political and aesthetic and an important tribute to activism.

Chapter Nine

1. Henry Louis Gates uses the figure of the signifying monkey who "dwells in the margins of discourse" and whose speech is always double-voiced to explain the features of African-American writing ("The 'Blackness of Blackness': A Critique of the Sign and the Signifying Monkey" *Critical Inquiry* 9 ([1983] 685–723). In *The Signifying Monkey* (New York: Oxford University Press, 1988) he finds the basis of the radical multiplicity of black writing and the denial of a singular self in the Yoruba god Esu. We need to recognize, however, that multiplicity is not a characteristic but an oft-used polemical strategy of African-American writing. There are, in fact, many

African-American writers whose reliance on patriarchal models of writing is extremely problematic. *The Autobiography of Malcolm X* is a good example of this problem. Haley presents the life of the radical Malcolm X almost in the manner of Benjamin Franklin, as a sort of manual for black youths, one that illustrates the exemplary conversion of the hero from a misguided dope peddler to a confident leader. The book is full of advice for black youth to better their lives and follow the exemplary life of Malcolm X. Episodes are presented with a view to instruction and correction of problems, like Franklin's "errata." The uncanny rhetorical similarity between the lives of two who could not have been more different points to the persistence of patriarchal thought even in the most radical of contexts.

2. Bell Hooks, *Feminist Theory: From Margin to Center* (Boston: South End Press, 1984), pp. 5–6.

3. Floya Anthias and Nira Yuval-Davis, "Contextualizing Feminism—Gender, Ethnic and Class Divisions," *Feminist Review* 15 (1983): 73.

4. On the problematic politics created by race and gender definitions, see Valerie Amos and Pratibha Parmar, "Challenging Imperial Feminism," *Feminist Review* 17 (Autumn 1984): 3–7. See also Barbara Johnson, *A World of Difference* (Baltimore, Md.: Johns Hopkins University Press, 1987), p. 170.

5. Maxine Hong Kingston, *The Woman Warrior: Memoirs of a Girlhood Among Ghosts* (New York: Vintage, 1976), pp. 3, 5. All subsequent references will be made parenthetically in the text (WW).

6. Gilbert and Gubar, *The Madwoman in the Attic*, p. 3.

7. Although it is her mother who admonishes her throughout the book, it is obvious that (in this role) the mother is the bearer of patriarchal values.

8. Until World War I unrestricted and unlimited immigration was the policy of the government, except for "Orientals, paupers, imbeciles, and prostitutes." Samuel Eliot Morison, *The Oxford History of the American People* (New York: Oxford University Press, 1965), p. 897.

9. Henry Louis Gates, *Figures in Black: Words, Signs, and the "Racial" Self* (New York: Oxford University Press, 1987), p. 4.

10. Carol Mitchell points out that Fa Mu Lan became a warrior "in order to save her elderly father from conscription and in order to right the wrongs that had been done in her village. Because she did her deeds out of filial respect, not just for personal glorification, she is an acceptable role model for a woman." Carol Mitchell, "'Talking Story' in *The Woman Warrior:* An Analysis of the Use of Folklore," *Kentucky Folklore Record* 27 (1981): 8.

11. For an excellent analysis of the questioning of gender oppositions, see Rabine. Of this vision, Rabine says," This couple is reminiscent of the Tao

in the I Ching where Yin, the masculine, and Yang, the feminine, are constantly in the process of changing into each other and where their changes engender chains of transformations similar to those Kingston expresses here in a poetic mode." Rabine, "No Lost paradise: Social and Symbolic Gender in the Writings of Maxine Hong Kingston" *Signs* 12 (1987): p. 476."

12. Lynn Z. Bloom also sees the mother-daughter relationship as a productive one. The narrator "realizes that she and her mother are much alike as mature women—intelligent, energetic, determined, courageous, analysts and conveyers of a complex culture in an alien land." Lynn Z. Bloom, "Heritages: Dimensions of Mother-Daughter Relationships in Women's Autobiographies," in *The Lost Tradition: Mothers and Daughters in Literature*, ed. Cathy M. Davidson and E. M. Broner (New York: Frederick Ungar, 1980), p. 301.

13. Virginia Woolf, *A Room of One's Own* (New York: Harcourt, 1929), p. 103. Musing about the realities and myths of revolutionary China, Kingston writes, "I've seen Communist pictures showing a contented woman sitting on a bunk sewing.... The woman looks very pleased. The Revolution put an end to prostitution by giving women what they wanted: a job and a room of their own" (WW 73).

14. The problem with this approach becomes painfully obvious when critics deny the very material with which Kingston works. Suzanne Juhasz, for example, suggests that *The Woman Warrior* is a particularly female form of autobiography in that "fantasy, the life of the imagination, creates female identity." Suzanne Juhasz, "Toward a Theory of Form in Feminist Autobiography: Kate Millet's *Flying* and *Sita*; Maxine Hong Kingston's *The Woman Warrior*," *International Journal of Women's Studies* 2 (1979): 63. Juhasz makes no mention of the fact that Kingston is in fact working with folklore, and gives little importance to the constant concern with the lives of Chinese immigrants.

15. See Edward Said, *Orientalism* (New York: Random House, 1978), pp. 308–10.

16. Reed Way Dasenbrock, "Intelligibility and Meaningfulness in Multicultural Literature in English," *PMLA* 102 (1987): 10.

17. Linda Morante accepts this division and equates the narrator's finding a voice with her becoming American. Morante says that "from childhood through adolescence, Kingston continues her quest for self-expression. As a teenager she is familiar with the English language and American culture, but her voice still squeals with ugly 'duck' like insecurity." Linda Morante, "From Silence to Song: The Triumph of Maxine Hong Kingston," *Frontiers* 9, No. 2 (1987): 79. She even interprets Chinese immigrants'secretiveness and changing of identities as a denial of (American) selfhood (p. 80). Such a reading completely ignores the very real fears of Chinese immigrants. Elaine H. Kim draws attention to some of these factors. From 1924 to 1943, for example,

any female American citizen who married a Chinese alien would automatically lose her citizenship. Only in 1952 were Chinese allowed to become naturalized U.S. citizens. And "anti-miscegenation legislation remained on the books in California until 1967." Elaine H. Kim, *Asian American Literature: An Introduction to the Writings and Their Social Context* (Philadelphia: Temple University Press, 1982), pp. 96–97.

18. Dasenbrock, "Intelligibility and Meaningfulness," p. 14.

19. Kim, *Asian American Literature*, p. 200.

20. I do not mean to suggest that all works by women and minority writers dialogically question oppositions and definitions. However, writers who write consciously from the margins and foreground this concern are likely to use such dialogic strategies.

21. Cited in Kim, *Asian American Literature*, p. xvi.

22. Cited in ibid., p. xvii.

23. Juhasz, "Toward a Theory of Form," p. 73. Although Kingston has found critical acceptance in the last decade, popular reviews of her works still reflect a not-so-hidden Orientalism. A two-column review of her most recent book, *Tripmaster Monkey*, concentrated first on why Chinese writing was being taken seriously (Nixon's China visit and subsequent American diplomacy); after devoting two paragraphs to the book itself, it concluded by assessing Kingston's literary merits: "Some of Tripmaster owes its atmosphere to Herman Hesse's overheated German vaudeville, Steppenwolf, and a few historical meditations are straight out of Saul Bellow.... But Kingston's humor and idiom are her own, and so is the message." Stefan Kanfer, review of *Tripmaster Monkey: His Fake Book* by Maxine Hong Kingston, *Time*, (May 1, 1989): 70, 72.

24. T. S. Eliot, *Selected Prose*, ed. Frank Kermode (London: Faber, 1975), pp. 177–78.

25. Roland Barthes in *Mythologies*, trans. Annette Lavers (New York: Hill & Wang, 1970), sees myths as traditional forms which oppose change and present themselves as complete (p. 117).

26. Leslie W. Rabine, "No Lost Paradise: Social and Symbolic Gender in the Writings of Maxine Hong Kingston," *Signs* 12 (1987): 484.

27. According to Robert Rorex and Wen Fong, the legend of Ts'ai Yen, with which the book ends, illustrates "the superiority of Chinese civilization over cultures beyond her borders; the irreconcilability of the different ways of life." Cited in Rabine, "No Lost Paradise," p. 485.

28. This fact is readily apparent when oppressive institutions are overt and sanctioned. Although slave narratives, for example, were used by abolitionists to argue against slavery, slaves were not encouraged to write their own narratives even when they could do so. Thus when Frederick Douglass

wrote his own narrative, he felt compelled to acknowledge the beneficence of white tutelage. He mentioned that he was moved to antislavery sentiment only after becoming a reader of the *Liberator,* the abolitionist paper edited by William Llyod Garrison. Frederick Douglass, *The Narrative and Selected Writings* (New York: Random House, 1984), p. 119. Douglass's *Narrative* had to be preceded by Garrison's preface certifying its authenticity. The irony, of course, is that Garrison, like most abolitionists, was opposed to blacks' (and Douglass's) visible participation in the antislavery movement.

Postscript

1. Walter L. Adamson, *Hegemony and Revolution: A Study of Antonio Gramsci's Political and Cultural Theory* (Berkeley: University of California Press, 1980), pp. 170–71.

2. Foucault, *Power/Knowledge,* p. 119.

3. Edward Said, *The World, The Text, and the Critic* (Cambridge: Harvard University Press, 1983), p. 246.

4. Foucault, *Power/Knowledge,* pp. 98–99. I have made a similar argument in "Questioning Race and Gender Definitions: Dialogic Subversions in The Woman Warrior," *Criticism* 31 (Fall 1989): 421–437.

5. M. M. Bakhtin, *The Dialogic Imagination,* p. 300.

6. Peter Dews has recently questioned what he calls the "logics of disintegration." He calls attention to the incompatibility of "progressive political commitments with the dissolution of the subject, or a totalizing suspicion of the concept of truth." See Peter Dews, *Logics of Disintegration: Post-structuralist Thought and the Claims of Critical Theory* (New York: Verso Press, 1987), p. xv.

Index

Adams, Henry, 65, 88, 94–96, 100, 104–6, 125, 140, 154–55, 159; *Education of*, 14, 65, 67–86, 105, 140; *Mont Saint Michel and Chartres*, 71, 85; different languages in, 11; woman as multiplicity in, 84; paradoxical structure of, 177
Adams, John, 21, 168
Adamson, Walter L., 157, 191n.1
Addams, Jane: 5, 11, 103–4, 106–108, 142, 144–46, 155, 159; *Democracy and Social Ethics*, 97; *Newer Ideals of Peace*, 95, 97; *Spirit of the Youth and the City Streets*, 97; *Twenty Years at Hull-House*, 87–102, 142; divided voices in, 101; socialism of, 180; women's franchise, 181
Advertisements for Myself, *see under* Mailer
Agee, James, 12, 88, 102, 124, 159; *Let Us Now Praise Famous Men*, 12, 103–22, 125; prophetic voice in, 114
Agnew, Jean Christophe, 175
Aesthetic ideology 12; emergence of in Thoreau, 32, 41; material and ideal split, 44–45
Alger, Horatio, 41, 47, 88,
Amacher, Richard E., 170
American identity: Franklin's creation of, 10; James's conflictual relation to, 11, 58; in American cultural studies, 13; as capitalism, 41; Adams's questioning of, 79
American Scene, The, *see under* James
Anderson, Charles R., 172

Anthias, Floya, 144
Aphorisms and ideology, 44, 45
Armies of the Night, The, *see under* Mailer
Austin, John L., 167
Autobiography, 14, 167–68
Autobiography of Benjamin Franklin, *see under* Franklin
Autobiography of an Ex-Colored Man, The, xi

Bailey, Jennifer, 186
Bakhtin, M. M: *Dialogic Imagination, The*, 162, 165, 178, 182, 183, 191; *Problems of Dostoevsky's Poetics*, 17, 165, 171;
    carnival, 34, 36; and community, 91;
    dialogism: defined, 6, 158; and feminine subjectivity, 197; and intersubjectivity; otherness, 165; and resistance to definition, 152–53; and social struggle, 158; ideology, 8–9;
    language and politics, 128; and Marxism, 8, 163–64; multivoicing, xi; and post–structuralism, 8, 163; voice: defined, 9–10;
Barson, Alfred T., 182
Barthes, Roland, 164
Bauer, Dale, 179
Beauvoir, Simone De, 96
Beidler, Philip D., 170

Bell, Daniel, 103, 181
Bercovitch, Sacvan, 2, 78–79
Berland, Alwyn, 174
Berthoff, Warner, 184
Bewley, Marius, 174
Bishop, Ferman, 178
Bloom, Lynn Z., 189
Boorstin, Daniel, 4, 162n.12
Bradford, William, 1, 22, 29
Bridgman, Richard, 173
Brownson, Orestes, 41
Buell, Lawrence E., 37
Bufithis, Peter, 186
Buitenhuis, Peter, 174
Burrows, Edwin G., 170
Burtner, William Thomas, 174

Caldwell, Erskine, 115,
Capote, Truman, 13
Cappon, Lester J., 168
Carroll, David, 8
Capitalism: and aesthetic ideology, 43; alienation, 36, 53, 162; and Americanism, 41; and class, 21; and commodification, 175; community, 4, 30; and consensus, x, 4, 78; and democracy, 46, 174–75; feminist subversion of, 100; and individualism, 4–5, 22, 88; and the work ethic, 40
Carnegie, Andrew, 88
Carnival: rhetoric in *Walden*, 34, 36
Carroll, David, 164
Cavell, Stanley, 39
Chesnick, Eugene, 182
Chodorow, Nancy, 5, 162
Cixous, Helene, 96
Clecak, Peter, 185
Cohen, Bernard, 169
Community, 91; in Marxism and feminism, 5 and capitalism, 30; and other voices, 149
Cotton, John, 18
Couser, Thomas G., 14–15

Cultural consensus, 68, 72, 81; Adams's questioning of, 76–78; and gender, 88, 99, 154; and myths, 153; and marginality, 155
Culture: emergence of aesthetic, 11; culture and masses in Addams, 12, 89; and class in Franklin, 21; linked with class and art by James, 48, 50, 64

Dasenbrock, Reed, 150, 152
Davidson, Cathy N., 13
Davis, Allen F., 179
Deauthoritative strategies, 64
Declaration of Independence, 2
DeCerteau, Michel, 117
Deegan, Mary Jo, 179
Deleuze, Gilles, 7, 139
DeMan, Paul, 7, 165
Democracy: as conformity, xi; and difference, 48; and culture, 49; and consensus, 51; and class, 61
Democracy and Social Ethics, see under Addams
Democratic capitalism, 48, 51, 52; and consensus, 47; and liberalism, xi, 54; and homogeneity, 55–56, 57, 60
Derrida, Jacques, 7–8, 39, 163
Dews Peter, 191
Dialogic Imagination, The, see under Bakhtin
Dickinson, Emily, 97
Dickstein, Morris, 132
Diggins, John P., 2, 16, 23
Documentary: and genre, 14; Depression writing, 88, 105, 183
Doctorow, E.L., 168
Donoghue, Denis, 177
Doty, Mark A., 183
Dougherty, James, 92, 180
Douglass, Frederick, 190–91
Dreiser, Theodore, 53
Du Bois, W. E. B., xi

Dusinberre, William, 178

East: in transcendental writing, 45, 50
Eagleton, Terry, 7
Eakin, John Paul, 168
Education of Henry Adams, see under
	Adams, Henry
Edwards, Jonathan, 2, 18
Eliot, T.S., 64, 153, 174
Ellison, Ralph, 146
Emerson, Caryl, 9, 163, 164
Emerson, Ralph Waldo, 31, 32, 33, 41,
	44, 111
End of Ideology, 103, 121, 126, 181
English Hours, see under James
Enlightenment, the, 23,
Evans, Walker, 107,

Fanon, Franz, 180
Feminism: class and repression, 179;
	feminine writing, 96; and human-
	ism, 104; as marginality, 98, 181;
	Marxism, 96–97, and race, 142–43;
	and repression of bourgeois
	women, 97; voicing, 97
Fetterly, Judith, 162
Foley, Barbara, 166, 167
Fong, Wen, 190
Foucault, Michel, 123, 126, 157–58:
	Discipline and Punish, 6;
Franklin, Benjamin, 5, 31, 36, 40, 42,
	65, 67, 70, 77, 79, 88, 96, 115, 133,
	144, 152, 158, 168, 169; *Autobiogra-
	phy of,* 10, 17– 30, 32, 45; diverse
	voices in, 22; control of other voic-
	es in, 22–23, 25–27; multivoicing
	and capitalist agenda, 10; Poor
	Richard, 39, 41; as revolutionary
	nationalist, 17
Frederickson, George M., 183
French, Warren, 186
Fuller, Margaret, *Woman in the Nine-*

teenth Century, xi, 41, 97
Furth, David L., 176

Gale, Robert L., 174
Gates, Henry Louis, 187
Geismar, Maxwell, 173
Gibson, Walker, 164
Gilbert, Sandra, 89
Gilded Age, The, 47, 49, 69
Gilligan, Carol, 5, 162
Gilman, Charlotte Perkins, 180
Gilmore, Michael T., 171
Godine, Amy, 183
Gold, Michael, 183
Goodman, Paul, 124
Gramsci, Antonio, 157
Granger, Bruce Ingham, 18, 169
Gray, Asa, 75
Gray, John, 2, 161–62
Greene, William B., 32
Guattari, Felix, 139
Gubar, Susan, 89
Gutman, Stanley, 140

Hall, William F., 175, 176
Hamilton, Alexander, 18, 67
Hammond, Bray, 31
Harbert, Earl N., 178
Hartz, Louis, xi, 4
Hawthorne, Nathaniel, 48
Hegemony, 157
Hellman, John, 14, 166
Heywood, Ezra, 32
Hofstadter, Richard, 75
Holder, Alan, 119
Holism in American studies, 13
Holowell, John, 14, 166
Hooks, Bell, 144
Howe, Irving, 174
Howells, William Dean, *Rise of Silas
	Lapham,* 49
Humanism: and language, 104

Hynes, Samuel, 112, 183

Ideology: Agee's attempt to transcend, 120–21; of form, 7, 161; and
language, 131, 133, 137–38; in
poststructuralist thought, 7;
Individualism: and capitalism 22;
and class, 87; and community, 29,
46; and liberalism, 21; Lockean, 2;
and marketplace, 20; noncon-
formist, 31; radical and transcendent, 2; and social consensus and
22;
Intertextuality: and dialogism, 165
Invisible Man, 146

Jackson, Andrew, 2
James, Henry, 12, 36, 46, 67, 69, 72, 79,
87, 88, 89, 91, 93, 100, 121, 125, 133,
158–59, 174; *The Ambassadors*, 53,
The American, 50; *The American
Scene*, 11, 47–65, 133; *English
Hours*, 48, *The Golden Bowl*, 53; *The
Wings of the Dove*, 53; on commod-
ification and reification, 52; con-
servatism and culture, 48–49; and
feminism, 176; and immigrants,
57, 59
Jameson, Fredric, 5, 7, 8, 161, 163
JanMohammed Abdul, 180
Jefferson, Thomas, 2, 168, 169
Jehlen, Myra, 13
Johnson, Stuart, 176
Johnson, Wendell, xi
Juhasz, Suzanne, 153

Kellog, Robert, 167
Kim, Elaine H., 189–90
King, Richard, 110, 182
Kingston, Maxine Hong, 98, 121,

158–59; *Woman Warrior, The*, 12,
98, 143–55; mother daughter rela-
tionships in, 189
Kramer, Victor, 182
Kristeva, Julia, 88, 98, 165, 185
Krupat, Arnold, 168

Laguiller, Arlette, 96–97, 180
*Let Us Now Praise Famous Men, see
under* Agee
Left, American, 103, 126
Lemay, J. A. Leo, 169
Lens, Sidney, 173
Leverenz, David, 171
Levine, Daniel, 179
Lewis, R. W. B., 166
Lewis, Sinclair, 127
Liberalism: and alienation, 4; and
community, 29; conflictual
creation of, 12; and consensus, 26,
72, 88, 123, 139; critique of, 139;
and democratic capitalism, 54;
emergence of, 2; Lockean, 32, 103,
105; in revolutionary America, 17;
in U. S. culture, 2–5; and owner-
ship, 18; and racial difference, 48,
65, 155; radical liberalism of
Thoreau, 32; and unified subject,
125; and universalism, 101
Life on the Mississippi, 13
Locke, John, 3, 17, 23, 32
Lukacs, Georg, 7, 52, 175n.15
Lynd, Staughton, 172
Lyon, Melvin, 177
Lyons, Richard S., 175
Lyotard, Jean Francois, 82
Magnalia Christi Americana, see under
Mather

Mailer, Norman, 5, 13, 76, 102, 121,
146, 149, 159; *Advertisements for
Myself*, 124, 126; *Armies of the*

Night, 12, 76, 123–42, 167; *Barbary Shore*, 129; *Cannibals and Christians*, 127; *The Naked and the Dead*, 136; *Presidential Papers*, 127; "The White Negro," 124; *Why Are We in Vietnam?*, 138

Marcuse, Herbert, 5, 124, 129–30

Marginality: and liberalism 12; and voicing, 99–100

Marginal writers: and patriarchal forms, 187–88

Marx, Karl, 36, 126; and alienation, 52, 172

Mather, Cotton, 2, 22

Matthiessen, F. O., 57

McCarthy, Mary, 168

McCormack, Peggy, 175

Medvedev, P. N., 163, 164

Mellard, James M., 76, 178

Mellon, Thomas, 19

Memoirs of a Catholic Girlhood, 168

Meredith, Robert, 129–30, 185

Miller, Perry, 2

Mills, J. S., 123

Minter, David L., 74, 177

Mitchell, Carol, 188

Moldenhauer, Joseph J., 35, 172

Mont Saint Michel and Chartres, see under Adams, Henry

Morante, Linda, 189

More, Paul Elmer, 84

Morson, Gary Saul, 163

Morison, Samuel Eliot, 174

Morrison, Toni, 180

A Moveable Feast, 168

Naked and the Dead, The, see under Mailer

Nash, Gary B., 170

Neufeldt, Leonard, 171, 172

New Journalism, 13, 14, 166

Newer Ideals of Peace, see under Addams

New Left, 12, 123–124, 126, 130, 132–33, 136, 139, 146, 184

Nietzsche, Friedrich, 43, 118, 125

Nonfiction Novel, 13–14

Ohlin, Peter, 111

Okhamafe, Imafedia E., 184

Olney, James, 167

Paine, Thomas, 2

Parker, David L., 170

Parrington, Vernon L., 18

Patriotism, 127–128, 187

Pechey, Graham, 163

Personal-political narratives, ix; and aestheticism, 108; and argumentation, 37; history of, 1–3; and liberal consensus, 103; and marginal writers, 142; opposed voices in, 52; persuasion in, 10; polemical impulse in, 124; of women, 97

Plymouth Plantation, Of, see under Bradford

Poirier, Richard, 134, 138, 161

Politics of difference, 125, 127, 133, 141, 159

Politics of form: and deconstruction, 7–8; defined x; in personal-political narratives, 6

Posnock, Ross, 175–76

Prince, Gerald, 164

Problems of Dostoevsky's Poetics, see under Bakhtin

Progressivism, 88

Puritanism: writing, persuasion in, 2; in American cultural history 2; used by Franklin 24

Rabine, Leslie, 188–89

Rabinowitz, Peter, 164

Radford, Jean, 126, 184–85

Reader response theories, 164–65
Reid, B. L., 177
Reising, Russell J., 13, 166
Republicanism, 23, 24
Reynolds, David S., 171
Rise of Silas Lapham, see under Howells
Rorex, Robert, 190
Ross, Morton, 184
Rousseau, Jean Jacques, 19
Rowe, John Carlos, 13, 74, 85, 166, 176, 177
Rubin, Jerry, 138
Ruland, Richard, 177
Ryan, Michael, 184, 185

Said, Edward, 150, 152, 158, 162
Samuels, Ernest, 71
Sanford, Charles, 169
Sartre, Jean Paul, 130
Sayre, Robert F., 14, 167, 170
Scholes, Robert, 167
Seed, David, 54, 175
Seib, Kenneth, 184
Shulman, Robert, 30, 162, 170
Social Darwinism, 41
Spanos, William V., 178
Spirit of Youth and the City Streets, see under Addams
Stein, Gertrude, 97, 168
Steinbeck, John, 168
Stinson, Peggy, 180
Stott, William, 105
Stewart, Susan, 9
Stone, Albert E., 14
Stott, William, 182
Subject: autonomous, 31, 62–63, 69; in capitalism, xi; dissolution of, and political action, 191; and intersubjectivity, 94; and material world, 43; and otherness, 136; questioning of autonomous self, 59, 136, 150; unified, in liberalism, 125
Sumner, William Graham, 41, 74

Tate, Cecil F., 12–13, 165
Thoreau, Henry David, 47, 65, 67, 69, 70, 71, 89, 100, 111, 115, 124, 130, 133, 152, 158–59, 171; "Civil Disobedience," 41;
  Walden, 10–11, 13, 31–46; aesthetic ideology in, 32; creation of reader-characters in, 35; carnival rhetoric used in, 34; parody of slogans in, 38; subversion of dominant culture in, 11; *A Week on the Concord and Merrimack Rivers*, 171
Tocqueville, Alexis de, 30, 51, 53, 127, 162; *Democracy in America*, xi, 3–4, 170
Todorov, Tzvetan, 163
Trachtenberg, Alan, 176
Transcendental: writing and conversation, 37
Transcendentalism, 111; and aesthetic ideology, 41–43; and capitalism, 31; East in, 50; material-ideal split in, 45–46
Trilling, Lionel, 183–84
Twenty Years at Hull-House, see under Addams

Updike, John, 127
Universalism, 3
Up From Slavery, 93

Voice: and authority in personal-political narratives; defined, 9–10; destabilization of authorial voice, 5, 68, 78; interrogative voices in *Walden*, 37; and marginality, 145–46; political, x; spoken, emphasis in personal-political narratives, 5; shifting voices in The American Scene, 54; women's, in personal-political

narratives, 89, 96–97
Volosinov, V. N., 161, 163

Wagner, Vern, 177
Walden, see under Thoreau
Walker, Alice, 144, 180
Wallace, Michael, 170
Warren, Austin, 167
Warren, Josiah, 32
Washington, Booker T., 93
Weber, Max, 18
Weber, Ronald, 14, 166
Webster, Noah, 19, 169
A Week on the Concord and Merrimack Rivers, see under Thoreau
Wellek, Rene, 167
Wenke, Joseph, 187
Whitman, Walt, 31, 111, 114
White, Allon, 163
White, Charles W., 168
White, Hayden, 167
Why Are We In Vietnam?, see under Mailer
Wiebe, Ronald, 49

Wigglesworth, Michael, 2
Wilcox, William B., 168
Williams, Raymond, 7, 32, 42, 161
Wilson, Woodrow, 47
Winthrop, John, 1, 22
Wittig, Monique, 98
Wolfe, Tom, 13
Woman in the Nineteenth Century, see under Fuller
Woman Warrior, The, see under Kingston
Woolf, Virginia, 150, 189
Woolman, John, 19
Wordplays: and subversion, 39, 137–39
Wright, Richard, 166
Wyatt, Jean, 179

Yaeger, Patricia, 179
Yuval–Davis, Nira, 144

Zall, P. M., 169
Zavarzadeh, Mas'Ud, 14, 166